C. S. Lewis—An Annotated Bibliography and Resource

C. S. Lewis—An Annotated Bibliography and Resource

P. H. Brazier

Foreword by Brian Horne

SERIES: C. S. LEWIS: REVELATION AND THE CHRIST

www.cslewisandthechrist.net

PICKWICK *Publications* • Eugene, Oregon

C. S. LEWIS—AN ANNOTATED BIBLIOGRAPHY AND RESOURCE

Series: C. S. Lewis: Revelation and the Christ 4

Copyright © 2012 Paul H. Brazier. All rights reserved. Except for brief quotations in critical publications or reviews, no part of this book may be reproduced in any manner without prior written permission from the publisher. Write: Permissions, Wipf and Stock Publishers, 199 W. 8th Ave., Suite 3, Eugene, OR 97401.

Pickwick Publications
An Imprint of Wipf and Stock Publishers
199 W. 8th Ave., Suite 3
Eugene, OR 97401

www.wipfandstock.com

ISBN 13: 978-1-61097-906-1

Cataloging-in-Publication data:

Brazier, Paul.

C. S. Lewis—an annotated bibliography and resource / P. H. Brazier.

Series: C. S. Lewis: Revelation and the Christ 4

xviii + 190 p. ; 23 cm. Includes bibliographical references and index.

ISBN 13: 978-1-61097-906-1

1. Lewis, C. S. (Clive Staples), 1898–1963—Bibliography. I. Title. II. Series.

BX5199.L53 B639 2012

Manufactured in the U.S.A.

All royalties from this series are donated to the University of Oxford C. S. Lewis Society

Typeset by P. H. Brazier, Ash Design
Minion Pro 10.75pt on 14pt

SERIES PREFACE
C. S. LEWIS: REVELATION AND THE CHRIST

This is a series of books that have a common theme: the understanding of Christ, and therefore the revelation of God, in the work of C. S. Lewis. These books are a systematic study of Lewis's theology, Christology, and doctrine of revelation; as such they draw on his life and work. They are written for academics and students, but also, crucially, for those people, ordinary Christians, without a theology degree who enjoy and gain sustenance from reading Lewis's work.

Book One
Revelation, Conversion, and Apologetics

Book Two
The Work of Christ Revealed

Book Three
The Christ of a Religious Economy

A fourth volume, consisting of an in-depth bibliography, plus an introductory essay on Christology as the study of Christ, and a glossary, completes the series:

C. S. Lewis—An Annotated Bibliography and Resource

There is a website to accompany (www.cslewisandthechrist.net) that provides material and downloads to complement these books. Those who feel somewhat bemused by the concepts in Christology (the study of Christ) may gain understanding from browsing the site, which will give an introduction to the series. In addition a full detailed contents, including all sections can be downloaded and printed as an aide-memoire and guide to each book in the series.

This series has been many years in the making. The serious writing of it started in 2007; however, sketches relating to some of the topics go back much further. With writing the work grew. Lewis was not a systematic theologian, nor did he attempt to write a systematic theology (though the aim of *Mere Christianity* gets close to it). What this work attempts is to present a systematic study of what Lewis understood about Jesus Christ, and the revelation of God, who is at the heart of orthodox, traditional, theology.

For Hilary

Contents

List of Illustrations / xi

Foreword by Brian Horne / xviii

Acknowledgements / xvii

Introduction / 1

1. Lewis . . . and the Christ / 5
2. C. S. Lewis: An Annotated Historical Bibliography of Primary Sources / 35
3. C. S. Lewis: Correspondent / 69
4. Helen Joy Davidman: An Annotated Historical Bibliography / 71
5. C. S. Lewis: Revelation and the Christ: Secondary Sources—Books / 75
6. C. S. Lewis: Revelation and the Christ: Secondary Sources—Articles and Essays / 89
7. Secondary Sources—Related to Lewis's Development / 119
8. Web Resources / 125
9. Glossary / 139

Index of Names / 167

Index of Subjects / 170

Index of C. S. Lewis's Works / 179

Sectional Contents / 185

List of Illustrations

Figure 1 (Chapter 1)
The Tensions that can affect all Christologies / 15

Figure 2 (Chapter 1)
The Apostles' Creed / 19

Figure 3 (Chapter 1)
The Nicene Creed / 21

Figure 4 (Chapter 1)
The Chalcedonian Creed / 25

Figure 5 (Chapter 1)
The Tensions inherent in the Doctrine of the Trinity / 27

Figure 6 (Chapter 1)
Christ Pantocrator—in the Patristic Tradition / 31

Figure 7 (Chapter 2)
The Three Periods of Lewis's Apologetics and Theology / 37

Foreword

In the opening pages of his vast, unfinished, work, the *Summa Theologica*, Thomas Aquinas declared, simply and incisively, that, "Since therefore grace does not destroy nature but perfects it, natural reason should submit to faith as the natural bent of the will ministers to charity."[1] With these few concise phrases one of the greatest minds of Christendom set forth his own understanding of the relationship between nature and grace—and by implication, reason and revelation—and thus established the foundation of his entire theological endeavor. The question of that relationship was to become one of the central issues of theological debate in the centuries that followed. It featured prominently as one of the defining differences between Catholic and Protestant interpretations of the faith, and it remains, just as controversially, with us today. One might go so far as to say that it is impossible to be a Christian theologian without having given serious thought to this most vital of issues.

There can be no doubt where C. S. Lewis's sympathies lay. Walter Hooper has pointed out that "the *Summa Theologica* was a work that Lewis used constantly."[2] This does not mean that he read the work of Thomas Aquinas uncritically, still less does it imply that he might be regarded as a crypto Roman Catholic, but it cannot be denied that he was profoundly influenced by Thomas Aquinas and that the issue of the relationship between Nature and Grace was regarded by him as being of fundamental importance to a Christian vision of life. (The frequency with which he returned to the subject of natural law, for example, is clear evidence of this). It is difficult to avoid the conclusion that he would have found in these words of the *Summa Theologica* a concise articulation of his own understanding of the nature of the world's relationship to its creator. However, if we are to say that he made this fundamental theological principle central to his own theology, we can also see that he made it his own in his own unique way—a way that would be true to his Anglican heritage. In doing so he became a successor to one of the architects of the Church of England itself, Richard Hooker (1554–1600), a thinker Lewis greatly admired and who, himself, had been deeply influenced by the thirteenth-century Dominican theologian.

---

1   Aquinas, *Summa Theologica* Q I. 8, ii.
2   Hooper, *C. S. Lewis. A Companion and Guide*, 595.

In his magisterial study of Hooker's *Laws of Ecclesiastical Polity*,[3] Lewis, having noted that "every system offers us a model of the universe" and that "Hooker's model has unsurpassed grace and majesty" he reveals the essence of that universe in a memorable phrase. "Few model universes are more filled—one might say, more *drenched with Deity*—than his."[4] Lewis sees Hooker's God as both "unspeakably transcendent, but also unspeakably immanent," and he enlarges on this observation by commenting: "It is this conviction which enabled Hooker, with no anxiety, to resist any inaccurate claim that is made for revelation against reason, Grace against Nature, the spiritual against the secular. . . . All good things, reason as well as revelation, Nature as well as Grace, the commonwealth as well as the Church, are equally, though diversely 'of God.' If 'nature hath need of grace,' yet also 'grace hath use of nature.'"[5] This book, *English Literature in the Sixteenth Century*, one of Lewis's major achievements, was published in 1954, but its genesis was in his Clark lectures of 1944 and he had, moreover, arrived at this conviction long before. It is the principle that permeates the theological and ethical teaching of his broadcast talks of 1941–42, *Mere Christianity*;[6] it is fundamental to the educational philosophy of the Riddell lectures of 1943, *The Abolition of Man*,[7] and it appears in a striking guise in a sermon he preached in Mansfield College chapel on the Feast of Pentecost in 1944.

The sermon was given the title: "Transposition"[8] and the notion of *transposition* is, indeed, the central theme of the homily: the transposition of the lower into the higher, the transformation of what is natural into the supernatural. Not, we must note, the disappearance or destruction of the lower or the natural, but a *transposition* of the ordinary into the extraordinary: "religious language and imagery, and probably religious emotion too, contain nothing that has not been borrowed from Nature."[9] The argument is articulated with characteristic trenchancy and vividness; and Lewis is aware of the clarity and subtlety that are needed to make his position convincing. Just as

3   In, Lewis, *English Literature in the Sixteenth Century*, Bk. 2, Ch. 2, 451–63. Richard Hooker (1554–1600), an Anglican priest and theologian who is attributed with the form of the Anglican *via media*, and—along with Thomas Cranmer and Matthew Parker—for the basis or ground of the Church of England after the Henrician Reformation. Hooker was born in the village of Heavitree, Devon; he became a fellow of Corpus Christi College, Oxford, 1577. He was ordained priest in 1584, and later served as Sub-dean of Salisbury Cathedral. Hooker's *Of the Laws of Ecclesiastical Polity* was highly influential on the development of the Church of England and was essentially a treatise on church-state relations, focusing on issues of biblical interpretation, soteriology, ethics and sanctification. Like Anselm, Hooker asserted that theology must be grounded in prayer.

4   Ibid., 459. (My italics.)
5   Ibid., 460, quoting Hooker, *Of the Laws of Ecclesiastical Polity*, III. viii, 6.
6   Lewis, *Mere Christianity*, 1952, based on the BBC Broadcast Talks, 1941–44: *Right and Wrong* (1941), and, *What Christians Believe* (1942), *Christian Behaviour* (1942), and, *Beyond Personality* (1944).
7   Lewis, *The Abolition of Man: or, Reflections on Education with Special Reference to the Teaching of English in the Upper Forms of Schools*, given as the University of Durham Riddell Memorial Lectures, fifteenth series, 1943.
8   Lewis, "Transposition," a sermon given in Mansfield College, Oxford on Whit Sunday, May 28, 1944, published (1st ed.) 1949. A reworked and extended 2nd edition of the sermon as an academic paper was published in 1962. Lewis, "Transposition." 2nd ed., 181. All subsequent references are to this second edition.
9   Ibid., 168.

we suspect that he might be leaning dangerously close to philosophical "naturalism" in drawing attention to the inherent capacities of Nature for conveying truth and beauty, he explicitly denies any possibility of there being a kind of inevitable development of the natural into the supernatural, of the lower into the higher. Reason is simply insufficient on its own and cannot by itself bring the human being to his or her true fulfillment without Revelation. The natural life of men and women needs the suffusion of grace to bring it to completion. As an illustration of this truth he offers these provocative thoughts on the doctrine of the resurrection at the close of the address: "May we not, by a reasonable analogy, suppose likewise that there is no experience of the spirit so transcendent and supernatural, no vision of Deity Himself so close and so far beyond all images and emotions, that there cannot be appropriate correspondence on the sensory level? Not by a new sense but by the incredible flooding of those very sensations we now have with a meaning, a transvaluation, of which we have no faintest guess?"[10]

Where did this come from? By what route did he arrive at this particular reading of the Christian story? It would not be unreasonable to suppose that it was by the way of philosophical argument, observation and speculation, arriving at the conclusion that this offered the best explanation for the facts of life as he had come to perceive them. Doubtless this is partly true; as I have already indicated, Lewis was capable of subtle philosophical debate, and intellectual clarity, the clarity that good philosophy gives, was always important to him. But it would be simplistic to suppose that this is an adequate answer; there is a deeper cause to be investigated and a richer seam to be mined: something that was rooted in his imagination as well as his intellect. The great love of his life—apart from his attachment to God, the church, and his friends—was literature. It was both his passion and his profession. And the literature that he loved was not confined to the texts of Medieval and Renaissance Europe in which he was so deeply read and of which he was so discerning an expositor. It included Homer and Sophocles, Virgil and Cicero, the literature of classical Greece and Rome as well as the Norse sagas and the pre-Christian writings of Old English. It would have been inconceivable that, on becoming a Christian, he could have abandoned the truth he had found in those great works of the human imagination for a version of the truth found only in the Bible or the teachings of the church. For him there was an inherent beauty and truth in these works that was not to be denied; they were in some real sense, precursors of the revelation that was to come in the incarnation of the Son of God. This was nature preparing the way for Grace

This is not to deny that there is something new—and shocking—about the appearance of Jesus Christ in history and this point is made vigorously in one of the most persuasive of all his essays, "Is Theology Poetry?" (1944) "If Christianity is only a mythology, then the mythology that I believe in is not the one I like best. I like Greek mythology better: Irish better still: Norse best of all."[11] And he goes on to draw a distinction between "imaginative enjoyment" (myth) and "intellectual assent" (fact);

10 Ibid., 182–83.
11 "Is Theology Poetry?" (1944), 152.

they are not in opposition to one another but they are not to be confused. "It is not the difference between falsehood and truth. It is the difference between a real event on the one hand and dim dreams and premonitions of that same event on the other."[12] What happens in the process of revelation is "the humiliation of myth into fact, of God into Man"[13] The essay ends with one of those perorations that is so characteristic of Lewis—a passage that not only marks him out as one the finest apologists for Christianity to have arisen in our era, but one that is singularly relevant to life at the beginning of the twenty-first century: "Christian theology can fit in science, art, morality, and the sub-Christian religions. The scientific point of view cannot fit in any of these things, not even science itself. I believe in Christianity as I believe that the Sun has risen not only because I see it but because by it I see everything else."[14]

Dr. Brian Horne
Lecturer in Systematic Theology (retired), King's College London
Chairman, The Charles Williams Society

BIBLIOGRAPHY

Aquinas, Thomas, *Summa Theologiae*. The complete paperback set: 60 volumes, plus one index volume; dual language, Latin–English. 1962–76. Reprint. Cambridge: Cambridge University Press, 2006.

Hooker, Richard, *Of the Lawes of Ecclesiastical Politie* (1593–1662) Vols. 1–4 published in 1594; Vol. 5 in 1597; Vols. 6–9 published posthumously. Modern edition: Richard Hooker, *Of the Laws of Ecclesiastical Polity*. Edited by A. S. McGrade. Cambridge: Cambridge University Press, 1989.

Hooper, Walter. *C. S. Lewis A Companion and Guide*. London: Harper Collins, 1996.

Lewis, C. S. "Is Theology Poetry?" In *They Asked for a Paper*. London: Geoffrey Bles, 1962, 150–65.

———. "Transposition." 2nd ed. In *They Asked for a Paper*. London: Geoffrey Bles, 1962, 166–82.

———. *English Literature in the Sixteenth Century Excluding Drama*. Oxford: Oxford University Press, Clarendon Press, 1954.

———. Mere Christianity. *A revised and amplified edition, with a new introduction, of the three books Broadcast Talks, Christian Behaviour, and Beyond Personality*. London: Geoffrey Bles, 1952.

———. *The Abolition of Man: or, Reflections on Education with Special Reference to the Teaching of English in the Upper Forms of Schools*. Oxford: Oxford University Press, 1943.

12 Ibid., 158.
13 Ibid., 159.
14 Ibid., 165.

Acknowledgements

My initial interest in C. S. Lewis started with a Sunday afternoon TV serialization of *The Lion, the Witch and the Wardrobe* in, I think, 1967. Crude by today's CGI standards, and in black-and-white, I only saw the first episode amidst a chaotic time of my life, yet a seed was sown, thoughts which I could not get out of my mind. Credit should also be given to a fellow student, Debbie Gould, when I was at art college, who commented pointedly to me that I should read Lewis's works. Something I started to do seriously when I became a Christian in 1980. Acknowledgement must be accorded to Dr. Murray Rae and Dr. Brian Horne (both formerly of King's College London) for engendering in me a serious study of Lewis from 1999, which culminated in this work. Thanks must also be given to Dr. Pat Madigan S. J. (Editor of *The Heythrop Journal*), for encouragement—and for publishing articles generated by this research; Judith and Brendan Wolfe (The University of Oxford C. S. Lewis Society); and also to John Field, a well-read Christian, for advice in reading early drafts. My thanks go to N. T. (Tom) Wright, for discussions (conducted by e-mailed message) on the nature of *the Christ* as presented in this work. Thanks go to Neil Hunter Raiford (Whitesburg Christian Academy) for perceptive and invaluable proof reading. My deepest thanks must go to Robin Parry (editor, Wipf and Stock) for countless ideas and advice, and his unrivaled expertise as a biblical scholar, particularly in his editing of this series. But ultimately acknowledgement and thanks must go to Hilary, my wife, without whom I would not be the person I am, and this work would never have existed.

My acknowledgement and thanks go to Owen Barfield for help with the web links regarding his father's work.

Extracts from the Bible used with permission:

Revised Standard Version of the Bible, copyright 1952 [2nd edition, 1971] by the Division of Christian Education of the National Council of the Churches of Christ in the United States of America. Used by permission. All rights reserved.

New Revised Standard Version Bible, copyright 1989, Division of Christian Education of the National Council of the Churches of Christ in the United States of America. Used by permission. All rights reserved.

New Revised Standard Version Bible: Anglicized Edition, copyright 1989, 1995, Division of Christian Education of the National Council of the Churches of Christ in the United States of America. Used by permission. All rights reserved.

THE HOLY BIBLE, NEW INTERNATIONAL VERSION®, NIV® Copyright © 1973, 1978, 1984, 2011 by Biblica, Inc.™ Used by permission. All rights reserved worldwide.

Nestle-Aland, Novum Testamentum Graece, 27th Revised Edition, edited by Barbara Aland, Kurt Aland, Johannes Karavidopoulos, Carlo M. Martini, and Bruce M. Metzger in cooperation with the Institute for New Testament Textual Research, Münster/Westphalia, © 1993 by Deutsche Bibelgesellschaft, Stuttgart. Used by permission.

Introduction
C. S. Lewis—An Annotated Bibliography and Resource

C. S. Lewis: Revelation and the Christ, is a series of books on Lewis's understanding of Jesus Christ. Jesus of Nazareth, the Christ, is of central importance to humanity. Jesus Christ is considered by orthodox Christians to be the unique revelation of God, the God above all gods, the God beyond all gods. This Jesus Christ was then crucified, died, and resurrected for our salvation, opening up heaven to humanity. These are strong, dynamic, and assertive claims, and at once appear to stand apart from, even contradict, most of the world's religions in their unique assertions. There are various ideas and interpretations of whom or what this Jesus of Nazareth, the Christ, *was* and *is*; these theories vary across the churches. However, down the centuries there has been a constant and steady seam of knowledge and understanding as to who Jesus Christ is, how he is God, and how this affects all of humanity. To talk about Jesus Christ is to speak of revelation—God's self-revelation, God's revealedness to humanity. Therefore God initiates both in our knowledge and understanding about these most important of matters, but also, crucially, in our salvation.

1. WHY C. S. LEWIS

This book is one of a series, it complements the three main volumes, which are about one man's understanding of, and his encounter with, Jesus Christ. That man is Clive Staples Lewis—C. S. Lewis, Jack, at his insistence, to all he knew—who wrote many, many books to defend Christianity and the witness of the churches. Lewis's aim was to defend Christianity itself, not Anglican or Roman Catholic, not Methodist or Baptist, not Presbyterian or Evangelical. Why? He sought to defend what he famously called "Mere Christianity," which was not his own personal religion, or his own personal selection from Christian theology and church history, but the faith set out in the creeds and explained by the church fathers living more than fifteen hundred years ago, the faith that originated with the apostles who knew this Jesus of Nazareth. Lewis sought to defend the faith that the martyrs died for. Being a "Mere Christian" for him represented the distilled basics of the faith rooted in the God-man Jesus Christ. This was to be distinguished, for Lewis, from watered-down Christianity, from human-centered religion.

Lewis's "Mere Christianity" was, therefore, polemical in its assertiveness. This "Mere Christianity" was there to a greater or lesser degree in all the churches of Lewis's day, but had been compromised by disputes between the churches; indeed the very fragmentation of the church into so many denominations or groupings weakened the basic core of the faith. Games of one-upmanship and power politics between bishops from competing denominations, or arguments over the finer points of worship, or in some instances a wholesale rejection of the beliefs set out in the creed, this all weakened the gospel: that God became incarnate as a human being in Jesus of Nazareth and died for our sins to open up a way for us into heaven. This was at the heart of the Christian faith. This Jesus of Nazareth, the Christ, did not simply live two thousand years ago leaving us alone in the world: the Holy Spirit of this Christ is active, alive, presses on us, seeks to convert us, to save us.

Lewis believed strongly in a basic core to the faith, a "mere" Christian core. All else could be considered to be an embellishment, details that are to a greater or lesser degree important to individual denominations, and are valid to a greater or lesser extent before God, but nonetheless these details and differences are culturally relative, they are in many ways subjective religion. Lewis therefore distinguished what he called "Mere Christianity" from this subjective religion. Lewis was an Anglican; he saw this "Mere Christianity" in the Church of England of his day, that it was at its strongest in the Catholic and Evangelical wings, as distinct from the liberal, modernist, central ground, which he believed marginalized this core of "Mere Christianity": Lewis could therefore be fairly described as a Catholic-Evangelical, indeed he described himself as such.

This book then is written for students and theologians, but also general readers familiar with Lewis's works. Because Lewis was an Anglican this is a work written to be appreciated by Anglicans; however, it can also be appreciated by Roman Catholics who in recent years have developed an interest more and more in the writings of C. S. Lewis; it is also aimed at Evangelicals who have long had a love of Lewis's work, but have been selective about what they agree with and disagree with in Lewis's presentation of the basic core of the Christian faith. Evangelicals may not like the way Lewis subscribed to what can be considered a traditional Catholic position on the sacraments and on purgatory, but he held these beliefs for good reason. And Evangelical readers would do well to think why he did. Likewise Roman Catholic readers would do well to see how Lewis could get beyond the external structure of religion to appreciate the immediacy of relationship any believer can have with the Lord Jesus, which in some ways by-passes the structures and authority of the church(es).

2. AIMS AND OBJECTIVES

The three main volumes in this series are related, but are written to be read independently of each other. The aim of this volume is to provide a bibliography and *resource* to the three main volumes in this series, with the emphasis on the word, resource. Some readers will be teachers of theology in higher education—including professors; others who value Lewis's work will be graduates (in other specialisms); still others will be knowledgeable Christians without formal higher education qualifications. This book as a resource should benefit all these groups, though not everything in this volume will be relevant to all of these readers.

As an annotated bibliography and resource this work opens with an explanation about *The Christ*, which then develops into an introductory essay on Christology (not everyone will be familiar with the technical terms and complex ideas that issue from the ancient Church in relation to what are sound ideas about Jesus). Having established this sound christological basis we can then briefly explore what Lewis's understanding of Jesus—the Christ—is. This is then followed by several chapters that form a chronological introduction to the development of Lewis's works, a copious bibliography of related secondary sources, and a guide to the study of Lewis. Then we have a guide to web resources on Lewis, and the Inklings. Finally a glossary for those unfamiliar with some of the background and terms to Lewis's understanding of revelation and the Christ.

Detailed and copious indexes at the end of this volume allow access to authors cited and writers referenced, also subjects cited in the chapters, in addition all of Lewis's works are listed alphabetically, and a detailed sectional contents assists navigation.

A work like this will never be absolutely up-to-date, and human frailty dictates that the author may overlook or inadvertently omit a reference: apology is offered for any unintentional oversight.

Essentially this is a volume that purports to answer some of the technical and detailed questions that readers of the three main volumes might come up with (though without fore knowledge of the questions, the answers may inevitably be general). Readers with specific questions to the main three books can contact through the "Contact" page on the dedicated website: www.cslewisandthechrist.net.

1

Lewis . . . and the Christ

In order to better understand the thinking of C. S. Lewis on Christology it is important to have a basic appreciation of the development of orthodox Christian thinking in this area. This chapter is intended to serve as just such an introduction.

Essentially this christological survey is for readers who have not undertaken a theology degree (though having said that, many Western university theology departments no longer run patristic—i.e. the church between, c.200–750 AD—courses generally, or specific courses on the development of orthodox Christology). General readers of C. S. Lewis's works—often graduates in their own specialism—may not have the background knowledge, often historical, to appreciate many of the terms and concepts, ideas and words cited in the three main volumes in this series. This chapter may be of use to them. This survey may give them the picture and context in which Lewis wrote: that is, the patristic basis of Lewis's theology generally, and his Christology specifically. These ideas may seem ancient, and to some irrelevant, yet when a "modern"/"liberal" American professor—W. Norman Pittenger—accused Lewis publically of christological heresy in 1958 (criticisms that were published in the leading American weekly, *The Christian Century*,[1] Lewis likewise publishing a reply.[2]) Pittenger drew on many of these patristic concepts about the nature of Jesus (Docetism, Gnosticism, Apollinarianism and Eutychianism) in his attack. Lewis, however, refuted the accusation and then proceeded to demolish Pittenger's Christology as dangerously "modern" and "liberal," and essentially heterodox.[3] Lewis and Pittenger's differences come down to two propositional questions: first, is Jesus Christ defined by the very nature of his being in and before God, or is he who he is because of humanely conferred status? Second, is what was established by the early and patristic church about the Christ as true today as it was then? These questions about Jesus may be ancient but are as pertinent today as fifteen hundred to two thousand years ago.

---

1 Pittenger, "Apologist versus Apologist," 1104–7.
2 Lewis, "Rejoinder to Dr Pittenger," 1369–71.
3 For the Pittenger-Lewis debate, see Book 1 in this series: *C. S. Lewis—Revelation, Conversion, and Apologetics*, Ch. 133–45.

1. WHO OR WHAT IS THE CHRIST?

i. The Messiah

Like many ancient names that had cultural or religious meanings, the name Jesus—in Hebrew, *Yeshua*, given to Mary by Gabriel, the angel at the annunciation—was known to those who heard it as signifying "God is savior," or "Jehovah is savior;" Christ means "anointed one," Messiah. The word Messiah was commonly used in the era between the two testaments, Old and New (i.e., the intertestamental period), the concept of messiahship having developed in later Judaism (from the early Hebrew *Mashiach*, the anointed one, derived from the ancient Hebrew tradition of anointing the king with oil). Messiah was not necessarily a name, but a label, an attribution, an office, a role, essentially a title. By the time of Jesus of Nazareth the title "Messiah" was often attributed to someone the people liked, whom they believed could fulfill, they hoped, a role for them. However, *the* Messiah was to be the one anointed at the end of days. Jesus is therefore taken by those around him to be *the* Messiah; hence the early attribution that he is the Christ. The word Christ is simply a translation from the Greek (χριστός) and the Latin (*Christus*) for Messiah. Therefore, Jesus Christ, in name and title, was God's salvation, the anointed one. This did not necessarily imply that he was the second person of the Trinity. The trinitarian perception is part of the dawning realization in the early church, with ample pointers and examples of Jesus's trinitarian nature in the books that became the New Testament (texts produced by the earliest church in the years after the resurrection and ascension).

ii. Expectations

Around the time of Jesus's birth messiahship carried expectations. Some saw the coming Messiah as a political leader who would expel the Romans; others expected a Messiah who would be a partisan revolutionary whose aims were unclear; to yet more the Messiah would return the Temple religion back to a happier time, he would oversee the restoration of Israel. To an extent these can be seen as purely human offices. During the intertestamental period there were many false Messiahs, men raised up to realize a revolutionary, political, or religious role supported by a group or sect to save Israel in some way or other. However, false Messiahs lapsed, disappeared, or were killed by the Romans or the Jewish religious authorities. The Jews were left still hoping.

The idea of redemption, salvation, was part of these multitudinous expectations of a Messiah figure during the intertestamental period—but saved *from what*, redeemed *to what*? The answers to those questions were as varied as the messianic expectations of these false Messiahs. As a redeemer figure, expected and foretold, Jesus does not necessarily live up to the expectations of his fellow Jews. However, on reflection, the clues were there all along in Jesus's life and ministry, and crucially in the Old Testament. The ancient Hebrews priests and kings were anointed, they were Messiahs (Exod 30:22–25); later, this messiahship entitled one anointed by God as a leader, a king from the line of David. Therefore, Jesus of Nazareth was perceived by many who saw and heard him to be *the* long awaited Messiah, with different and often subjective expectations as to his role. What is important is that *a posteriori*, after the event, the proto early church interpreted this messiahship in the context of Jesus's role as God descended to earth to judge and forgive humanity, hence the use of the Greek word χριστός, Christ, by the writers of the New Testament. Jesus is then the final Messiah of Messiahs.

iii. Trinitarian

Messiah, Christ, is then revealed to be trinitarian: God anoints God to descend to save his chosen people: the Father gives the Son in the Holy Spirit. Salvation is in potential: along with humanity, Christ reascends into the divine life. Only in the fullness of the incarnation-cross-resurrection and the ascension is messiahship finally defined by Jesus. Then his life and ministry, his sayings and actions, take on new meaning, a significance and understanding veiled to many during his lifetime. Whatever the expectations of messiahship, Jesus of Nazareth is *the* Messiah (therefore, *the* Christ), not *a* Messiah, political or otherwise. It is fair to say that some of the Hebrew expectations were blown away by God's revelation; whatever people expected, it fell short of what was given by God in this Jesus. People couldn't see or fully understand what Messiah was to be, even though the evidence was there in the Old Testament.

iv. Witness

The witness of the apostles, disciples, and the early church is then a form of revelation equal to Scripture (indeed their witness forms much of the New Testament). The early church tradition replaces the old Hebrew categories of messiahship; the expectations of Jesus's contemporaries were fulfilled by God's revelation, but not necessarily in accordance with what they desired or expected. This divergence also extended to the interpretation of messiahship that the Jewish religious authorities held to in Jerusalem. For many years the Western church concentrated only on the early church tradition and the conclusions of the church councils in the fourth and fifth centuries, often, in effect, ignoring the Hebrew tradition that Jesus of Nazareth was born into. In recent years many theologians and Bible scholars, for example the orthodox Christian N. T. Wright, derive most of their conclusions about Jesus of Nazareth from an understanding of the New Testament's Jewish background, a setting in the life of the times in some ways. Perhaps the answer is to hold in balance the Hebrew tradition and categories, the perceptions of the earliest church, and also the conclusions of the later church councils, about the person and nature of Jesus. This is how to see and understand the term Messiah, *the Christ*.

2. A DEVELOPING CHRISTOLOGICAL TRADITION

C. S. Lewis: Revelation and the Christ is a work, in many ways, of Christology; that is, a study of the work and person of Christ, Jesus of Nazareth. Christology is thinking about Christ, explaining using the faculty of reason, mostly in written form, so as to explicate who and what Jesus Christ was and is. Lewis's work was very much in the context of the developed understanding of who and what Christ was; an understanding that took shape in the first seven centuries of the Christian era. As with the Bible, this understanding became something of a compass, a guide, or lodestone, as to what counts as sound doctrine about Christ and what does not. It is this body of knowledge and understanding about the Christ that judges Lewis's theology and apologetics, as it does also those of his critics. This body of knowledge of what is a traditional and orthodox understanding of Jesus Christ developed gradually during the early church, and then through the following centuries, and was complete by around the year 750 AD. Christology is therefore seen to be the study of the person and work of Christ, fully human and fully divine, historical and universal, and his significance for humanity: this systematic study is therefore the doctrine of Christ, but it must always understand the Hebrew roots into which Jesus of Nazareth was born and lived.

3. THE STUDY OF THE CHRIST

If Christology is the study of the person and work of Christ, asserting who *he* was and is, and what *he* did and continues to do, then the first books of the New Testament to be written down (Paul's epistles, specifically 1 and 2 Thessalonians, written around 50 AD to the fledgling church) give us a picture at the very beginning of this christological tradition. They are in many ways about who Jesus of Nazareth, Mary's son, was:

> For since we believe that Jesus died and rose again, even so, through Jesus, God will bring with him those who have died. For this we declare to you by the word of the Lord, that we who are alive, who are left until the coming of the Lord, will by no means precede those who have died. For the Lord himself, with a cry of command, with the archangel's call and with the sound of God's trumpet, will descend from heaven, and the dead in Christ will rise first. Then we who are alive, who are left, will be caught up in the clouds together with them to meet the Lord in the air; and so we will be with the Lord forever.
>
> 1 Thess 4:14–17

> For God has destined us not for wrath but for obtaining salvation through our Lord Jesus Christ, who died for us, so that whether we are awake or asleep we may live with him.
>
> 1 Thess 5:9–10

These documents asserted that the Jewish carpenter Jesus of Nazareth was *the* Christ, *the* Messiah, *the* Anointed One, who had come to save us; so straight away Paul was making strong assertions, doctrinal assertions about Jesus Christ. Those hearing Paul's words, his assertions, could only really understand what he was saying if they were familiar with the Jewish Scriptures. What Paul was saying would have struck a chord with them if they knew the book of Isaiah, Hosea, the Psalms, and the writings of the prophets; if they knew about the *fall* into original sin recorded and presented in Genesis 3 then what he said would have made sense to them, it would have resonated with their religious background. Without the Jewish Scriptures as shared background between Paul and his audience (for instance, when writing to converted pagans in, say, Rome, or the sea ports of Corinth and Ephesus around twenty-five years after the resurrection) it became more and more necessary for Paul to *explain* what had happened on Calvary in its historical context. This historical context is not Roman or Greek history, or Persian or Celtic history: this is Jewish salvation history. In a related vein the writer of the Letter to the Hebrews placed emphasis on the nature of Jesus as Messiah and high priest when writing to Jews who believed that Jesus was the Son of God, the Christ. Given that they were very familiar with the Jewish background the Letter to the Hebrews demonstrated to them how their Jewish heritage came together, culminated in Jesus of Nazareth. The Letter to the Hebrews presents a very high, very strong Christology; it presents an understanding of Jesus of Nazareth, as the great high priest rooted in Jewish salvation history, whose blood is the one atoning sacrificial offering for our sins, through which we are reconciled to God the Father. And in case any were in doubt as to this interpretation in the years to come, the writer of the Letter to the Hebrews asserts that, "Jesus Christ is the same yesterday and today and forever" (Heb 13:8; cf. Mal 3:6a).

This is the early church developing a way of establishing who and what this Christ was from the beginning, which in turn is the beginning of church tradition. When writing to non-Jews Paul's letters become more and more elaborate as to who this person Jesus of Nazareth is, what he did for us on the cross, what he continues to do for us, and how we should respond. Paul assumed that those hearing his letters read out in the fledgling churches believed that this Jesus was the Christ, the long-expected Messiah, the Anointed One, the Son of the Living God, the Most High descended to earth, he was crucified and rose from the dead for our salvation. The earliest Christians, many of whom had known this Jesus of Nazareth, followed him, saw him heal people, saw him preach, saw him lay down his life in one of the cruelest and most humiliating ways possible, and personally were witnesses to his resurrection, many of them formed the beginning of the church and knew that without the Spirit of this dead and resurrected Christ Jesus living in them then they could do nothing. So what they said about this Jesus of Nazareth and how they operated as the church were intimately intertwined. Paul would soon assert that the church, the followers of the Way,[4] were in fact the body of Christ.[5]

i. Trinitarian Considerations

The Christ is a person: God reveals to us; God reveals himself as trinitarian: Father, Son and Holy Spirit. This is paradoxical to humanity: how can God be simultaneously

---

4   See Acts of the Apostles 9:2, 19:9, 19:23, 24:14, 24:22.
5   "Now you are the body of Christ and individually members of it." 1 Cor 12:27. See also: "In the same way, my friends, you have died to the law through the body of Christ, so that you may belong to another, to him who has been raised from the dead in order that we may bear fruit for God." Rom 7:4; "The cup of blessing that we bless, is it not a sharing in the blood of Christ? The bread that we break, is it not a sharing in the body of Christ?" 1 Cor 10:16; and "To equip the saints for the work of ministry, for building up the body of Christ." Eph 4:12.

one and three? The Trinity is probably something humanity would not have come up with by itself because it cuts against the ingrained capacity in humanity to invent a "god" which is a singularity, a single unity (the ancient Greeks and pagans had dozens of "gods," but each was a singularity, a single unified entity to itself). The Trinity is one God: God is one holy and indivisible unity of three persons who subsist in each; three persons who exist in perpetual love.

What does this mean?—and what does it have to do with Christ? The mutual indwelling of the persons within the triune God, the very being of God, is love (Greek, αγάπη—self-giving, self-denying love); this love is the very nature of God. This communion of being within the godhead is perichoretic: that is all three persons of the triune God mutually inhere in one another, draw life from one another; they are what they are by relation to one another, and that relation is of self-giving, self-denying, love. This love is personhood and is intimate, pure and unadulterated with no loss of identity or confusion. Therefore, God is love and love is God, and this God is the coinherence of the triune persons in the divine essence and in each other. That these three persons are love implies that within the immanent Trinity[6] each ever focuses on the other and never on itself. Therefore, God cannot be a single entity, a singularity. This ever focusing on the other within the immanent Trinity is an essence of love that indwells us, flows through humanity, if humanity will allow it to. This is a dynamic and active relationship with the believer because this God comes to us: the second person of this holy and indivisible Trinity stoops in humility to come to us, be born of a virgin, suffer and die, yet be resurrected and ascend, to return to the Godhead. Why?—for our redemption. This is Christ: the second person of this holy and indivisible Trinity: God in Christ.

So, straightaway in trying to understand who Christ is, humanity must acknowledge the perilous state it is in because of the *fall* into original sin, while humanity deludes itself into believing it is whole and healthy, that it controls everything, that the measure of humanity is not God but humanity itself. God the Son comes to us to saves us from our perilous willful fallenness: we are not as we should have been, and the fault lies with us (Gen 3). We willfully disobeyed God and ate of the fruit of the knowledge of good and evil—convinced we would be gods. But all it brought us was death; enslaved to sin we ever seek to find a way out for ourselves ignoring what God in Christ has done for us on the cross. But there are those who respond: the church. And those who do respond, who acknowledge what *he* has done, are indwelt by the Holy Spirit of God the Son, the Christ.

It is important to remember that the term "Christ" is a title: Messiah, the Anointed One. The Anointed One was Jesus of Nazareth. Jesus was both fully human and fully divine: God incarnated as a human being. Jesus Christ is therefore prophet, priest, and king. Jewish expectations of the coming Messiah were mixed and varied, and it was only in the fullness of time that many realized who and what this Jesus of Nazareth was in terms of his nature and his mission. He was both Son of God and Son of Man:

---

6   The *immanent* Trinity is God within God's self, how the three persons cohere within the Godhead in themselves; the *economic* Trinity is how God deals with, relates to, humanity and creation.

1. Lewis . . . and the Christ

the second person of the Trinity proceeding from the Father, but also, equally, the Son of humanity, the new man the new creation raised from the ashes of the old Adam. As such he is not only acknowledged as God, he is God and is referred to as the Lord (in the New Testament Greek, κυρίος; in Aramaic, *mar*), this is because in the Old Testament God is revealed as the Lord. Lordship requires submission: we submit to the authority of the Lord. Jesus Christ is then not simply a "god" of speculation: lordship requires submission, obedience, servanthood on our part. The "I am" sayings in John's Gospel point to the fact that Jesus Christ is eternally begotten with the Father, that he always was, always is, and always will be, it is Christ the second person of the Trinity who was instrumental in creation, but who also bows down to be part of creation simply to save creation: the act of salvation is then part of creation. What are we to God in Christ? We are the object of his love; therefore we should simply turn and worship in love this one God in three persons, for in that worship lies our ultimate happiness.

ii. "But, Who do You Say I Am?"

The precise nature of Jesus, the Christ, is paramount and central to Lewis's apologetics and philosophical theology. What we say about this Jesus is of consequence, it is part of our faith. Lewis confronted his critics with a simple question. Given the importance of what this Jesus said and did, given the reliability of the record (the gospels) written under threat of martyrdom, then we must decide: is this Jesus God? If not then we must see him as a mad, or bad, man. So Christology is humanity trying to understand what God is and does when God is incarnated as a human being in Jesus, the Christ. Straight away Christology is about two things: *who this man is* (the person of Christ) and *what he does* (the work of Christ—primarily, the salvation of humanity, but also creation as cited in John 1). When does Christology start? It starts during Jesus's ministry here on earth. The Gospels are full of people speculating as to who he is because of what he does. During his ministry, addressing the disciples, Jesus asks who do people say that the Son of Man is. Simon Peter comments that some people think he is John the Baptist, others Elijah, and so on, but Jesus presses Peter-

> but who do you say I am?
> Simon Peter answered, "You are the Messiah, the Son of the living God."
> And Jesus answered him, "Blessed are you, Simon son of Jonah!
> For flesh and blood has not revealed this to you,
> but my Father in heaven."
>
> Matt 16:15–17; See also, Mark 8:29; Luke 9:20

What Peter is doing is making a profound christological statement: this man Jesus of Nazareth is the Messiah, the Son of the Living God, the one sent to save Israel. Jesus does not force his true identity onto the people he meets, he does the work of the Father, but it is important for people to come to a realization of who he is. Jesus of Nazareth is God incarnate, but *incognito*. So, critical observations and factual statements about Jesus of Nazareth were part of the church from the moment Peter uttered what is in later centuries to be at the heart of the creed that Christians recite in churches all over the world. Peter is therefore in many ways the father of all theologians. But, when pressed again, on the night of Jesus's arrest, he fails; worse, he denies Jesus; denies that he ever knew him. Peter could have risen to Jesus's defense, he could have drawn some of the flak away from Jesus onto himself and the other disciples—but he did not, and the others had fled. And his despair is complete. But, Peter does not drown in his despair—he repents. Peter having denied the Christ could so easily have taken his own life like Judas, who also denied Christ. Despair is therefore worse than denial, yet, like Peter, none of us should when pressed deny Christ. If Peter had in his despair committed suicide and Judas repented how different would Christian history have been? Peter, after the Ascension, when the church was at its most vulnerable, left alone—or so it seemed—in the world, is placed on the spot again: "All were constantly devoting themselves to prayer, together with certain women, including Mary the mother of Jesus, as well as his brothers: In those days Peter stood up among the believers (together the crowd numbered about one hundred twenty persons) and spoke . . ." (Acts 1:15); then when the Day of Pentecost came, Peter is fired with the Holy Spirit of this resurrected and ascended Christ and can speak, testifies, bear witness, in front of many, many strangers, from different lands and nations. It is this that is in many ways at the heart of all theology and all Christology: owning who Christ was and is.

If Peter is the father of all theologians Mary Magdalene is in many ways the mother of all theologians who try to expound on who Jesus is, for it is she who looked at the resurrected Jesus, recognized him, and called him *Rabbouni*—teacher! From that point on the church will speak of Jesus as the Christ, the savior for all humanity, but also this resurrected Christ will teach them, his Spirit will teach them and lead them into all truth: what they say will be an explication and illumination, a clarification and an exposition of the self-revelation of God in Jesus of Nazareth. They will reason about the person and work of Christ, they will write treatises, many books, many long books, millions of words. But the reality remains unchanged: who Christ was and what he did for our salvation on the cross. They will speak of the person and the saving work of Christ. They will speak of the person as human and divine, historical and universal. If Mary and Peter founded theology—or more pertinently Christology—perhaps Thomas, doubting Thomas, can also be considered as having his place in the debate about who Christ is because if all humanity simply accepted Jesus for who he is then Christology would not be necessary.

Thirty years after the Resurrection the oral tradition amongst the church of the sayings of Jesus, the accounts of the witness—those who saw Jesus—is beginning to be written down by the Gospel writers. Around thirty-five years after the Resurrection Jews in Jerusalem rebel, and the Romans stamp down ruthlessly, exiling many, destroying the Temple (fulfilling many of the prophecies of Jesus), and forcing Christians to stand on their own, no longer in the shadow of Judaism. Sixty years after the Resurrection we have important early theologians, such as the writer of the

Didache,⁷ or Ignatius of Antioch and Polycarp of Smyrna who will explicate and set out who Christ is in contrast to pagan Roman religion. These churchmen also wrote to correct error (heterodoxy, or heresy) amongst some Christians. And many of these defenders of the faith will die horribly at the hands of the Romans for doing so. Why? Because in asserting who Christ is—God incarnate, the second person of the Trinity descended to earth, born of a virgin to die for our salvation—they are marginalizing all other religions, particularly the pagan Roman religion that regarded the Emperor as divine, as a god, above all other gods. The church will grow, built on the blood of the martyrs who shared in the sufferings of Christ. After all, this Jesus Christ did leave to us the command to take up the cross and to follow him.⁸

So, from the very moment of Peter's perception of who Jesus is, from the moment of Mary Magdalene's recognition of the risen Christ we have Christology: setting out who Jesus of Nazareth was and is, that is, we have the explication of the person and work of Christ Jesus. This has been going on for nearly two thousand years and it is at the heart of the church because the church is the body of this risen and ascended Christ. So if we are going to talk about Jesus Christ, if we are going to study him, as Lewis did, so as to explain to people who he was and what he did and continues to do then we will need at some point to explain about the very nature of the church. Christology is about the self-revelation of God in Jesus of Nazareth, Jesus the Christ, it is reasoning about the person and work of Christ. Ecclesiology is about the nature of the church (*ecclesia*, for church). It relates closely to Christology because the church is the body of Christ. So what has the church said about Christ Jesus? What, if you like, is the history of Christology, the tradition Lewis wrote in?

iii. The Gospels

The Gospels are full of references to people speculating about who Jesus was. These speculations reach their peak in Peter's assertion that Jesus is the anointed Messiah, the Son of the living God. In all instances these reactions do not separate the identity of Jesus from his work. Indeed it is because of what he does—exorcisms, healing, preaching—that people begin to perceive his identity; who he is. So from the beginning

---

7   The *Didache* (from the Greek—Διδαχή—for "teaching") was the name of a short treatise (c.100–120 AD) which set-out instructions for Christian communities. It consists of three main parts: Christian instruction; forms of baptism and Eucharist; organization of the church, and authority. During the second century it was considered by some Christians as Scripture but was eventually excluded from the biblical canon. See: Louth, *Early Christian Writings*, 185–99.

8   Ignatius of Antioch (c.35–107), saint and martyr, was the third Bishop of Antioch and a student and disciple of the Apostle John, the author of the Fourth Gospel, John the Evangelist. Ignatius was arrested for being a Christian, convicted and sentenced, and transported to Rome, to the arena. Many Christians gathered around him on his journey; he wrote many letters to the churches in the region that he passed through on this journey (to the Ephesians; to the Magnesians; the Trallians; the Romans; the Philadephians; the Smyrnaeans; and to Polycarp, Bishop of Smyrna). These early documents, theological treatises, are very important for our understanding of the development of Christian theology and how the understanding of Christ was developing. Polycarp of Smyrna (c.69–c.155), saint and martyr, was Bishop of Smyrna (Izmir in Turkey). He was martyred by being stabbed whilst being burnt alive at the stake. He was also a disciple of the Apostle John. Both knew the Apostle John, studied under him, and therefore provide a first-hand connection with the Christ.

theological thinking about Jesus focused jointly on his identity (the Christ) and his function (salvation). His identity is seen, as the years pass and the church develops, as both fully human and fully divine—equally man and equally God. If either is watered down then his character and work/function suffer and our salvation is in peril. This is the crucial litmus test of all christologies: this man Jesus of Nazareth is fully human and fully divine. If you had lived two thousand years ago and saw him walking around Palestine you would have seen a man, an ordinary fully human man, but you also saw God incarnate walking the earth and healing people, exorcising demons, preaching and teaching. And if you were in Jerusalem around the year 31 AD then you might have been privileged to witness him suffer and die for your salvation. Perhaps you might have been fortunate enough to have seen him, as did many, after his resurrection, in the flesh, the very same flesh that had healed with its touch and then had been so cruelly tortured and wasted.

The New Testament was and is still the primary source for our understanding of Jesus Christ. The Gospel record shows not just how people who saw Jesus, or came into contact with him, came to the conclusion that he was the Christ, Jesus gives himself away: Jesus's action and words also incriminate him, they reveal him as God. What he says and does is what God alone should do: the culmination of this is the audacity with which he declares that people's sins are forgiven. This is tantamount to blasphemy for the Jews—particularly noted by the Pharisees (See, Matt 9:2–8; Mark 2:3–12; Luke 5:17–26 and Luke 7:36–50).

4. THE DEVELOPMENT OF PATRISTIC CHRISTOLOGY

A full and proper Christology did not arrive complete in the years after the resurrection. This understanding developed gradually, often in response to what can only be termed heresy, bad doctrine. Doctrine is important. Doctrine is about what we believe: doctrine is a set of beliefs and principles, axioms, truths, held by the church. Doctrine is about ideas and ideas lead us to form value judgments about how we behave: right doctrine leads to right behavior, in principle. Heretical doctrine is doctrine that contradicts to a greater or lesser degree this body of axiomatic truth, of belief and ethics. Christological heresy is wrong ideas about Christ, about how we behave in relation to Christ and to one another. There is therefore a gradual givenness about a sound Christology, but men and women had to struggle with their reason and the Hebrew Scriptures to defend the truth about Jesus Christ. Church tradition gradually develops as do the very books of the New Testament over the coming years: church tradition and the books of the New Testament develop simultaneously during the first decades and centuries of the church. Often the stimulus to doctrinal development is bad doctrine. That is, what Jesus was not. In contrast to the bad doctrine of heresy, orthodoxy develops. This is a constant battle that has been waged for two thousand years to keep alive the truth of what Jesus Christ was and is.

The immediate years after Christ's resurrection is the apostolic era—the era or period of the apostles, essentially the people who knew Jesus of Nazareth or were

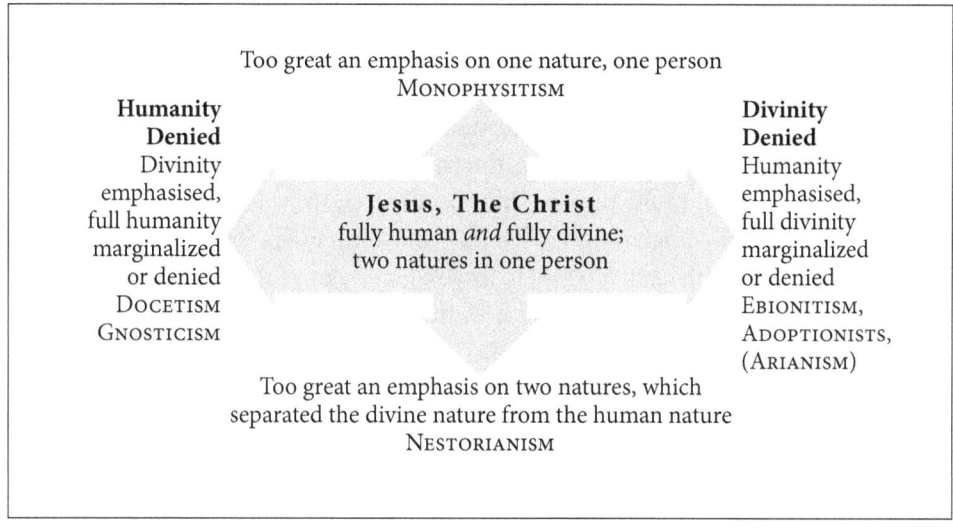

Figure 1: The Tensions That Can Affect All Christologies.

of his generation, all of whom had died by around the year 100 AD. We then have the sub-apostolic era, which is essentially the second century, then fully the patristic era. The development of this understanding of Christ in the subsequent centuries is called patristic Christology. The church leaders and theologians of this period are called patristic—from the Greek for fathers πατήρ, πατρός, *patēr, patros*—hence the theology of these centuries is patristic, formed by the early church fathers.

i. Humanity and Divinity

The earliest debates in a developing doctrine of the person of Christ centered on his humanity and his divinity. Two of the earliest heresies that had to be challenged and overcome were Ebionitism and Docetism. The Ebionites (from the Greek, Ἐβιωναῖοι, *ebionaioi*, for poor ones, derived from the Hebrew, *ebyonim*) were an early Jewish Christian sect that followed Jewish religious rituals and law; crucially they regarded Jesus as fully human but not divine, they also revered him as a messianic prophet, that is one who was inspired by hope for the Messiah, by belief and expectation of the Messiah, but who was not himself divine. Therefore the Ebionites saw Jesus as an ordinary human being, that he was not really divine (in the intertestamental period messiahship did not necessarily carry with it claims of divinity). The Ebionites were regarded by the early church fathers as heretics in not accepting the divinity of Jesus, but also for contradicting what they thought the Apostle Paul had established with regard to the relationship between law and faith (in the Epistle to the Romans and to the Galatians), by seeking to re-establish the centrality of the Jewish law. On the other hand, the Docetists believed Jesus was not really human, his humanity was only an appearance—hence the title, Docetism (from the Greek verb δοκέω, *dokeō*, which meant to appear or to seem to be). The Docetists believed that Jesus's human body of flesh was a chimera, and so in the crucifixion he only *seemed* to suffer and die, that he was really incorporeal, a pure spirit, and hence could not physically die. So, to the Docetists, Jesus only appeared to suffer, and therefore from an orthodox perspective we are still lost in original sin: the atonement was not really real. In both instances whether a Docetic or an Ebionite Christ, the true nature is out of balance: Christ is not equally fully human and fully divine. These tendencies, these heresies, are perennial. For example, many theologians, philosophers, and churchmen in nineteenth-century Germany wrote at length in an attempt to forge a picture of a fully human Jesus, a Jesus of history that denied the Christ of faith as they saw it, who was solely human, but who had a special sense of God as his father, a sense of the divine to a greater degree than other people. This was in effect a Germanic version of the Jewish Ebionite Jesus. This non-Christian, solely human, Jesus was celebrated in German civic religious art where Jesus was often reduced to a mere human presented with neo-Classical imagery derived from Greek and Roman culture: for example, the early painting of Max Klinger, *Christ on Mount Olympus*, where Jesus is portrayed as a pale-skinned, blonde-haired wise Germanic religious leader conversing with young Greek men and women.[9]

ii. Justin Martyr and Logos Christology

Born around the year 100 AD in Flavia, Neaplois in Samaria, Justin Martyr was so named because he was martyred by the Romans in the year 165 AD for not believing in god (i.e., the Emperor as god to whom Justin was required to sacrifice), and worshiping a man as God: Jesus Christ. Justin sought to show how Jesus was the Christ and was truly man and truly God. Raised as a pagan he studied philosophy, taught philosophy (he wore the pallium, the philosopher's gown), then converted to Christianity, thereafter he dedicated his life to teaching Christianity as the true philosophy. He continued to wear the pallium to point out that he had reached the Truth in Christ. He sought to teach the rationality of the gospel, how Jesus was the Messiah, God's word, his Logos because as the opening chapter of John's Gospel asserted, "the word became flesh and dwelt among us" (John 1:14). The Logos was seen as the enveloping principle of rationality in the universe in Greek philosophy (an idea essentially derived from the Stoics). John knew this when he wrote his Gospel: "In the beginning was the Word (Greek, λόγος) . . ." (John 1:1). Justin Martyr therefore claimed that Christ Jesus was not only or merely human, but was the eternal and universal Word/Logos of God. This was why there was a virginal conception: he was human yet also equally God. Therefore he should be worshipped and named Lord for he was the Logos of God. Justin thus founded in many ways what is called Logos Christology, which was a way of explicating how Jesus was the Christ and was both fully human and fully divine.[10] The one Logos of God is known, said Justin, by Greek pagan philosophers as *reason*, by Christians as *Lord*, and by the ancient Hebrews in the *law*. Christ was therefore known

---

9   Max Klinger, *Christ on Mount Olympus* (1897).
10   See, Justin Martyr's *First Apology*, specifically §§. 1–12. Justin is essentially drawing on Stoic philosophy and Middle Platonism in asserting Jesus as the *Logos* (exactly the word in the opening of John's Gospel), but Jesus was also not just the *Logos* but also the *nomos* (νόμος: Greek, for the law) of the ancient Hebrews.

implicitly amongst the ancient Hebrews and the ancient philosophers; however, Christians have the fullest and the most profound understanding because of their encounter with Christ both historical (the Jesus of history) and universal (the Spirit of the resurrected Christ that indwells his people, his followers, his church). For Justin the Greek pagan philosophers had only an incomplete and fragmented understanding of Christ the Logos (Lewis saw Plato's suffering servant as just such an intimation), however, for Justin the Logos had sowed seeds (he used the term *logos spermatikos*—λόγος σπερματικὸς—derived from Middle Platonism) throughout human history and therefore Christ was known in part, implicitly, and in fragments of revelation, amongst different peoples at different times. (Again, a strong point of confluence with Lewis—his doctrine of christological prefigurement highlighted the evidence of elements of the incarnation-resurrection narrative in North European Pagan myths, amongst other world religious traditions.) Christianity is therefore the culmination and conclusion of all these philosophies and religions, many of which anticipated the Truth. So, Justin Martyr is presenting not reason or law alone, but a person—both fully human and fully divine—as the fullest revelation of God, a revelation that the ancient Hebrew law makers and the ancient pagan philosophers could point towards, could glimpse.[11]

iii. Irenaeus and the Gnostics

Irenaeus of Lyons whose life spanned the second century (c.110–c.190) was the second Bishop of Lugdunum in Gaul (now Lyon, France) whose writings were crucial in establishing the sound doctrinal basis of the faith.[12] In terms of the early development of Christian theology he is an important father of the church, notable as a Christian apologist. He was also a disciple of Polycarp, which gave him a spiritual and doctrinal connection to John (the Gospel writer), and hence Jesus. Irenaeus wrote many works but the most important is the five-volume *Against Heresies* (*Adversus Haereses*, often called *On the Detection and Overthrow of the So-Called Gnosis*), which was a systematic refutation of the Gnostic heresy. The Gnostic heresy was a complex mythology with various levels of gods or aeons. Irenaeus stressed the unity of God, the indivisibility, equality yet distinctiveness as persons of the Father, the Son, and the Spirit: the Holy Trinity. He referred to the Son and the Spirit as the hands of God. Christ the Son was fully God and fully human, not a lesser god, or only partially human in varying degrees as different Gnostic sects emphasized. He also stressed how Christian knowledge and truth was not esoteric and secretive, it was not complex and individualistic. Salvation is not therefore available only to an elite with special access to secret knowledge (Greek: γνῶσις, *gnōsis*—knowledge) as the Gnostics believed. At the centre

---

11   This was brought out at its clearest in Justin Martyr's *Second Apology*, which was a supplement to his first apology and was written specifically for a Roman Senator by Justin in an attempt to justify his beliefs as a Christian. It was written probably ten years before his martyrdom, therefore around 154–57 AD.

12   Irenaeus of Lyons was born a Greek in Polycarp's home town of Smyrna who was raised a Christian rather than being an adult convert. See: Roberts, *et al* (eds.) *The Early Church Fathers: Ante-Nicene Fathers*, Vol. 1.

of Irenaeus's apology is his understanding of Christ. Irenaeus argued that Christ would always have come even if people had not been subject to original sin. However, because of the *fall* sin determines his role as the savior; Jesus Christ is the new Adam, who overcomes original sin through obedience in contrast to Eve and Adam's disobedience (eating the fruit of the tree of the knowledge of good and evil). Therefore, Christ was obedient even to death on the cross, the wood of a tree. In addition he compares Eve and Mary, developing Mariology in the process, contrasting Eve's disobedience with Mary's obedience. In addition Christ is seen by Irenaeus as the sum of human life, by living a fully human life, Christ sanctifies humanity. Therefore, the incarnation of God as a man—Irenaeus places a very high emphasis on Christ as fully God and fully man—is crucial to our salvation. The Gnostic Christ was essentially Docetic because the full humanity of Jesus was denied. In contrast to the Gnostics, Irenaeus asserted that humanity received corruption and death as a penalty for original sin; God is incorruptible and immortal: incarnation is essential for atonement, the uniting of God with humanity.

5. CREEDAL CHRISTOLOGY

i. The Proto Creed

Creeds—definitions of faith—are an important part of the work of the church in the world; they were also the chief weapon, in many ways, for the early church against error, false belief, and corruption. Creeds start as statements of recognition. Statements of belief have always been, from earliest days of infant church. When the followers huddled in secret groups in upper rooms in Jerusalem, Damascus, Emmaus, they did not have a creed as such. However, doubting Thomas's declaration, "my Lord and my God," (John 20:28) is, if not creedal, doctrinal as it is rooted in a recognition of a reality and truth outside of an individual human ego. Creeds are a test of belief, a declaration of faith. They are axiomatic statements, propositions; they are a declaration that serves as a test of belief, of what is, what had happened, and what is to come. Paul writing to the church in Rome in his famous epistle quotes what is probably a proto-creed at the very beginning of his letter—to show his credentials. Paul quotes what was probably known to the early church in Rome as an acceptable definition of the faith:

> Paul, a servant of Christ Jesus, called to be an apostle, set apart *for the gospel of God, which he promised beforehand through his prophets in the holy Scriptures, concerning his Son, who was descended from David according to the flesh and was declared to be the Son of God in power according to the Spirit of holiness by his resurrection from the dead, Jesus Christ our Lord*, through whom we have received grace and apostleship to bring about the obedience of faith for the sake of his name among all the nations, including you who are called to belong to Jesus Christ, To all those in Rome who are loved by God and called to be saints: Grace to you and peace from God our Father and the Lord Jesus Christ.
>
> Rom 1:1–7 (My emphasis.)

The Apostles Creed

I believe in God, the Father almighty,
  creator of heaven and earth.

I believe in Jesus Christ, his only Son, our Lord.

He was conceived by the power of the Holy Spirit
  and born of the Virgin Mary.

He suffered under Pontius Pilate,
  was crucified, died, and was buried.

He descended into hell.

On the third day he rose again.

He ascended into heaven
  and is seated at the right hand of the Father.

He will come again to judge the living and the dead.

I believe in the Holy Spirit,
  the holy Catholic Church,
  the communion of saints,
  the forgiveness of sins,
  the resurrection of the body,
  and the life everlasting.

Amen.

Figure 2: The Apostles' Creed

So, we have the prophecy of the Old Testament, the eternal Sonship of the Messiah Jesus, his lineage from David as Son of Man, his revelation as Son of God through his resurrection, the Holy Spirit of holiness encompassed in the title, "Jesus Christ our Lord." This Christ Jesus whom Paul serves is equally Son of Man and Son of God: he is fully human and fully divine. This proto creed is also implicitly trinitarian.

ii. The Apostles' Creed

The Apostle's Creed is the first proper creed as such—the *symbolum apostolorum* as it was often known. The exact origins of it are lost in the mists of time, but it is referred to from early on as the statement of faith of the apostles, therefore it probably grew from the time of the apostles from a basic assertion of the incarnation, crucifixion, and resurrection. It is therefore a relatively simple statement of faith and outlines the barebones of Christology, beliefs that were present in and amongst the disciples and apostles from the resurrection and from the time they met in the upper room. The Apostle's Creed is the first of such creeds and it probably assumed the form we now have it in from some time in the early second century, around the time of the church's initial counter measures against Gnosticism: The Apostle's Creed lacked the christological sophistication that we find in later creeds, however, most of the later creeds are expansions of the Creed of the Apostles. That it is a refutation of Gnosticism is written into the creed throughout: this is why it emphasizes that Jesus was the Christ and that he was born, suffered, crucified, and died; he did not materialize as an apparition, he did not only *seem* to suffer, he did not only *appear* to die. The Christ of the Apostle's Creed was fully human and fully divine; he really did suffer and die: this was in the tradition of the apostles' and was pronounced to defend the gospel.[13]

6. ARIANISM

Irenaeus' work is very much a reaction against the popularity of Gnosticism. This is often how doctrine gets formulated in the church: as apologetics in response to heresy. Arianism—probably one of the most widespread and insidious of christological heresies to emerge—is typical of popular false beliefs: they are usually, say, around 90 percent right, with just a few components wrong, enough to create a false picture but not enough for most Christians to see the whole as bogus or counterfeit, spurious or corrupting. As with so many early heresies Arianism is characterized by an imbalance between Christ as fully God and fully man. In this instance, Christ's divinity is compromised. So what was Arianism about? Arius (c.256–336) was a Christian priest in Alexandria who became embroiled in a dispute that escalated. This was a doctrinal dispute about the nature of Jesus Christ. Arius argued that the Son was not consubstantial (that is, of the same substance or essence) as the Father; but he also argued that the Son was not coeternal (that is, that he had always been) with the Father. The controversy became, in a word, global: i.e., it affected the whole Christian world. In his defense Arius and his supporters claimed that the Word/Logos and the Father were not of the same essence/substance (Greek: οὐσία, ousia), in addition that the Son was created; created before the universe, created before anything that exists was created, for all was created through him, but—and Arius was very careful here—there was when the Son was not. Essentially Arius argued that there was when Christ was not. Note—he carefully avoided any word to do with time. He argued that there was a once when the Logos of God, the second person of the Trinity, did not exist. He was therefore not eternally begotten of the Father but created, for once he was not: the Logos had a beginning. Traditional Christology had established that the relation of the Son to the Father had no beginning, that the three persons of the Trinity were coeternal—existed from and through eternity without beginning—that the Son was

---

13   Most scholars see the Apostle's Creed developing from what was termed "The Old Roman Symbol" of the first and second centuries, and the earliest extant copies are in Latin, which is unusual when Greek was the language of the scriptures and of the early church until the later fourth century, therefore the Apostle's Creed may, or probably, originated amongst the Christians of the church in Rome, perhaps it was even begun to be formulated around the time Peter and Paul were in Rome: "*Credo in Deum Patrem omnipotentem, Creatorem caeli et terrae. Et in Iesum Christum, Filium Eius unicum, Dominum nostrum, qui conceptus est de Spiritu Sancto, natus ex Maria Virgine, passus sub Pontio Pilato, crucifixus, mortuus, et sepultus, descendit ad ínferos, tertia die resurrexit a mortuis, ascendit ad caelos, sedet ad dexteram Dei Patris omnipotentis, inde venturus est iudicare vivos et mortuos. Credo in Spiritum Sanctum, sanctam Ecclesiam catholicam, sanctorum communionem, remissionem peccatorum, carnis resurrectionem, vitam aeternam. Amen.*"

THE NICENE CREED

We believe in one God, the Father Almighty,

Maker of all things visible and invisible.

And in one Lord Jesus Christ, the Son of God, begotten of the Father, the only-begotten;

that is, of the substance/essence (Greek homoousios) *of the Father,*

God of God, Light of Light, very God of very God, begotten, not made, being of one substance with the Father;

by whom all things were made both in heaven and on earth;

who for us men, and for our salvation, came down and was incarnate and was made man;

he suffered, and the third day he rose again, ascended into heaven; from thence he shall come to judge the quick and the dead . . .

Figure 3 : The Nicene Creed

eternally begotten and therefore uncreated (John 1:1–3). Arianism effectively made Christ less than fully divine, not fully God. One of the most insidious elements of Arianism was that it claimed to read this from Scripture—from a highly selective reading of certain verses in the New Testament, often taken out of context. To Arius and his followers the Son is a creature, the term Son is then to be seen as a metaphor which gives him status over all other creatures, this is from the will of the Father, not because the Son is a person: to many of Arius' opponents this reduced Christ to no more than a Gnostic aeon, a lesser "god".

7. CHURCH COUNCILS

i. *The Nicene Creed*

Athanasius of Alexandria (293–373 AD) emerged as the champion of an orthodox, traditional, Christology and with it our understanding of the Trinity. The Arian controversy affected all of the church. This was in the early fourth century, by which time the Emperor Constantine had approved of Christianity and elevated it to the status of the official religion in the Roman Empire: from this point on the Emperor is not divine—Christ Jesus is. Constantine convened a Council of bishops and leaders to sort out the controversy: The Council of Nicaea, held initially in 325 AD. The history, decisions, and conclusions of Nicaea led to Arius being repudiated, and a traditional orthodox statement about the Trinity, about Christ, a summary of the faith, was produced by the Council—The Nicene Creed—which is still recited communally in a later form in churches today as a declaration of faith. The creed was the sum of the long detailed debates at the Council, it also became the means by which orthodoxy was defined, peace regained in the church, and the Arian controversy eventually dealt with. As Lewis's debate with W. Norman Pittenger proved, the issues involved and these deliberations are not obscure theological discussions over hair-splitting details, which have no relevance to the lives of the faithful; these debates dealt with what is at the heart of the faith and therefore at the heart of redemption—our salvation! It is very important to realize just how important these debates were, and how important they are today as well, how relevant they are to today's church because these erroneous beliefs have not gone away, heresy is perennial. And what we believe is important: intellectual sins, that is sins of ideas, are at the root of all sin. We are saved by faith in Christ's sacrifice. And faith is built on, defined by, what we believe.

Athanasius became the focus of opposition to Arius and Arianism. Athanasius' logic stated that no creature could redeem; if according to Arius Jesus Christ had been created, was a creature, then Jesus Christ could not redeem/save. Furthermore Athanasius argued that only God can save; Jesus Christ saves, therefore Jesus Christ is God. This is only a sketch of the Arian controversy and the work of the Council of Nicaea—which was as heavily recorded by scribes as a government committee is today—but it is at the heart of traditional/orthodox creedal Christianity to this day

ii. "What has not been assumed has not been healed"

Needless to say there were disputes even within the traditional/orthodox peace established at Nicaea, but distinction then was essentially focused on details; thus we find Antiochene (i.e., based on the city of Antioch, in Asia Minor—modern Turkey) and Alexandrian (based on theologians in the city of Alexandria in Egypt) schools of Christology. The Alexandrians—with whom Athanasius was associated—emphasized the importance of the incarnation because redemption means *being taken up* into God, into the divine life (Lewis's motif of Christ descending to reascend with humanity); therefore it was essential that the Word became flesh, that God became incarnate with humanity, which changes the very nature of all of humanity, through faith. Therefore questions about the relationship between Christ's divinity and Christ's humanity became important. Cyril of Alexandria wrote on how the Logos became enfleshed at the incarnation, creating one nature both human and divine in Christ. By comparison the Antiochene school of Christology emphasized two natures—the human and the divine. So what kind of nature did Christ have? What effect did human weaknesses have on the nature of Jesus Christ? Apollinarius of Laodicea (c.310-390 AD) argued that the Son of God could not be allowed to be tainted, contaminated by sinful human nature: the sinlessness essential for our salvation would be affected. For Apollinaris, the mind of Christ must have been replaced by a divine will, so that there was a divine mind and soul. The problem was that on this account only part of human nature was assumed at the incarnation. The Christ therefore was not fully human (the old heresy raising its ugly head again). Gregory of Nazianzus (329-389) countered with the proposition that all of human nature had to be appropriated at the incarnation otherwise our salvation is imperiled: "What has not been assumed has not been healed"[14] was in many ways his rallying cry, which has been a principle of Christology down the centuries to today.

iii. Antioch and Alexandria

Alexandrian Christology (which strongly relied on Greek philosophy) emphasized the importance of salvation and an understanding of Christ, which ensured the full, unimpeded redemption of humanity through the incarnation. Antiochene Christology by comparison with the Alexandrian school emphasized moral aspects: obedience. Christ gained our salvation because he was obedient, obedient even unto death. Humanity could not redeem itself through an act of will, it was too corrupt. But with the coming of Christ a new obedient people of God is established. Therefore it is important to recognize the two natures in Christ: a perfect divine nature and a perfect human nature, there is still a perfect unity of the two. This perfect unity in the incarnation allows for the obedience of the human will without it being blotted out by the divine. However, critics still argued that this led to two Sons, a split personality? Debates about the *person* in Christ, one nature or two, were never fully resolved, questions remained. Lewis alludes to the difficulties early on in his apologetics,[15] which Pittenger tries to use against him—unsuccessfully.[16]

iv. The Council of Ephesus

The Council of Ephesus in 431 AD dealt, amongst other things, with the relation of Mary to the Christ and her status, affirming the Greek title *Theotokos* (θεοτόκος); literally, "God-bearer" (Greek: θεος, *theos*: God; τόκος, *tokos*: bearer), though most often translated as "Mother of God." The Council insisted that the holy Fathers were right in calling the holy virgin *Theotokos*. At the end of this particular session of the Council, historians record that large crowds of men, women, and children marched through the streets of Ephesus calling-out: "Praise be to the *Theotokos*!" Those who objected to the title Mother of God arguing that it was impossible for a woman to create and give birth to God had to accept the innate paradox of the title, or reject the full divinity of Christ: either Jesus born of Mary was the Christ, was God incarnate, therefore our redemption was secure, or he was not God, was not divine and thus our salvation is in peril. The Council of Ephesus also dealt with Nestorianism, which had been seen to over separate the two natures of Christ—the divine and human natures—into two separate persons.

8. CONSTANTINOPLE, AUGUSTINE, AND PELAGIANISM

Discussion about the nature of the divine and human elements within Christ was to dominate christological debate for some considerable time. The Council of Nicaea established, it may be said, the parameters of what was acceptable traditional/orthodox

---

14 Gregory of Nazianzus, Letter no. 101, to Cledonius.
15 Lewis, *The Problem of Pain* (1940), 110.
16 Pittenger, "Apologist versus Apologist", 1107.

thought, and what was not. The Council of Constantinople in 360 AD focused on the question of whether the Son was of the same substance as the Father or only similar: in the Greek, ὁμοούσιος (homoousios—the same substance or essence) or ὁμοιούσιος (homoiousios—of similar substance or essence). This was taken further by the Council of Constantinople in 381 AD, which reaffirmed and ratified the Nicene Creed as well as making clearer what was and was not acceptable Christology.

During the early fifth century the work of Christ was imperiled by an insidious belief known as Pelagianism. Pelagianism was named after a British monk, Pelagius (c. 354–c. 430). Pelagius argued that Adam's *fall*, that original sin, did not contaminate and infect human nature, therefore Adam and Eve's *fall* was a bad example for the rest of humanity but Adam's deed did not lead to the infected corruption of all of humanity: a human will is still capable of choosing good or evil without God's aid in the form of grace. We can, therefore, pull ourselves up by our own shoelaces or bootstraps, so to speak! Pelagians see Jesus as a role model; he sets a good example for humanity. Therefore humanity can save itself, rendering Christ's propitiating (to win, or regain favor, to appease) and atoning (reconciling) sacrifice on the cross as unnecessary. The great church father Augustine of Hippo (354–430) was the champion of orthodoxy in asserting that because of the corrupting effects of *fallen* and willful human nature we can do nothing for ourselves: for our own salvation.

> I do not understand my own actions. For I do not do what I want, but I do the very thing I hate. Now if I do what I do not want, I agree that the law is good. But in fact it is no longer I that do it, but sin that dwells within me. For I know that nothing good dwells within me, that is, in my flesh. I can will what is right, but I cannot do it. For I do not do the good I want, but the evil I do not want is what I do. Now if I do what I do not want, it is no longer I that do it, but sin that dwells within me. So I find it to be a law that when I want to do what is good, evil lies close at hand. For I delight in the law of God in my inmost self, but I see in my members another law at war with the law of my mind, making me captive to the law of sin that dwells in my members. Wretched man that I am! Who will rescue me from this body of death? Thanks be to God through Jesus Christ our Lord! So then, with my mind I am a slave to the law of God, but with my flesh I am a slave to the law of sin.
>
> Rom 7:15–25

Only through the cross and through Christ's Spirit indwelling in grace can we achieve anything. Christ's work is essential for our salvation. Augustine established our utter dependence on Christ's propitiating and atoning sacrifice, and that only through God's grace working in us can we do anything of value.

9. THE CHALCEDONIAN CREED

The Council of Chalcedon in 451 AD was important because it finally came up with a formula to deal with the "two natures/one nature" dispute. Chalcedon rejected the Eutychian doctrine of monophysitism, which stressed the single nature of Christ, that the two natures were assimilated so that the human side was deified forming a new

The Chalcedonian Creed

Wherefore, following the holy Fathers, we all with one voice confess our Lord Jesus Christ one and the same Son,

the same perfect in Godhead, the same perfect in manhood, truly God and truly man, the same consisting of a reasonable soul and a body,

of one substance with the Father as touching the Godhead,

the same of one substance with us as touching the manhood,

ike us in all things apart from sin;

begotten of the Father before the ages as touching the Godhead,

the same in the last days, for us and for our salvation,

born from the Virgin Mary, the Theotokos,

as touching the manhood, one and the same Christ, Son, Lord,

Only-begotten, to be acknowledged in two natures, without confusion, without change, without division, without separation;

the distinction of natures being in no way abolished because of the union, but rather the characteristic property of each nature being preserved, and concurring into one Person and one subsistence (Greek: hypostasis),

not as if Christ were parted or divided into two persons, but one and the same Son and only-begotten God, Word, Lord, Jesus Christ;

even as the Prophets from the beginning spoke concerning him, and our Lord Jesus Christ instructed us, and the Creed of the Fathers has handed down to us.

Figure 4 : The Chalcedonian Creed

hybrid nature: this was called Eutychianism (more commonly called Monophysitism). The Council also set forth the Chalcedonian Creed asserting the full humanity and full divinity of Jesus Christ, the incarnate Son of God, fully God and fully human, the second person of the holy Trinity: the divine nature and the human nature created *one person*, the Christ. The Chalcedon declaration of faith—for such is a creed—is often seen as a compromise, the statement about two natures in one person is seen as a compromise, it is seen as a play on words, but it did settle the dust so to speak, it did appear to end most of the arguments. After Chalcedon attention focused onto details, the basic framework for sound Christology had been established. An inordinate amount of time and energy was focused on the *Anhypostasia/Enhypostasia* issue, most of which, while establishing a sound relationship between flesh and spirit, often seems obscure today.[17] For example:

---

17   *Anhypostatis/enhypostatis* (ἀνυπόστασις –ἐνυπόστασις): in patristic Christology the Greek word *hypostasis* (ὑπόστασις) is used to denote *being, a state of being*, and theologically is closely related to the use of the Greek word, *ousia* (ουσία)—essence. The prefix *an-* (ἀν-) denotes a state of being without a *hypostasis*, and represents the doctrine that although Jesus had two natures, divine and human, these are united in a single person (*hypostasis*); this implied that the human *hypostasis* is replaced by the divine *hypostasis*. The prefix *en-* (ἐν-)denotes a teaching after Chalcedon that claimed that Jesus Christ did indeed have a human *hypostasis* that was taken up into the *hypostasis* of the divine *Logos*, the second person of the Trinity.

> Anhypostasia (the word means literally the "state of being without a hypostasis") is the doctrine that although Jesus Christ had two natures, a divine and a human (as Chalcedon teaches), these "concur" or are united in a single person (hypostasis), and this person is the divine Logos, so that the human hypostasis is superseded and replaced by the hypostasis of the divine Logos. Jesus Christ therefore is without a human hypostasis. Enhypostasia, a doctrine which arose later as a modification of anhypostasia, concedes that Jesus Christ did indeed have a human hypostasis, but it was taken up and included in the hypostasis of the Logos. Thus baldly stated, these notions are not only hard to understand, but it may be even less clear how they can help us towards a better understanding of the God-man. Yet these are stages through which the search for understanding has historically moved . . .[18]

The question is therefore raised as to how much value there is in this detailed argumentation, post-Chalcedon.

10. THE MOMENT OF THE INCARNATION

During the sixth and seventh centuries there was still further development focused on very particular detail—which maintained the balance between Christ Jesus being fully divine and fully human, even if such decisions flew in the face of ancient Greek scientific theories: for example, the question of ensoulment. Maximus the Confessor (c.580–662 AD) wrote on and established Christ's human beginning. The principle of human ensoulment had been established according to rather spurious grounds by Aristotle and ancient Greek philosopher-scientists centuries earlier (that the soul is only given to a human after several weeks of development in the womb), but they were deemed wrong in the light of the revelation of God. The full predicament of humanity becomes clear in the Word incarnate—only in the light of what God does in Christ Jesus do we fully appreciate our predicament, our *fallen* status. Maximus the Confessor asked what the moment of the incarnation reveals: "It confirmed what he already believed on other grounds, namely, that the rational soul of man, which is not generated by his parents, is created immediately by God and infused into the body at the *moment of conception* (in modern jargon, the doctrine of 'immediate animation')."[19]

For Maximus, contrary to a drift amongst many church theologians who were beginning to see a human as a soul using a body, all men and women are a unity of soul

---

18 John Macquarrie, *Christology Revisited*, 44–45.
19 Saward, *Redeemer in the Womb*, 8. On the question of the moment at which soul and body are united, Maximus wrote in the *Second Ambigua* to contradict earlier teachings (for example, the Origenist teaching that the soul exists before the body, also, the Aristotelian teaching that the body exists before the soul) and to deal with certain ambiguities in Gregory of Nazianzus' writings. Maximus rejected both Origen and Aristotle's teachings, asserting that soul is created by God and infused into the body in the very instant of conception. See: Maximus the Confessor, *Ambigua* 2.42, in, Migne, *Patrologia Graeca*, Vol. 91, 1324C; see also, *Ambigua* 2.7, in, Vol. 91, 1101A; also, references to Maximus in Migne, Vol. 3 & 4. For a modern translation see, Berthold, *Maximus Confessor: Selected Writings*. For modern scholarship on Maximus and these issues see, Von Balthasar, *Cosmic Liturgy*, and, Cooper, *The Body in St Maximus Confessor*.

TRINITARIAN TENSION

Modalism		Polytheism
The danger with Modalism is that the Trinity is just a way of saying that God appears or does things in three different modes. The Son is only an appearance—or mode—of God. The three persons of the Trinity do not therefore co-exist in or as the One God.	The Trinity is one God in three persons, not three separate gods, and not one god expressed in three different ways or modes. Christ Jesus, the Logos, is the second person of the Trinity, eternally begotten from all eternity, incarnated as a human being	Too great a degree of individuality leads to three separate "gods" making Jesus Christ either human or a lesser "god". It also means that the father "god" brutalises and kills the son, the lesser "god".

Figure 5: The Tensions Inherent in the Doctrine of the Trinity

and body.[20] This wholeness is from the beginning, from the moment of conception: what is true for humanity is true for the Christ; what is true for Jesus born of Mary is true for all men and women. If Christ Jesus's soul was not the result of immediate animation, then his humanity is optional; if Jesus Christ was not fully human from the point of his conception then, again, our salvation is in peril. If Jesus Christ was fully human (ensouled—immediate animation) from the point of his conception, but we are not (delayed ensoulment), then this separates humanity from the Christ and, again, our salvation is incomplete, in peril. Furthermore, Maximus identified that behind the theory of later ensoulment was a Manichee aversion, a loathing, a repugnance, for associating the higher elements of the human—the intellect, and so on—with the messiness of sex (mating) and bodily fluids. This begins to deny the Incarnation, deny that the Word was made flesh: delayed ensoulment points to a Docetic Christ, which seems to be human, fleshly, but is really only inhabiting a human form temporarily.

11. MODERN CHRISTOLOGY

The consensus of agreement on the person and nature of the Christ in whose person lies our salvation that was laid out by the first six ecumenical councils (including Nicaea, Constantinople, and Chalcedon) established the faith of the church. None of this was really questioned in any detail even during the fraught and fought over times of the

---

20 The Greek concept and word is *holos, holon.*, Maximus uses the term εἶδος ὅλον (*eidos holon*—a complete whole), a complete entity, or, ἐκπλέρθσις (*ekplerosis*—completeness). The Greek word ὅλος (*holos*) implies that something is simultaneously a whole and a part, hence Maximus's use of the term evokes dialectic and paradox—the soul and body are simultaneously parts and a whole, a complete entity, yet separately divisible and identifiable. In terms of twentieth century philosophy, a *holon* is simultaneously a whole and a part and refers to phenomena that are whole in themselves, but are also part of a larger system, a *holon* is embedded in larger *holons*, which influence it whilst it influences the greater. A model of this is sub-atomic particles, molecules, matter and objects, and the universe.

Reformation: all sides in the sixteenth century (the Protestant Reformation churches and Rome's Counter Reformation, essentially the Council of Trent) accepted the canon of Scripture, the Creeds, and the ecumenical councils. These Creeds, councils, and Scriptures represented the givenness—given by God—of the truth; this was revealed truth. It was with the Age of Reason and the dawn of the period of the Enlightenment in the seventeenth and eighteenth centuries that this consensus was challenged. Many intellectuals—historians, philosophers, and theologians—sought to reduce the divine status of Jesus Christ, in many instances to deny Jesus as God incarnate completely.[21] Many sought to redefine the Christ as an ordinary human being. This mirrors the rise of Deism and Theism, a return to the concept of God as a monist singularity, a distant "god," unified and pure in oneness. Much of this critique came from central European theologians while the Church of England reduced itself, in many ways, to a cultural wing of the British establishment and ignored such questions. In this context it was left to the Roman Catholic, the Eastern Orthodox, and the Non-Conformist and Evangelical churches to witness to Christ's truth, along with lone prophets such as the Danish philosopher Søren Kierkegaard and the Russian writer Fyodor Dostoevsky. The ground of this Enlightenment critique claimed to be rationalist but was essentially humanist: humanity was at the centre, humanity was the measure of all; "god"—if there was one—was allowed to exist if humanity deemed, approved, "god" to be. Within this a distinction is driven between the Jesus of history and the Christ of faith. There was then, particularly in nineteenth-century theology, a desire, a quest, to find out who this man Jesus of Nazareth was if the church's witness was to be rejected? Within this quest for the historic Jesus many even sought to deny that Jesus was a Jew: Jesus was recast, redefined, as a bourgeois, cultured, enlightened white European. The writer George Tyrrell S. J. said about this Jesus that it "is only the reflection of a Liberal Protestant face, seen at the bottom of a deep well."[22] The authority of the Bible was demolished; historians claimed that the Gospels were inaccurate and unreliable and sought to try paint what they saw to be a "true" portrait of Jesus: the historical Jesus which the Christ of faith had smothered over. However, after two hundred years no one has managed to recapture/reconstruct this merely human Jesus of a Western liberal mindset. During this time Bishops and theologians, priests and clergy were effectively split into two broad, overlapping, camps: those who subscribed to the Creeds, the Scriptures, and church authority, and those who did not. There have been good creedal orthodox/traditional bishops and priests, theologians, and ordinary Christians in this modern era, but their witness was so often drowned out by the skeptics, by the zeitgeist, the spirit of the age, in a world that sought ever more and more to define truth in its own *fallen* and willful image.

---

21 For a survey of how Enlightenment and post Enlightenment thinkers in, essentially, Western Europe and North America have critiqued traditional Christology see: Macquarrie, *Jesus Christ in Modern Thought*.

22 Tyrrell, *Christianity at the Cross-Roads*, 45–49, see specifically, 46.

1. Lewis . . . and the Christ

It was into this cultural and theological context that C. S. Lewis spoke. His passions and concerns can only be fully appreciated when understood against the background of the theological narrative set out in this chapter. He spoke as one calling the church back to the "faith once for all delivered to the saints."

12. LEWIS'S CHRIST; LEWIS'S CHRISTOLOGY

Therefore, we may ask, what do we make of Lewis's understanding of Jesus Christ, the incarnation of the one true living God, against the background of the theological/christological narrative set out in this chapter? How do we assess the rare accusations by some professional theologians/writers that there are elements of christological heresy in some of Lewis's writings? How do we define/categorize Lewis's objective understanding of Christ, and likewise his subjective appropriation? What christological model does Lewis draw in our minds? Lewis's Christ, that is the picture he gives us in his Christology, is essentially a picture in words, narrative that generates an understanding in our minds. This is a Christ from below, not primarily from above because it starts with Immanuel, God with us, with the human, Jesus of Nazareth. This is balanced, initiated, by a shift (a Platonic shift for Lewis) from eternity into our reality: the Christ descends to raise us up; in doing so we are drawn into the divine life. However, humanity is not overwhelmed by Christ, for *he* is the loving servant, but *he* is authoritative in *his* divine claim on all creation, a creation that, for Lewis, Christ sang into being, into existence, *ex nihilo* (out of nothing).[23] Lewis's Christology is therefore high—this is God incarnate, not a wandering preacher/healer who was super-religious, or a Palestinian carpenter who was a good moral teacher, or an eccentric Jewish holy man.

i. Christ Pantocrator

Lewis knew his patristic heritage. His Christology is orthodox, traditional: it concurs with Chalcedon, and with the earlier framework that refuted the emerging heresies. The key to Lewis's Christology is in the authority of Christ in majesty, in the Last Judgment. This was represented in patristic art by the Pantocrator, the risen and ascended Christ enthroned in majesty, surveying, sustaining and judging creation: Christ as the ruler of the universe. This was seen especially in Byzantine art (for example, The Christ Pantocrator, a mosaic in the apse of Monreale Cathedral in Sicily, see: www.cslewisandthechrist.net). Christ, the second person of the Trinity was most often shown in paintings and mosaics of the Pantocrator in the form of a Jewish man, God descended to be the humble servant, though reigning in the future, on high (see figure 6). Lewis's understanding of Christ is grounded in many ways in the future, the pure transcendent action of the loving God, the God of love, manifested in and with humanity that comes to us: Immanuel. This is the timeless breaking into space-time rather than an anticipation, though it is prophetically foretold, amongst the ancient Hebrews, and witnessed to implicitly in intimations of the gospel narrative amongst

---

23   See Lewis's account of Aslan's creation of Narnia. Lewis, *The Magician's Nephew*, Ch. 9, "The Founding of Narnia" 97f.

myths of pagan religion. It is not possible to understand this without appreciating Lewis's personal relationship with God in Christ. For Lewis, the conscious start of this relationship is in his conversion, which was both emotional and reasoned. The reasoning was very much pressed on him by J. R. R. Tolkien, the Roman Catholic Oxford Professor of Anglo-Saxon, in bringing Lewis to accept the truth of what is stated in the creed: that Jesus Christ is God incarnate and that this Christ died because of our sins and for our redemption. Though he could then reason this out, for Lewis acceptance was very much through the Holy Spirit, which pressed upon him, possessed and converted him.

ii. Christ in the Shadowlands

Therefore, Lewis's Christology is read initially from below in the light of the evidence of the self-revelation of the one true living God in Jesus of Nazareth: this is the ground, the reality behind his conversion experience and his assertive apologetics. This points repeatedly to Christ from above, the Universal Christ of the Trinity, uncreated, eternally begotten with the Father, the Universal Light of the world that comes down to redeem in (as Tolkien and Lewis Platonically termed our world) "the shadowlands." Reasoning comes after this has happened, after the event, but is revealed to a degree in our minds because God has put this knowledge, this understanding, in our hearts and minds: such knowledge is, in effect, retained as a fragment of the *imago Dei* (the image of God) despite our *fallen* state, our willfulness to deny God and God's claims on our lives. Christ is within as well as without. For Lewis's this is characterized by an immediate relation with Christ, through the Holy Spirit. Where there is such religious understanding/knowledge it is after the event, after the incarnation, cross, and resurrection, which reveals the absolute—God—drawing us all towards eternity from above. This is Immanuel's descent to raise us up, to draw us into God, to bring us home; therefore it is the *potential* salvation of all, subject to our appropriation of Christ's atonement through faith (we are perfectly free to reject our salvation as many do). Holiness/sanctification, for Lewis and for the patristic tradition, is the key here: we are to be perfect—whatever it takes (even a purifying after death, if needed—purgation). Lewis often presents this using nature metaphors; therefore it is, in many ways, an organic Christology. Because there is a dialectical balance between the humanity and humility of Jesus Christ as compared to the authority and freedom of the Father from above we are not overwhelmed—despite the direction of God's actions. This is shown in Lewis's writings and his Christian analogical (symbolic) narratives (for example, *The Chronicles of Narnia*, *Till We Have Faces*, *The Space Trilogy*, *The Screwtape Letters*, and *The Great Divorce*), and concurs with what we have seen of the patristic christological tradition. In Lewis's writings Christ is characterized often by beauty, a beauty that comes to us from the future. This is a beauty that simultaneously judges and forgives, that is, if the human accepts in repentance this judgment and forgiveness. Despite the religious upbringing and education, even religious prejudices, of many of the characters in these Christian symbolic narratives each and every individual must at

1. Lewis . . . and the Christ

Top Left: An early depiction. Christ, alpha to omega, the beginning and the end, a Jewish Jesus, wall painting in the Catacombs below Rome where the early church used to meet, circa. 3rd Century

Top Right: Christ Pantocrator, mosaic, Hagia-Sophia, from 532AD, in Byzantium (modern-day Istanbul), in the style of a formal Jewish Jesus.

Bottom: Christ Pantocrator, mosaic, Monreale Cathedral, 1174–82, Sicily, in the style of a Jewish Jesus, the Christ of the *eschaton*, residing in judgement.

Figure 6: Christ Pantocrator—in the Patristic Tradition
Pen and ink drawings by P. H. Brazier.

some point meet with the Aslan-Christ, the embodiment of the love and salvation of the Father; these meetings represent a crisis in each individual's life: they must choose one way or the other. Subject to the vagaries and vicissitudes of the Narnian reality (i.e., he can be killed by the White Witch on the stone table), the Aslan-Christ changes not as we do, our perception changes as we grow spiritually in Christ.

Lewis's picture of Christ in his writings is not simply a restatement of orthodox, classic or high Christology in the form of apologetics, philosophical theology, and analogical narratives—it is orthodox in that it concurs with what we have established of patristic Christology—Lewis's Christology is important in its vibrant balance between the humanity of Immanuel and the power and authority of the shift from the above, the timeless, to here below, into to the world of shadows. Lewis's Christ is significant and important and has often been overlooked in the history of twentieth-century theology.

BIBLIOGRAPHY

Anon. *The Didache*. In, *Early Christian Writings*, edited and translated by Andrew Louth, 185–99. Harmondsworth, UK: Penguin, 1987.

Balthasar, Hans Urs Von. *Cosmic Liturgy: The Universe according to Maximus the Confessor*. San Francisco, CA: Ignatius Press, 2003.

Barnard, L. W., editor. *Justin Martyr: First and Second Apologies*. Ancient Christian Writers. Mahwah, NJ: Paulist, 2004.

Berthold, George C., editor. *Maximus Confessor: Selected Writings*. Classics of Western Spirituality. Mahwah, NJ: Paulist, 1985.

Bettenson, Henry, translator and editor. *The Early Christian Fathers: A Selection from the Writings of the Fathers from St Clement of Rome to St Athanasius*. Oxford: Oxford University Press, 1969.

———, translator and editor. *The Later Christian Fathers: A Selection from the Writings of the Fathers from St Cyril of Jerusalem to St Leo the Great*. Oxford: Oxford University Press, 1972.

Cooper, Adam G. *The Body in St Maximus Confessor: Holy Flesh, Wholly Deified*. Oxford Early Christian Studies. Oxford: Oxford University Press, 2005.

Gregory of Nazianzus. "Letter no. 101, to Cledonius," 161–63. In *On God and Christ: The Five Theological Orations and Two Letters to Cledonius*, edited and translated by John Behr, Lionel Wickham, Frederick Williams. Popular Patristics Series. Yonkers, NY: St Vladimir's Seminary Press, 2011.

Hall, Stuart. G., editor. *Doctrine and Practice in the Early Church*. London: SPCK, 1991.

Klinger, Max. *Christ on Mount Olympus* (1897). Oil on canvas, 70cm x 34cm. Leipzig, Museum of the Fine Arts.

Lewis, C. S. *The Chronicles of Narnia: The Magician's Nephew*. Ch. 9, "The Founding of Narnia." London: Bles, 1955.

———. *The Problem of Pain*. London: Bles, 1940.

———. "Rejoinder to Dr Pittenger." In *Christian Century* LXXV (Nov. 26, 1958) 1369–71.

Macquarrie, John, *Christology Revisited*. Harrisburg, PA: Trinity, 1998.

———. *Jesus Christ in Modern Thought*. London: SCM, 1990.

Migne, J. P., editor. *Patrologia Graeca*. 161 Vols. Paris: Imprimerie Catholique, 1857–66.

O'Dell Bullock, Karen. *Shepherd's Notes: Writings of Justin Martyr*. Nashville, TN: Broadman and Holman, 1999.

Pittenger, W. Norman, "Apologist versus Apologist: A Critique of C. S. Lewis as 'Defender of the Faith.'" In *Christian Century* LXXV (Oct 1, 1958) 1104–7.

1. Lewis . . . and the Christ

Roberts, Alexander; James Donaldson, Philip Schaff, and Henry Wace, editors and translators. *The Early Church Fathers: Ante-Nicene Fathers: Translations of the Writings of the Fathers Down to A.D. 325; The Nicene and Post-Nicene Fathers of the Christian Church-First and Second Series.* 38 Vols. Vol. 1: Apostolic Fathers, Justin Martyr, Irenaeus. Grand Rapids: Eerdmans, 1979.

Saward, John. *Redeemer in the Womb.* San Francisco, CA: Ignatius, 1993.

Stevenson, J., editor. *Creeds, Councils and Controversies: Documents Illustrating the History of the Church, AD 337-461.* Revised edition by W. H. C. Frend. London: SPCK, 1989.

———, editor. *A New Eusebius: Documents Illustrating the History of the Church to AD 337.* Revised by W. H. C. Frend. SPCK Church History. London: SPCK, 1957.

Tyrrell S. J., George, *Christianity at the Cross-Roads.* London: Longmans Green, 1909.

2

C. S. Lewis: An Annotated Historical Bibliography of Primary Sources

The following is a brief a chronological bibliography of books, novels and short stories, essays and academic papers, addresses and sermons. The works cited here give as complete a bibliography of primary sources as possible relating to Lewis's Christology. This is a general chronological bibliography of the development of Lewis's writings—orientated towards his doctrine of revelation and his understanding of the Christ.

Since Lewis's death there never ceases to be a year when fresh compilations and reprints are published. Generally these are not included here. The exception is with expanded collections produced in the years after Lewis's death; also included are the volumes of correspondence and essays published between 2000 and 2007 (these are included because of their comprehensive nature) and recent volumes that may contain an essay not before published. Locating academic papers in journals is relatively straight forward; however, many of the essays published in Lewis's lifetime, particularly in the 1940s, appeared in rare journals, newspapers, or obscure local periodicals. These were, by and large, re-printed after Lewis's death in four volumes: *Christian Reflections* (1967) *Undeceptions* (1971) *Present Concern: Ethical Essays* (1986) and *Christian Reunion* (1990). In addition, there have been numerous reprints published of most of Lewis's essays, papers, sermons, and reviews in abundant paperback volumes from the mid-1980s on.

In compiling this chronological bibliography all dates given are the year of composition of a work, or of its first publication. Many essays were re-printed several times, particularly in the decades following Lewis's death; however, the purpose of this list is to illustrate the chronological development of Lewis's thinking as evidenced by his various works. Therefore the key date is the date of publication, or, if earlier, the date of writing/composition, or, the date of delivery of an address/sermon. The volume of essays cited is then the first re-printing. Subsequent re-prints may be found in the many paperback volumes published in the last twenty years.

There can be confusion caused by the multitudinous volumes of essays and lectures, short pieces, sermons, letters, and addresses published since Lewis's death.

Some essays were re-titled after Lewis's death. In all instances the original title Lewis gave a work is given (with the subsequent title, and its consequent publication date given in parentheses). In some instances it is noted that a work was not published in the same year as its composition; in some cases publication followed years later. In addition, there are two volumes entitled *God in the Dock*: a large volume of essays published in America—*God in the Dock: Essays on Theology and Ethics* (1970) which was then published in Britain under the title *Undeceptions: Essays on Theology and Ethics*, the following year; a smaller volume of different essays was published under the name *God in the Dock* in the Britain in 1979.

In rare instances the date of original composition or delivery as a sermon or academic paper is lost, unknown, particularly in the case of posthumously published works. These works are listed at the end.

Please note that references to *The Guardian* are not to the British daily national newspaper (often called The Manchester Guardian) but to a Church of England Anglo-Catholic weekly newspaper published in London by George Bell & Sons from 1846 to 1951, which Lewis often contributed to.

Lewis's apologetics, philosophical theology, and other Christian writings, where they relate broadly to Christology and his doctrine of revelation, can be sub-divided according to how his work develops, in relation to the maturity of his faith, the events in his life, and the approach he took to apologetics and for that matter philosophy. Therefore, there are broadly three periods bounded by his conversion in 1931, the wartime *Broadcast Talks* (1941–44) the Anscombe-Lewis debate in 1948, and his death in 1963: the early works 1931 to 1944; the middle works 1941 to 1947 (a deliberate overlap is implied in these two periods); and the later works 1948 to 1963.

The Early Works: 1931–44

Lewis's *The Pilgrim's Regress*, published in 1933 two years after his final conversion to belief in Christ as the Son of God, the revelation of God, was in some ways an intellectual apology for his conversion. In it he rejected the multivarious nineteenth- and twentieth-century philosophies and neo-Gnostic religious systems he had been seduced by. In the 1930s he published many academic papers relating to his work as a lecturer on English literature, however, during this period he was identifying and considering, gradually, his vocation as an orthodox biblical and creedal Christian, evidenced by his correspondence. His primary witness, initially, was in the common rooms of Oxford colleges. This led, in part, to the publication of his first implicitly Christian work: *Out of the Silent Planet* (1938). Further academic works in English literature followed, then in 1940 (instigated by Ashley Samson of the Centenary Press) *The Problem of Pain* was published. A clear work of apologetics this tackled one of the most difficult subjects for a Christian apologists: pain and affliction, anguish and suffering, and thereby theodicy: how do you justify God as good in the face of pain and suffering? The book was popular, and in effect, brought Lewis to the attention of the public. It led to the BBC radio broadcasts on the essence of the Christian faith.

The Middle Works: 1941–47

Lewis is arguably at his most productive and confident as a preacher, apologist, and philosophical theologian during the period of the middle works. This period overlaps the early period in that the radio broadcasts were initiated in 1941, and the early talks truly represent the learning and emerging confidence of Lewis as he found his feet, so to speak, in the 1930s. The later talks, from 1944, display the maturity and confidence that we find in many of his sermons, addresses, and works in the 1940s. This assertive confidence, the ability to present a profound understanding in defence of the Christian faith and the truth of the gospel, is found in the sermon, "The Weight of Glory," and apologetic narratives such as *The Screwtape Letters*, these typify the self-assurance of the middle period works, and originate in 1941, whilst Lewis was still working on the early broadcast talks. Before the radio broadcasts were over he had produced *The Great Divorce* and begun writing his seminal definition of the relationship between Platonism and the gospel (which in effect defined in limited terms the mechanism whereby the Holy Spirit relates to and acts in our world, our reality): an address entitled, "Transposition" (delivered at Mansfield College just after the conclusion of the final series of broadcast talks). There are many essays and sermons which characterise the self-assured argumentative nature of Lewis's apologetics during this period, which culminates with the first edition of *Miracles*, still one of Lewis's most cogent arguments for the supernatural nature of the Christian faith.

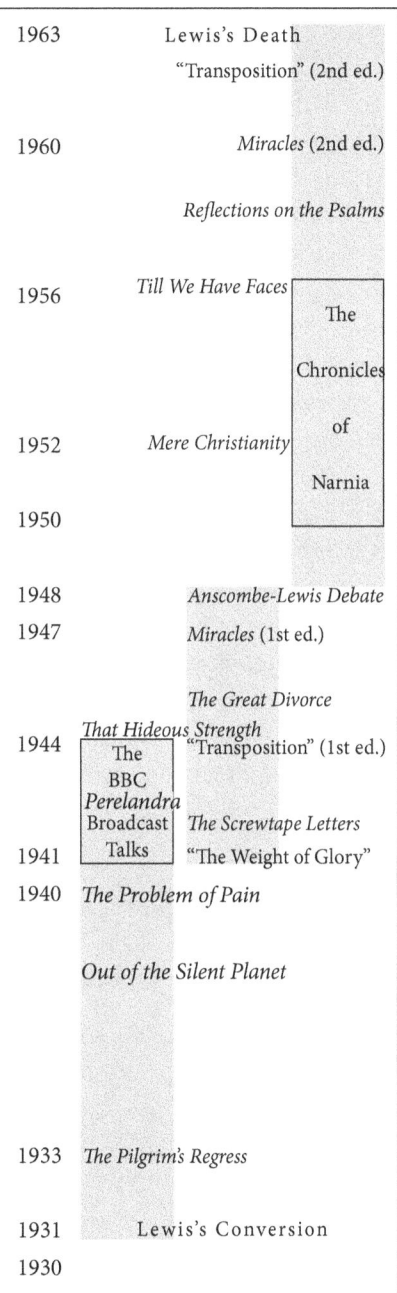

Figure 7 The Three Periods of Lewis's Apologetics and Theology

The Later Works: 1948–63

In 1948 Lewis had what was to many a bruising encounter with a young philosophy don at the Oxford Socratic Club: Elizabeth Anscombe. An analysis of this along with the nature of Lewis as a philosopher, raises complex issues about revelation and reason, the use of language and how we "know"; however, this debate in effective marks a slowly developing change in his work, with less of an emphasis on assertive apologetics. Foremost, indeed characteristic of, this later period are *The Chronicles of Narnia*. There are also many devotionally based works, which also characterise a developing interest in Lewis's mature work: Christlikeness. For example, *Till We Have Faces* (1956) *Reflections on the Psalms* (1958) and the posthumously published, *Letters to Malcolm: Chiefly on Prayer* (1964). There is also a wealth of essays of philosophical theology, and important correspondence that develop Lewis's mere Christology.

There is, as yet, no *Complete Works of C. S. Lewis* published, however approximately 95 percent of his writings are in print, with the remainder being accessible through second-hand copies (one does not need to trawl through second-hand bookshops any longer, there are plenty of web sites that bring together the electronic databases of resellers). The only difficulties are rare works such as *Rehabilitations and Other Essays* (1939) though most of these essays were re-published in later volumes, and copies of *The Socratic Digest* (the journal of the Oxford Socratic Club that Lewis was heavily involved in) which if available command very high prices.

What follows therefore is a chronology of relevant works—books and novels, essays and academic papers, sermons and addresses, and short stories

1. THE EARLY PERIOD WORKS

1919
Books

Clive Hamilton (pseudonym for C. S. Lewis,) *Spirits in Bondage*. London: Heinemann, 1919.

1920s
Essays, Academic Papers, and Short Stories

"The Man Born Blind."
>Written in the 1920s, published in *The Dark Tower and Other Stories* (1977) 89–94. For a complete discussion and history of "The Man Born Blind" and a later draft of the story, "Light," see Charlie W. Starr, *Light: C. S. Lewis's First and Final Short Story*, Winged Lion Press, 2012.

1926
Books

Clive Hamilton (pseudonym for C. S. Lewis) *Dymer*. London: J. M. Dent, 1926. Hamilton was the maiden name of Lewis's mother. There was a tradition of anonymity amongst soldiers returning from WW1.

1932
Essays, Academic Papers, and Short Stories

"A Note on Comus."
> In *The Review of English Studies*, VIII.30 (1932). Re-printed in *Studies in Medieval and Renaissance Literature* (1966) 175–81.

"What Chaucer Really did to Il Filostrato."
> In *Essays and Studies*, Vol. XIX (1932). Re-printed in *Selected Literary Essays* (1969) 27–44.

1933
Books

The Pilgrim's Regress: An Allegorical Apology for Christianity, Reason and Romanticism. London: J. M. Dent and Sons, 1933.

1935
Essays, Academic Papers, and Short Stories

"The Alliterative Metre."
> In *Lysistrata*, Vol. II (May 1935). Reprinted in *Rehabilitations and Other Essays* (1939); and in *Selected Literary Essays* (1969) 15–26.

1936
Books

The Allegory of Love: A Study in Medieval Tradition. Oxford: Clarendon Press, 1936.

Essays, Academic Papers, and Short Stories

"Genius and Genius."
> In *The Review of English Studies*, XII.46 (1936). Re-printed in *Studies in Medieval and Renaissance Literature* (1969) 169–74.

1937
Essays, Academic Papers, and Short Stories

"William Morris."
> A paper read to The Martlet Society on Nov. 5, 1937. Published in *Rehabilitations and Other Essays* (1939. Reprinted in *Selected Literary Essays* (1969) 219–31.

1938
Books

Out of the Silent Planet. London: Bodley Head, 1938.

Essays, Academic Papers, and Short Stories

"Donne and Love Poetry in the Seventeenth Century."
> In *Seventeenth Century Studies Presented to Sir Herbert Grierson*, edited by John Dover Wilson. Oxford: Clarendon Press, 1938. Reprinted in *Selected Literary Essays* (1969) 106–25.

"The Dark Tower."
> Written c. 1938–40, published, in *The Dark Tower and Other Stories* (1977) 3–88.

1939
Books

Rehabilitations and Other Essays (1939). Oxford: Oxford University Press, 1939.

C. S. Lewis and E. M. W. Tillyard, *The Personal Heresy: A Controversy*. Oxford: Oxford University Press, 1939.

Essays, Academic Papers, and Short Stories

"Variation in Shakespeare and Others."
> Presented by Lewis to the Mermaid Club in 1939. Printed in *Rehabilitations and Other Essays* (1939). Reprinted in *Selected Literary Essays* (1969) 74–87.

"The Fifteenth-Century Heroic Line."
> Initially published in *Essays and Studies*, XXIV (1937). Reprinted in *Selected Literary Essays* (1969) 45–57.

"Christianity and Literature."
> Initially published in *Rehabilitations and Other Essays* (1939). Reprinted in *Christian Reflections* (1967) 1–11.

"The Hobbit"
>   In *The Times Literary Supplement* (Oct. 2, 1939). Reprinted in C. S. Lewis, *Of This and Other Worlds* (1982) 93–94.

"Shelley, Dryden, and Mr Eliot."
>   An academic paper presented at Bedford College, London. Published in *Rehabilitations and Other Essays* (1939). Reprinted in *Selected Literary Essays* (1969) 187–208.

"Bluspels and Flalansferes: A Semantic Nightmare."
>   An academic paper presented at Manchester University. Published in *Rehabilitations and Other Essays* (1939). Reprinted in *Selected Literary Essays* (1969) 251–63.

"High and Low Brows."
>   A paper presented to the English Society at Oxford. Published in *Rehabilitations and Other Essays* (1939). Reprinted in *Selected Literary Essays* (1969) 266–79.

Addresses, Lectures, and Sermons

"None Other Gods: Culture in War Time."
>   A sermon preached in the University Church of St Mary the Virgin, Oxford, Dec. 22, 1939. Published as a pamphlet, *The Christian in Danger*. London: SCM Press, 1939. Reprinted as "Learning in War-time," in *Transposition and Other Addresses* (1949) 45–54.

1940
Books

The Problem of Pain. London: Centenary Press, 1940.

Essays, Academic Papers, and Short Stories

"Dangers of National Repentance."
>   In *The Guardian* (Mar. 15, 1940). Re-printed in Undeceptions (1971) 151–53.

"Christianity and Culture," in *Theology* XL (Mar. 1940) 166–79.
>   Lewis's article generated a discussion and several responses. See: S. L. Bethell and E. F. Carritt, "Christianity and Culture: Replies to Mr Lewis." *Theology* XL (May 1940) 356–66; Lewis, "Christianity and Culture." *Theology*, Letters Section, XL (Jun. 1940) 475–77; and, George Every, "In Defence of Criticism." *Theology* XLI (Sept. 1940) 159–65. Lewis's reply to these various responses closed the debate. See: Lewis, "Peace Proposals for Brother Every and Mr Bethell." *Theology* XLI (Dec. 1940) 339–48. Lewis's contributions to the debate were re-printed in *Christian Reflections* (1967) 12–36.

"Notes on the Way." in *Time and Tide*, XXI (Aug. 17, 1940).
> Re-printed as, "The Importance of an Ideal," in *Living Age* (1940) and as "The Necessity of Chivalry," in *Present Concern: Ethical Essays* (1986) 13–16.

"On Ethics." written c. 1940–42
> Published in *Christian Reflections* (1967) 44–56.

"The Kappa Element in Romance."
> Paper presented to Merton College Undergraduate Literary Society in 1940, published as, "On Stories," in *Essays Presented to Charles Williams* (1947).

"The Pains of Animals."
> An academic correspondence between Lewis and the philosopher C. E. M. Joad in 1940–41, published in *The Month* CLXXXIX (1950).

"Two Ways with the Self."
> In *The Guardian* (May 3, 1940). Reprinted in *Undeceptions* (1971) 154–56.

"Dante's Similes."
> A paper presented to the Oxford Dante Society, Feb. 13, 1940. Published in *Studies in Medieval and Renaissance Literature* (1966) 64–77.

"Tasso."
> Probably written during the 1940s. Published in *Studies in Medieval and Renaissance Literature* (1966) 111–20.

Addresses, Lectures, and Sermons

"Why I am not a Pacifist."
> An address written and presented in 1940 to the Pacifist Society in Oxford. Published in *The Weight of Glory and Other Addresses* (1949). N.B: this was a US edition of *Transposition and Other Addresses* (1949) expanded with additional material. The first UK publication was in *Timeless at Heart* (1987).

2. THE MIDDLE PERIOD WORKS

1941
Essays, Academic Papers, and Short Stories

"Evil and God."
> *The Spectator* CLXVI (Feb. 7, 1941).

"Meditation on the Third Commandment."
> *The Guardian* (Jan. 10, 1941). Re-printed in *Undeceptions* (1971) 157–60.

"Notes on the Way."
> *Time and Tide*, XXII (Mar. 29, 1941). Re-printed in an expanded form as "'Bulverism' or The Foundation of Twentieth Century Thought," *The Socratic Digest* 2 (1944) later in *Undeceptions* (1971) 223–28.

"Psycho-Analysis and Literary Criticism."
> A paper first delivered at Westfield College in 1941 to a Literary Society, published by The English Association in *Essays and Studies* XXVII (1941). Subsequently published in *They Asked for a Paper: Papers and Addresses* (1962) 120–38; and in *Selected Literary Essays* (1969) 286–300.

"Religion: Reality or Substitute?"
> Written and published in *World Dominion*, XIX (Sept-Oct 1943). An expanded edition (with the addition of paragraphs 4 and part of 9 written in all probability in the 1950s) was published in *Christian Reflections* (1967) 37–43.

"Edmund Spenser."
> In *Fifteen Poets Chaucer; Spenser; Shakespeare; Milton; Dryden; Pope; Cowper; Coleridge; Wordsworth; Shelley; Byron; Keats; Browning; Tennyson; Arnold*, edited by T. S. Eliot. Oxford: Clarendon Press, 1941. Re-printed in *Studies in Medieval and Renaissance Literature* (1966) 121–45.

"On Reading The Faerie Queene."
> In *Fifteen Poets Chaucer; Spenser; Shakespeare; Milton; Dryden; Pope; Cowper; Coleridge; Wordsworth; Shelley; Byron; Keats; Browning; Tennyson; Arnold*, edited by T. S. Eliot. Oxford: Clarendon Press, 1941. Re-printed in *Studies in Medieval and Renaissance Literature* (1966) 146–48.

Addresses, Lectures, and Sermons

"The Weight of Glory"
> One of the most important, if not the most significant, sermons of Lewis's given relatively early on in his career as an apologist and theologians, "The Weight of Glory," was preached in the University Church of St Mary the Virgin on Sunday, June 8, 1941. This was initially published as, C. S. Lewis, "The Weight of Glory," *Theology* XLIII (Nov. 1941). The sermon-essay was then reproduced as a pamphlet by SPCK in 1942: C. S. Lewis, *The Weight of Glory*. Little Books of Religion, no. 189. London: SPCK, 1942. It was later included in a volume of essays, C. S. Lewis, "The Weight of Glory," in *Transposition and Other Addresses* (1949). One of the most recent volumes it appeared in is probably *Screwtape Proposes a Toast* (1998).

Radio Broadcasts

The Broadcast Talks.
The First Series, *Right and Wrong*. Radio talks transmitted live on the BBC Home Service, c. 15 mins, duration.
> First Talk, 1. "Common Decency," 6 August 1941.
> Second Talk, 2. "Scientific Law and Moral Law," 13 August 1941.
> Third Talk, 3. "Materialism or Religion," 20 August 1941.
> Fourth Talk, 4. "What Can We Do About It?," 27 August 1941.
> Fifth Talk, 5. "Answers to Listeners' Questions," 6 September 1941.

1942
Books

Broadcast Talks. Reprinted with some alterations from two series of Broadcast Talks "Right and Wrong: A Clue to the Meaning of the Universe" and "What Christians Believe" given in 1941 and 1942. London: Geoffrey Bles, The Centenary Press, 1942.

A Preface to Paradise Lost. Oxford: Oxford University Press, 1942.
> The Ballard Matthews Lectures, delivered at University College North Wales 1941.

The Screwtape Letters. London: Geoffrey Bles, The Centenary Press, 1942.

Essays, Academic Papers, and Short Stories

"Notes on the Way."
> In Time and Tide XXIII (Jun. 27, 1942) 512–20. Re-printed in *Undeceptions* (1971) 229–32.

"The Founding of the Oxford Socratic Club."
> Preface to *The Socratic Digest* 1 (1942). Re-printed in *Undeceptions* (1971) 96–98.

Addresses, Lectures, and Sermons

"Hamlet: the Prince or the Poem."
> The Annual Shakespeare Lecture of the British Academy. Published in *Proceedings of the British Academy*, 28 (1942) 139–54. Subsequently published in *They Asked for a Paper: Papers and Addresses* (1962) 51–71.

"Miracles."
> A sermon preached in St Jude on the Hill Church, London. Published in *St Jude's Gazette*, 73 (Oct. 1942) 4–7. A shorter version was published in *The Guardian*, Oct. 2, 1942. Re-printed in *Undeceptions* (1971) 5–16.

Radio Broadcasts

The Broadcast Talks.
The Second Series, 1942, *What Christians Believe*. Radio talks transmitted live on the BBC Home Service, c. 15 mins, duration.
>First Talk, 1. "The Rival Conceptions of God," 11 January 1942.
>Second Talk, 2. "The Invasion," 18 January 1942.
>Third Talk, 3. "The Shocking Alternative," 1 February, 1942.
>Fourth Talk, 4. "The Perfect Penitent," 8 February 1942.
>Fifth Talk, 5. "The Practical Conclusion," 15 February 1942.

1943
Books

Christian Behaviour. London: Geoffrey Bles, The Centenary Press, 1943.

Perelandra. London: Bodley Head, 1943.

The Abolition of Man: or, Reflections on Education with Special Reference to the Teaching of English in the Upper Forms of Schools. Oxford: Oxford University Press, 1943.
>Given as the University of Durham Riddell Memorial Lectures, fifteenth series.

Essays, Academic Papers, and Short Stories

"Dogma and the Universe" and "Dogma and Science."
>In *The Guardian* (Mar. 19 and 26, 1943) 96, 104, and 107. Re-printed as "Dogma and the Universe," in *Undeceptions* (1971) 17–25.

"Equality."
>In *The Spectator* CLXXI (Aug. 27, 1943). Reprinted in *Present Concern: Ethical Essays* (1986) 17–20.

"Notes on the Way."
>In *Time and Tide* XXIV (Sept. 4, 1943). Re-printed as "My First School," in *Present Concern: Ethical Essays* (1986) 23–26.

"The Poison of Subjectivism."
>In *Religion in Life* XII (Summer 1943). Re-printed in *Christian Reflections* (1967) 72–81.

"Three Kinds of Men."
>In *The Sunday Times*, (Mar. 21, 1943). Reprinted in *Present Concern: Ethical Essays* (1986) 21–22.

Addresses, Lectures, and Sermons

"De Futilitate."
>An address written and presented, c. 1943, at Magdalen College, Oxford, at the invitation of the President, Sir Henry Tizard. Published in *Christian Reflections* (1967) 57–71.

Radio Broadcasts

The Broadcast Talks.
The Third Series, 1943, *Christian Behaviour*.
>Radio talks transmitted live on the BBC Home Service, c. 15 mins, duration.

>>First Talk, 1. "The Three Parts" Sept. 20, 1942.
>>Second Talk 2. "Social Morality" Sept. 27, 1942.
>>Third Talk 3. "Morality and Psychoanalysis," Oct. 4 1942.
>>Fourth Talk 4. "Sexual Morality" Oct. 11, 1942.
>>Fifth Talk 5. "Forgiveness," Oct. 18, 1942.
>>Sixth Talk 6. "The Great Sin" Oct. 25, 1942.
>>Seventh Talk 7. "Faith," Nov. 1, 1942.
>>Eighth Talk 8. "Faith," Nov. 8, 1942.

1944
Books

Beyond Personality: the Christian Idea of God. London: Geoffrey Bles, The Centenary Press, 1944.

Essays, Academic Papers, and Short Stories

"Preface to Third Edition."
>In *The Pilgrim's Regress: An Allegorical Apology for Christianity, Reason and Romanticism*, 3rd ed. London: Geoffrey Bless, 1944. Note that in some American reprints this "Preface" is placed at the end of the book and called an "Afterword". For example, *The Pilgrim's Regress*. Illustrated by Michael Hague. Grand Rapids, MI: Eerdmans (1992), 200–209.

"A Dream."
>In *The Spectator* CLXXIII (Jul. 28, 1944). Reprinted in *Present Concern: Ethical Essays* (1986) 37–40.

"Answers to Questions on Christianity."
>Originally published as a pamphlet by the Electrical and Musical Industries Christian Fellowship, Hayes, Middlesex, UK, 1944. Re-printed in *Undeceptions* (1971) 26–38.

"Blimpophobia."
: In *Time and Tide* XXV (Sept. 9, 1944). Reprinted in *Present Concern: Ethical Essays* (1986) 41–45.

"Christian Reunion."
: Written at the invitation of Roman Catholic friends, this essay was discovered after Lewis's death amongst notes for the broadcasts made in 1944. Published in *Christian Reunion and Other Essays* (1990) 17–21.

"Horrid Red Things."
: Published in *The Church of England Newspaper*, LI (Oct. 6, 1944). Re-printed in *Undeceptions* (1971) 44–47.

"Introduction."
: In *St. Athanasius, The Incarnation of the Word. Being the Treatise of St Athanasius, De Incarnatione Verbi Dei*. Translated by Sr. Penelope CSMV. London: Geoffrey Bles, The Centenary Press, 1944. Re-printed as "On the Reading of Old Books," in *Undeceptions* (1971) 161–66.

"Is English Doomed?"
: In *The Spectator* CLXXII (Feb. 1, 1944). Reprinted in *Present Concern: Ethical Essays* (1986) 27–31.

"Is Theology Poetry?"
: A paper presented to the Socratic Club in Oxford 1944. Published in *The Socratic Digest*, 3 (1945). Reprinted in *They Asked for a Paper* (1962) 150–65.

"Myth Became Fact."
: In *World Dominion* XXII (Sept-Oct. 1944),. 267–70. Re-printed in *Undeceptions* (1971) 39–43.

"Notes on the Way."
: In *Time and Tide* XXV (11 Mar. 11, 1944). An expanded edition was published as "The Parthenon and the Optative," in *Of This and Other Worlds* (1982) 123–26.

"Private Bates."
: In *The Spectator* CLXXIII (Dec. 29, 1944). Reprinted in *Present Concern: Ethical Essays* (1986) 46–49.

"The Death of Words."
: In *The Spectator* CLXXIII (22 Sept. 22, 1944). Reprinted in *Of This and Other Worlds* (London: Collins, 1982) 119–22.

"Notes on the Way."
: In *Time and Tide* XXV (Apr. 29. 1944). Reprinted as "Democratic Education" in *Present Concern: Ethical Essays* (1986) 32–36.

Addresses, Lectures, and Sermons

"Transposition." 1st ed.
> A sermon given in Mansfield College, Oxford on Whit Sunday, May 28, 1944. It was then published five years later in *Transposition and Other Addresses* (1949) 9–20. A reworked and extended edition of the sermon as an academic paper was published in *They Asked for a Paper: Papers and Addresses* (1962) 166–82.

"New Learning and New Ignorance."
> Originally part of The Clark Lectures, delivered by Lewis at Trinity College Cambridge, 1944. This was later reworked to form the "Introduction" to *English Literature in the Sixteenth Century* (1954) 2–65.

"The Inner Ring."
> An address, a memorial oration, given at King's College London in 1944. Subsequently published in *They Asked for a Paper: Papers and Addresses* (1962) 139–49.

Radio Broadcasts

The Broadcast Talks.
The Fourth Series, 1944, *Beyond Personality: The Christian View of God.*
> Radio talks transmitted live on the BBC Home Service, c. 15 mins, duration.
> First Talk 1. "Making and Begetting," Feb. 22, 1944.
> Second Talk 2. "The Three-Personal God, Feb. 29 1944.
> Third Talk 3. "Good Infection," Mar. 7, 1944.
> Fourth Talk 4. "The Obstinate Toy Soldiers," Mar. 14, 1944.
> Fifth Talk 5. "Let's Pretend," Mar. 21, 1944.
> Sixth Talk 6. "Is Christianity Hard or Easy?," Mar. 28, 1944.
> Seventh Talk 7. "The New Man," Apr. 4, 1944.

> Extracts from the third and seventh talks, the last surviving from the BBC archives, can be heard at:
> www.youtube.com/watch?v=JHxs3gdtV8A.

> N.B. the title of the third talk is changed to "Time and Beyond Time" in the published edition of this series: *Beyond Personality: the Christian Idea of God* (1944).

1945
Books

The Great Divorce: A Dream. London: Macmillan, 1945.

That Hideous Strength. A Modern Fairytale for Grown-Ups. London: Bodley Head, 1945.

Essays, Academic Papers, and Short Stories

"After Priggery—What?"
> In *The Spectator* CLXXV (7 Dec. 7 1945). Reprinted in *Present Concern: Ethical Essays* (1986) 56–60.

"Hedonics."
> In *Time and Tide* XXVI (Jun. 16, 1945). Reprinted in *Present Concern: Ethical Essays* (1986) 50–55.

"Meditation in a Toolshed."
> In *The Coventry Evening Telegraph* (Jul. 17, 1945). Reprinted in *Undeceptions* (1971) 171–74.

"Religion and Science."
> In *The Coventry Evening Telegraph* (Jan. 3, 1945) 4. Reprinted in *Undeceptions* (1971) 48–51.

"Scraps."
> In *St James' Magazine*, the parish magazine of St James's Church, Birkdale, Southport (Dec 1945). Reprinted in *Undeceptions* (1971) 175–76.

"The Laws of Nature."
> In *The Coventry Evening Telegraph* (Apr. 4, 1945) 4. Reprinted in *Undeceptions* (1971) 52–55.

"The Sermon and the Lunch."
> In *The Church of England Newspaper* (Sept. 21, 1945). Reprinted in *Undeceptions* (1971) 233–37.

"Who was Right – Dream Lecturer or Real Lecturer?"
> In *The Coventry Evening Telegraph* (Feb. 21, 1945). Reprinted as "Two Lectures," in *Undeceptions* (1971) 167–70.

"Work and Prayer."
> In *The Coventry Evening Telegraph* (May 28, 1945). Reprinted in *Undeceptions* (1971) 77–80.

"Addison."
> In C. S. Lewis, Herbert J. Davis, David Cecil and Edmund Blunden, *Essays on the Eighteenth Century presented to David Nichol Smith*. Oxford: Clarendon Press, 1945. Reprinted in Selected Literary Essays (1969) 154–68.

Addresses, Lectures, and Sermons

"Christian Apologetics."
> An address to the Church of England Carmarthen Conference for Youth Leaders and Junior Clergy, Easter 1945. Published in *Undeceptions* (1971) 64–76.

"Membership."
> An address to The Society of St Alban and St Sergius, Oxford, in Sobornost, 31 (Jun. 1945). Reprinted in *Transposition and Other Addresses* (1949) 34–44.

"The Grand Miracle."
> A sermon, published in *The Guardian*, (Apr. 27, 1945) 161 and 165. Reprinted in *Undeceptions* (1971) 56–63.

"The Grand Miracle."
> An address, an expansion of the kernel of material initially presented in a sermon ("Miracles") in 1942 at St Jude on the Hill Church and the sermon "The Grand Miracle" (above). Published in *Miracles* (1st ed. 1947) Chapter 14. 113–138.

Radio Broadcasts

"An Introduction to The Great Divorce"
> Lewis introduces his *The Great Divorce*. An extract from a BBC programme first broadcast on May 9, 1948:
>
> www.lewissociety.org/audios.php

1946
Books

George MacDonald: *An Anthology*. Edited by C. S. Lewis. London: Geoffrey Bles, 1946.

Essays, Academic Papers, and Short Stories

"A Reply to Professor Haldene."
> Written c. 1946–47 in reply to J. B. S. Haldene, "Auld Hornie, FRS," in *Modern Quarterly*, 1.4 (Aut. 1946). Published in *Of Other Worlds. Essays and Stories* (1966) 74–85.

"A Christian Reply to Professor Price."
: A paper presented to The Oxford Socratic Club on May 20, 1946, in answer to a paper of Professor H. H. Price, "The Grounds of Modern Agnosticism," (delivered on Oct. 20, 1944). Both papers were later published in *The Phoenix Quarterly* 1.1 (Autumn 1946) 31–44.

: "A Christian Reply to Professor Price," was re-printed as, "Religion without Dogma?" in *The Socratic Digest* 4 (1948) 82–94. Amendments and responses from the floor are in the minutes' book of The Socratic Club. "Religion without Dogma," related notes, amendments and responses were all published in *Undeceptions* (1971) 99–114.

"Man or Rabbit?"
: Published as a pamphlet by the Student Christian Movement for distribution in schools, London: SCM Press, 1946. Re-printed in *Undeceptions* (1971) 99–114.

"Modern Man and his Categories of Thought."
: An essay written at the request of Bishop Stephen Neill for the World Council of Churches Assembly, Commission II, as discussion material for, God's Design and Man's Witness. Part of this essay, the section on, The Emancipation of Women, was published in *CSL: The Bulletin of the New York C. S. Lewis Society* 17.4 (Feb. 1986). The complete essay was published in *Present Concern: Ethical Essays* (1986) 61–66.

"Notes on the Way."
: In *Time and Tide*, XXVII (May 25, & Jun. 1, 1946). Re-printed as the first part of "Different Tastes in Literature," in *Of This and Other Worlds* (1982) 132–39.

"Notes on the Way."
: In *Time and Tide* XXVII (Nov. 9, 1946). Re-printed as "Period Criticism," in *Of This and Other Worlds* (1982) 127–31.

"Preface."
: In G. B. Sandhurst, *How Heathen is Britain?* London: Collins, 1946. Re-printed as "On the Transmission of Christianity," in *Undeceptions* (1971) 86–90.

"Preface."
: In *George MacDonald: An Anthology* (1946.) xxi–xxiv.

"Talking about Bicycles."
: In *Resistance* (Oct. 1946). Reprinted in *Present Concern: Ethical Essays* (1986) 67–72.

"The Decline of Religion."
: In *The Cherwell*, Oxford XXVI (Nov. 29, 1946). Reprinted in *Undeceptions* (1971) 177–81.

Addresses, Lectures, and Sermons

"Miserable Offenders."
> A sermon preached at St Matthew's Church, Northampton, on Apr. 7, 1946 and published by St Matthew's in a pamphlet entitled *Five Sermons by Laymen* (Apr.–May 1946) 1–6. It was subsequently published as *Miserable Offenders: An Interpretation of Prayer Book Language*. Series: Advent Paper No 12. Boston, MA: Church of the Advent, 1950. Re-printed in *Undeceptions* (1971) 91–95

1947
Books

Miracles. A Preliminary Study. 1st ed. London: Geoffrey Bles, 1947.

Essays Presented to Charles Williams. Edited by C. S. Lewis. London: Geoffrey Cumberlege, 1947.

Vivisection. Boston: New England Anti-Vivisection Society, 1947.
> A pamphlet published by The New England Anti-Vivisection Society, 1948. Reprinted in *Undeceptions* (1971) 186–87.

Essays, Academic Papers, and Short Stories

"Preface."
> In *Essays Presented to Charles Williams* (1947) v–xiv.

"On Forgiveness."
> Written, dated, 1947, published posthumously in *Fern Seed and Elephants* (1975) 26–30.

"Preface."
> In J. B. Philips's, *Letters to Young Churches: A Translation of the New Testament Epistles*. London: Geoffrey Bles, 1947, vii–x. Re-printed as "Modern Translations of the Bible," in *Undeceptions* (1971) 187–90.

"The Morte D'arthur."
> A review of Eugene Vinaver, *Works of Sir Thomas Malory*, in *The Times Literary Supplement* (Jun. 7, 1947).

3. THE LATER PERIOD WORKS

1948
Books

C. S. Lewis and Charles Williams, *Arthurian Torso, Containing the Posthumous Fragment of The Figure of Arthur and a Commentary on the Arthurian Poems of Charles Williams and C. S. Lewis*. Oxford: Oxford University Press, 1948.
> Two essays, the first by Williams is a history of the development of the Arthurian legend, the second by Lewis is a guide to Williams' Arthurian poems.

Essays, Academic Papers, and Short Stories

"Difficulties in Presenting the Christian Faith to Modern Unbelievers."
> In *Lumen Vitae* III (Sept. 1948) 411–16. Reprinted as "God in the Dock," in *Undeceptions* (1971) 197–201.

"Notes on the Way."
> In *Time and Tide* XXIX (Aug. 14, 1948) 830–31. Re-printed as "Priestesses in the Church?," in *Undeceptions* (1971) 191–96.

"On Living in an Atomic Age."
> In *Informed Living* IV (1948) 78–84. Reprinted in *Present Concern: Ethical Essays* (1986) 73–80.

"Some Thoughts."
> In *The First Decade: Ten Year's Work of the Medical Missionaries of Mary, 1937–1947*. Dublin: Sign of the Three Candles, 1948, 91–94.
>
> Written for the Medical Missionaries of Mary, Our Lady of Lourdes Hospital, Drogheda, Ireland. Re-printed in *Undeceptions* (1971) 115–18.

"The Trouble with 'X' . . ."
> In *The Bristol Diocesan Gazette* XXVII (Aug. 1948) 3–6. Re-printed in *Undeceptions* (1971) 119–22.

"Imagery in the Last Eleven Cantos of Dante's Comedy."
> Paper presented to the Oxford Dante Society, Nov. 9, 1948. Published in *Studies in Medieval and Renaissance Literature* (1966) 121–45.

Addresses, Lectures, and Sermons

"Kipling's World."
> An address to The English Association, in Guy Boas, Osbert Lancaster, C. S. Lewis, and I. H. Bell, Literature and Life: Addresses to the English

Association, Vol. 1. London: Harrap, 1948. Reprinted in *They Asked for a Paper: Papers and Addresses* (1962) 72–92.

1949
Books

Transposition and Other Addresses. London: Geoffrey Bless, 1949.
    Published in the USA: *The Weight of Glory and Other Addresses*. New York: Macmillan, 1949.

    N.B. this contains the 1st ed. (1944) of "Transposition."

Essays, Academic Papers, and Short Stories

"On Church Music."
    In *English Church Music*, XIX (Apr. 1949). Reprinted in *Christian Reflections* (1967) 94–99.

"The Humanitarian Theory of Punishment."
    In *20th Century: An Australian Quarterly Review* III.3 (1949) 5–12. This paper instigated a debate in print. See, Norval Morris and Donald Buckle, "Reply to C. S. Lewis," in *20th Century: An Australian Quarterly Review* VI.2 (1952) 20–26. Both Lewis's article and this reply were reprinted in *Res Judicatae*, VI (Jun. 1953) 224–30 and 231–37. See also, Professor J. J. C. Smart's "Comment: The Humanitarian Theory of Punishment," in *Res Judicatae* VI (Feb. 1954) 368–71. Lewis concluded the exchange: "On Punishment: A Reply," in *Res Judicatae*, VI (Aug. 1954) 519–23.

Radio Broadcasts

"The Novels of Charles Williams."
    Broadcast on BBC Radio, the Third Programme, Feb. 11, 1949. Published in *Of This and Other Worlds* (1982) 34–41.

    An extract from this recording can be heard on YouTube: www.youtube.com/watch?v=Z5w134gYz04

1950
Books

The Chronicles of Narnia. The Lion, the Witch and the Wardrobe. London: Geoffrey Bles, 1950.

Essays, Academic Papers, and Short Stories

"Avant-Propos a l'édition Française"
> In *Le Problème de la Souffrance*, 11–12. Translated by Marguerite Faguer. Paris: Desclée de Brouwer, 1950.

"Historicism."
> In *The Month* IV (Oct. 1950). Re-printed in *Christian Reflections* (1967) 100–113.

"What Are We to Make of Jesus Christ?"
> In *Asking Them Questions*, edited by Ronal Selby Wright. Third series. Oxford: Oxford University Press, 1950, 95–104. Re-printed in *Undeceptions* (1971) 123–27.

Addresses, Lectures, and Sermons

"The Literary Impact of the Authorized Version."
> The Ethel M. Wood Lecture, the University of London, 1950. Published in pamphlet form as, *The Literary Impact of the Authorized Version: The Ethel M. Wood Lecture Delivered before the University of London on Mar. 20, 1950*. London: The Althone Press, 1950. Reprinted in *They Asked for a Paper: Papers and Addresses* (1962) 26–50. Reprinted in *Selected Literary Essays* (1969) 126–45.

1951
Books

The Chronicles of Narnia. Prince Caspian: The Return to Narnia. London: Geoffrey Bles, 1951.

Essays, Academic Papers, and Short Stories

"Christian Hope—Its Meaning for Today."
> In *Religion and Life*, XXI (Winter 1951–52). Reprinted as, "The World's Last Night," in *The World's Last Night and Other Essays* (1960) 93–113.

1952
Books

Mere Christianity. A revised and amplified edition, with a new introduction, of the three books Broadcast Talks, Christian Behaviour, and Beyond Personality. London: Geoffrey Bles, 1952.

The Chronicles of Narnia. The Voyage of the Dawn Treader. London: Geoffrey Bles, 1952.

Essays, Academic Papers, and Short Stories

"Is Theism Important? A Reply."
>In *The Socratic Digest* No. 5 (1952) 48–51. Reprinted as, "Is Theism Important?" in *Undeceptions* (1971) 138–42.

"The Empty Universe."
>"Preface" to D. E. Hardings, *The Hierarchy of Heaven and Earth: A New Diagram of Man in the Universe*. London: Faber and Faber, 1952. Reprinted in *Present Concern: Ethical Essays* (1986) 81–86.

Addresses, Lectures, and Sermons

"Hero and Leander."
>The Warton Lecture on English Poetry. This was presented to the British Academy in 1952. Published in *The Proceedings of the British Academy* XXXVIII (1952). Reprinted in Selected Literary Essays (1969) 38–73.

"On Three Ways of Writing for Children."
>An address given to The Library Association. Published in *Proceedings, Papers and Summaries of Discussion at the Bournemouth Conference, Apr. 29, to May 2, 1952*. Reprinted in *Of Other Worlds. Essays and Stories* (1966) 22–34.

1953
Books

The Chronicles of Narnia. The Silver Chair. London: Geoffrey Bles, 1953.

Addresses, Lectures, and Sermons

"Petitionary Prayer."
>An address presented in to The Oxford Clerical Society, 8 December 1953. Published as "Petitionary Prayer: A Problem without an Answer," in *Christian Reflections* (1967) 142–51.

1954
Books

English Literature in the Sixteenth Century Excluding Drama. Oxford: Oxford University Press, Clarendon Press, 1954.

The Chronicles of Narnia. The Horse and His Boy. London: Geoffrey Bles, 1954.

Essays, Academic Papers, and Short Stories

"The Gods Return to Earth."
> Review of the first part of Tolkien's *The Lord of the Rings*, in *Time and Tide* (Aug. 14, 1954). Combined with "The Dethronement of Power" (1955) as, "Tolkien's The Lord of the Rings," in *Of This and Other Worlds* (1982) 95–103.

"Edmund Spenser, 1552–1599."
> In *Major British Writers*, edited by G. B. Harrison. London: Harcourt, 1954.

"A Note on Jane Austen."
> In *Essays in Criticism* IV (Oct. 1954). Reprinted in *Selected Literary Essays* (1969) 175–86.

Addresses, Lectures, and Sermons

"De Descriptione Temporum."
> Lewis's inaugural lecture at Cambridge, November 1954, published in pamphlet form 1955, by Cambridge University Press. Published subsequently in *They Asked for a Paper: Papers and Addresses*. London: Geoffrey Bles, 1962, 9–25; and in Selected Literary Essays (1969) 1–14.

1955
Books

Surprised by Joy: The Shape of My Early Life. London: Geoffrey Bles, 1955.

The Chronicles of Narnia. The Magician's Nephew. London: Geoffrey Bles, 1955.

Essays, Academic Papers, and Short Stories

"George Orwell."
> In *Time and Tide* XXXVI (Jan. 1955). Re-printed in *Of This and Other Worlds* (1982) 114–18

"Lilies that Fester."
> In *Twentieth Century* CLVII (Apr. 1955). Reprinted in *The World's Last Night and Other Essays* (1960) 31–50.

"On Obstinacy in Belief."
> A paper presented to the Oxford Socratic Club 1955, published in *The Sawanee Review* LXIII (Autumn 1955). Reprinted in *The World's Last Night and Other Essays* (1960) 13–30.

"On Science Fiction."
> A paper presented to the Cambridge University English Club, 24 Nov. 1955, Published in *Of Other Worlds. Essays and Stories* (1966) 59–73.

"Prudery and Philology."
> In *The Spectator* CXVIV (Jan. 21, 1955). Reprinted in *Present Concern: Ethical Essays* (1986) 87–91.

"The Dethronement of Power."
> Review of the second and third part of Tolkien's *Lord of the Rings*, in *Time and Tide* (Oct. 22, 1955). Combined with "The Gods Return to Earth" (1954) as, "Tolkien's *The Lord of the Rings*," in *Of This and Other Worlds* (1982) 95–103.

"Xmas and Christmas: a Lost Chapter from Herodotus."
> In *Time and Tide* XXXV (Dec. 4, 1955) 1607. Re-printed in *Undeceptions* (1971) 250–52.

1956
Books

The Chronicles of Narnia. The Last Battle. London: Geoffrey Bles, 1956.

Till We Have Faces. London: Geoffrey Bles, 1956.

Essays, Academic Papers, and Short Stories

"Behind the Scenes."
> In *Time and Tide* XXXVII (Dec. 1, 1956). Re-printed in *Undeceptions* (1971) 202–6.

"Interim Report."
> In *The Cambridge Review* (Apr. 21, 1956). Reprinted in *Present Concern: Ethical Essays* (1986) 92–99.

"Sometimes Fairy Stories May Say Best What's to be Said."
> In *The New York Times Book Review*, Children's Section, (Nov. 18 1956). Reprinted in *Of Other Worlds. Essays and Stories* (1966) 35–38.

"The Shoddy Lands."
> In *The Magazine of Fantasy and Science Fiction* 10. 2 (Feb. 1956) 68–74. Reprinted in *Of Other Worlds. Essays and Stories* (1966) 99–106.

Addresses, Lectures, and Sermons

"Thoughts of a Cambridge Don."
> A sermon preached in Magdalene College Chapel, Cambridge, 1956, published in *The Lion: The Magazine of St Mark's Dundela, Belfast* (Jan. 1963). Re-printed as, "A Slip of the Tongue," in *Screwtape Proposes a Toast and other Pieces* (1965) 113–18.

"Imagination and Thought in the Middle Ages."
> A pair of lectures presented to the Zoological Laboratory Cambridge, Jul. 17 and 18 1956. Published in *Studies in Medieval and Renaissance Literature* (1966) 41–63.

"Sir Walter Scott."
> An address given to the Edinburgh Sir Walter Scott Club, 1956, published in *The Edinburgh Sir Walter Scott Club Forty-ninth Annual Report*, 1956. Reprinted in *They Asked for a Paper: Papers and Addresses* (1962) 93–104.

1957
Essays, Academic Papers, and Short Stories

"Delinquents in the Snow."
> In *Time and Tide* XXXVIII (Dec. 7, 1957) 1512–22. Re-printed in *Undeceptions* (1971) 255–58.

"Is History Bunk?"
> In *The Cambridge Review* LXXVIII (Jun. 1, 1957) 647 and 649. Reprinted in *Present Concern: Ethical Essays* (1986) 100–104.

"The Psalms."
> Written c. 1957–58. Published in *Christian Reflections* (1967) 114–28.

"What Christmas Means to Me."
> In *Twentieth Century* CLXII (Dec. 1957) 517–18. Re-printed in *Undeceptions* (1971) 253–54.

"Dante's Statius."
> Published in *Medium Aevum* XXV.3 (1957). Reprinted in *Studies in Medieval and Renaissance Literature* (1966) 94–102.

1958
Books

Reflections on the Psalms. London: Geoffrey Bles, 1958.

Essays, Academic Papers, and Short Stories

"A Tribute to E. R. Eddison."
> Probably written sometime in the mid-1950s, this short piece was published on the dust jacket of E. R. Eddison's *The Mezentian Gate* in 1958. Re-printed in *Of This and Other Worlds* (1982) 42.

"Ministering Angels."
: In *The Magazine of Fantasy and Science Fiction*, XII (Jan. 1958). Reprinted in *Of Other Worlds. Essays and Stories* (1966) 107–18. Written in reply to an article by Robert S. Richardson, "The Day after We Land on Mars," in *The Saturday Review* XXXVIII (May 28, 1958) 28.

"On Juvenile Tastes."
: In *The Church Times*, Children's Supplement CXLI (Nov. 28, 1958). Reprinted in *Of Other Worlds. Essays and Stories* (1966) 39–41.

"Rejoinder to Dr Pittenger."
: In *Christian Century* LXXV (Nov. 26, 1958) 1369–71. Re-published in *Undeceptions* (1971) 143–48. Lewis's rejoinder was in response to W. Norman Pittenger, "Apologist versus Apologist: a Critique of C. S. Lewis as 'Defender of the Faith,'" in *Christian Century* LXXV (Oct. 1, 1958) 1104–7.

"The Genesis of a Medieval Book."
: A draft chapter for a proposed book written c. 1958–60, published in *Studies in Medieval and Renaissance Literature* (1966) 18–40.

"Revival or Decay?"
: In *Punch*, CCXXXV (9 July 1958) 36–38. Reprinted in *Undeceptions* (1971) 207–10.

"Religion and Rocketry."
: Written in 1958. First published as, "Will We Lose God in Outer Space?" in *The Christian Herald* LXXXI (Apr. 1958). Reprinted as a pamphlet, *Shall We Lose God in Outer Space?* London: SPCK, 1959. Then as, "Religion and Rocketry," in *The World's Last Night and Other Essays* (1960) 83–92.

"Willing Slaves of the Welfare State."
: The second in a series, "Is Progress Possible?" in *The Observer* (Jul. 20, 1958) 6. Reprinted in *Undeceptions* (1971) 259–64.

Addresses, Lectures, and Sermons

"A Panegyric for Dorothy L. Sayers."
: Oration written for the memorial service for Dorothy L. Sayers in St Margaret's Church London, Jan. 15 1958. Published in *Of This and Other Worlds* (1982) 104–5.

1959
Essays, Academic Papers, and Short Stories

"After Ten Years."
>In Of Other Worlds. *Essays and Stories* (1966) 127–45. Written in 1959, this is the fragment of an unpublished novel, which Lewis discussed with Roger Lancelyn Green and Alastair Fowler at the time of composition. Notes from this conversation are published, 146–48. Reprinted in *The Dark Tower and Other Stories* (1977) 129–53; Lancelyn Green/Fowler notes, 154–57, with a contextual explanation of the unfinished novel by Walter Hooper, xii–xiv.

"Good Work and Good Works."
>In *The Catholic Art Quarterly* (1959). Reprinted in *Good Work*, XXIII (Christmas 1959) then in *The World's Last Night and Other Essays* (1960) 71–82.

"Modern Theology and Biblical Criticism."
>A paper read at Westcott House, Cambridge, May 11, 1959, first published in *Christian Reflections*, (1967) 152–66. In later editions this essay is re-named "Fern Seeds and Elephants": see, *Fern Seed and Elephants* (1975). 86–105.

"Screwtape Proposes a Toast."
>In *The Saturday Evening Post* (USA) CCXXXII Dec. (19, 1959). Re-printed in *The World's Last Night and Other Essays* (1960) 51–70, and, in *The Screwtape Letters and Screwtape Proposes a Toast* (1961) 1–18.

"The Efficacy of Prayer."
>In *The Atlantic Monthly*, CCIII (Jan. 1959). Reprinted in *The World's Last Night and Other Essays* (1960) 3–12.

"De Audiendis Poetis."
>An early draft chapter for a proposed book c. 1959. Published in *Studies in Medieval and Renaissance Literature* (1966) 1–17.

1960
Books

Miracles. 2nd ed. London: J. M. Dent, 1960.

The Four Loves. London: Geoffrey Bles, 1960.

Studies in Words. Cambridge: Cambridge University Press, 1960.

The World's Last Night and Other Essays. New York: Harcourt, Brace and World, 1960.

Essays, Academic Papers, and Short Stories

"It All Began with a Picture..."
In *The Radio Times*, Junior Section CXLVIII (Jul. 15, 1960). Re-printed in *Of Other Worlds. Essays and Stories* (1966) 42.

"The Language of Religion."
In *Christian Reflections* (1967) 129–41. An address written for the Twelfth Symposium of the Colston Research Society, held at the University of Bristol, March 1960, which Lewis was unable to attend due to ill health.

"Haggard Rides Again."
A review of Morton Norton Cohen, *Rider Haggard: His Life and Works* (1960) in Time and Tide XLI (Sept. 3, 1960). Reprinted as, "The Mythopoeic Gift of Rider Haggard," in *Of This and Other Worlds* (1982) 109–13.

"Metre."
In *A Review of English Literature* I (Jan. 1960). Reprinted in *Selected Literary Essays* (1969) 280–85.

1961
Books

An Experiment in Criticism. Cambridge: Cambridge University Press, 1961.

N. W. Clerk (pseudonym for C. S. Lewis), *A Grief Observed*. London: Faber & Faber, 1961.

Essays, Academic Papers, and Short Stories

"Four-Letter words."
>In *The Critical Quarterly* III (Summer 1961). Reprinted in *Selected Literary Essays* (1969) 169–74.

"On Myth."
>In *An Experiment on Criticism*. Cambridge: Cambridge University Press, 1961, 40–49.

"Before We Can Communicate."
>In *Breakthrough* 8 (Oct. 1961) 2. Reprinted in *Undeceptions* (1971) 211–15.

"Neoplatonism in the Poetry of Spenser."
>In *Etudes Anglaises* XIV.2 (1961). Re-printed in *Studies in Medieval and Renaissance Literature* (1966) 149–63.

1962
Books

They Asked for a Paper: Papers and Addresses. London: Geoffrey Bles, 1962.

Essays, Academic Papers, and Short Stories

"Sex in Literature."
    In *The Sunday Telegraph* 87 (Sept. 30, 1962) 8. Reprinted in *Present Concern: Ethical Essays* (1986) 105–8.

"Transposition." 2nd ed.
    A reworked and extended edition of the sermon from 1944, as an academic paper, in *They Asked for a Paper: Papers and Addresses* (1962), 166–82.

"The Anthropological Approach."
    In *English and Medieval Studies*. Presented to J R. R. Tolkien on the Occasion of his Seventieth Birthday, edited by Norman Davis and C. L. Wrenn. London, George Allen and Unwin, 1962.

Radio Broadcasts and Audio Presentations

"The Vision of John Bunyan."
    Broadcast by the BBC. Published in *The Listener* LXVIII (Dec. 13, 1962). Reprinted in *Selected Literary Essays* (1969) 146–53.

"'The Establishment Must Die and Rot . . .', C. S. Lewis Discusses Science Fiction with Kingsley Amis."
    A discussion recorded on Dec. 4, 1962 between C. S. Lewis, Kingsley Amis, and Brian Aldiss, published in *SF Horizons* 1 (Spring 1964). Reprinted as, "Unreal Estates," in *Encounter*, XXIV (Mar. 1965) and in *Of Other Worlds. Essays and Stories* (1966) 86–96.

1963
Essays, Academic Papers, and Short Stories

Sherwood E. Wirt and C. S. Lewis, "I was Decided Upon."
Sherwood E. Wirt and C. S. Lewis, "Heaven, Earth and Outer Space."
    In *Decision* II (Sept., 1963) 3, and, *Decision* II (Oct. 1963) 4. The Interviews were conducted in Lewis's rooms at Magdalen College Cambridge on Tuesday, May 7, 1963, by Sherwood E. Wirt of the Billy Graham Evangelistic Association. The two parts were reprinted together as, "Cross-Examination," in *Undeceptions* (1971) 215–21.

"Must Our Image of God Go?"
> In *The Observer* (Mar. 24, 1963) 14. Reprinted in David L. Edwards, *The Honest to God Debate: Some Reactions to the Book 'Honest to God' with a New Chapter by its Author, J. A. T. Robinson, Bishop of Woolwich*. London: SCM Press, 1963, 91–92, and, in *Undeceptions* (1971) 149–50.

"Onward, Christian Spacemen."
> In *Show* III (February 1963). Reprinted as, "The Seeing Eye," in *Christian Reflections* (1967) 167–76.

"We Have No 'Right to Happiness.'"
> Written shortly before Lewis's death in November 1963, and published in *The Saturday Evening Post*, CCXXXVI (Dec. 21–28, 1963) 10 and 12. Re-printed in *Undeceptions* (1971) 265–69.

"Spenser's Cruel Cupid."
> A draft chapter for a book on Spenser, written in 1963, a few months before Lewis' death, and published in *Studies in Medieval and Renaissance Literature* (1966) 164–74.

C. S. Lewis died on November 22, 1963

4. C. S. LEWIS: PUBLICATIONS—*POST MORTEM*

1964
Books

Letters to Malcolm: Chiefly on Prayer. London: Geoffrey Bles, 1964.

The Discarded Image: An Introduction to Medieval and Renaissance Literature. Cambridge: Cambridge University Press, 1964.

Poems. Edited by Walter Hooper. London: Geoffrey Bles, 1964.

1965
Books

Screwtape Proposes a Toast, and Other Pieces. London: Collins, Fontana Paperbacks, 1965.

1966
Books

Letters of C. S. Lewis. Edited, with a memoir, by W. H. Lewis. London: Geoffrey Bles, 1966.

Studies in Medieval and Renaissance Literature. Cambridge: Cambridge University Press, 1966.

Of Other Worlds. Essays and Stories. Edited by Walter Hooper; London: Geoffrey Bles, 1966.

Essays, Academic Papers, and Short Stories

"Forms of Things Unknown."
> First publication—date of composition unknown—in, *Of Other Worlds. Essays and Stories.* Edited by Walter Hooper. London: Geoffrey Bles, 1966, 119–26.

"On Criticism"
> First publication—date of composition unknown—in *Of Other Worlds: Essays and Stories*, edited by Walter Hooper. London: Geoffrey Bles, 1966, 43–58.

1967
Books

Spenser's Images of Life. Edited by Alastair Fowler. Cambridge: Cambridge University Press, 1967.

Letters to an American Lady. Edited by Clyde S. Kilby. Grand Rapids: Eerdmans, 1967.

Christian Reflections. Edited by Walter Hooper. London: Geoffrey Bles, 1967.

Essays, Academic Papers, and Short Stories

"The Funeral of a Great Myth."
> First publication—date of composition unknown—in, *Christian Reflections*, edited by Walter Hooper. London: Geoffrey Bles, 1967, 82–93.

1969
Books

Selected Literary Essays. Cambridge: Cambridge University Press, 1969.

Narrative Poems. Edited by Walter Hooper. London: Geoffrey Bles, 1969.

1970
Books

God in the Dock: Essays on Theology and Ethics. Grand Rapids: Eerdmans, 1970.
>Published as, *Undeceptions* (1971) in UK.

1971
Books

Undeceptions: Essays on Theology and Ethics. Edited by Walter Hooper. London: Geoffrey Bles, 1971.
>Published as, *God in the Dock: Essays on Theology and Ethics* (1970) in US.

1975
Books

Fern Seed and Elephants: and Other Essays on Christianity. Edited by Walter Hooper. London: Collins, Fontana, 1975.

1977
Books

The Dark Tower and Other Stories. London: Collins, 1977.

1979
Books

They Stand Together: The Letters of C. S. Lewis to Arthur Greeves 1914–1963. Edited by Walter Hooper. London: Collins, 1979.

God in the Dock. Edited by Walter Hooper. London: Fount, 1979.

1982
Books

Of This and Other Worlds. Edited by Walter Hooper. London: Collins, Fontana, 1982.

1985
Books

Boxen: The Imaginary World of the Young C. S. Lewis. Edited by Walter Hooper. London, Collins, 1985.

1986
Books

Present Concerns: Ethical Essays. Edited by Walter Hooper. London: Collins, Fount, 1986.

1987
Books

Timeless at Heart. Edited by Walter Hooper. London: Collins, Fount, 1987.

1988
Books

Letters of C. S. Lewis. Revised and enlarged, edited by Walter Hooper. London: Fount, 1988.

1990
Books

Christian Reunion and Other Essays. Edited by Walter Hooper. London: Collins, Fount, 1990

1991
Books

All My Road Before Me: The Diary of C. S. Lewis 1922–27. London: Harper Collins, 1991.

1994
Books

The Collected Poems of C. S. Lewis. Edited by Walter Hooper. London: Fount Paperbacks, 1994.

1998
Books

Screwtape Proposes a Toast. London: Fount, Harper Collins, 1998.

2000
Books

Essay Collection and Other Short Pieces. London: Harper Collins, 2000.
> N.B. : hardback edition containing most, but not all, of Lewis's essays, academic papers, etc. Most, but not all, of the missing material can be found in *Christian Reflections* (1967) and *Undeceptions* (1971).

Essay Collection: Literature, Philosophy and Short Stories. London: Harper Collins, 2000.
> Paperback edition, containing half of the material in the hardback *Essay Collection and Other Short Pieces*.

Essay Collection: Faith, Christianity and the Church. London: Harper Collins, 2000.
> Paperback edition, containing the other half of the material in the hardback *Essay Collection and Other Short Pieces*.

2004
Books

Collected Letters, Vol. I: Family Letters 1905–1931. San Francisco: Harper San Francisco, 2004.

Collected Letters, Vol. II: Books, Broadcasts and War 1931–1949. San Francisco: Harper San Francisco, 2004.

2007
Books

Collected Letters, Vol. III: Narnia, Cambridge and Joy 1950–1963. San Francisco: Harper San Francisco, 2007.

3

C. S. Lewis: Correspondent

Lewis was a voluminous letter writer. For decades he answered all letters himself, by hand (he was a master of the fountain pen). Late in life Warnie, his brother, helped him in the role of amanuensis. In terms of correspondence three very large volumes of Lewis's letters were published between 2004 and 2007 (totalling around 4,000 pages), however, these are not complete. Some of the missing letters may be found in earlier smaller volumes.

1966
Lewis, C. S. *Letters of C. S. Lewis*. 1st edition. Edited by W. H. Lewis. London: Geoffrey Bles, 1966.
> Compiled by his brother (Warren Hamilton Lewis) three years after Lewis's death, this is a thematic selection, chronologically arranged with a memoir by "Warnie:" A rare edition, but containing some letters not published elsewhere.

1967
———. *Letters to an American Lady*. Edited by Clyde S. Kilby. Grand Rapids: Eerdmans, 1967.
> A collection of letters, correspondence (1950–63) between Lewis and an American lady—Mary—whom he never met The correspondence is very human, revealing of the ordinary, and characterized by Christian advice.

1979
———. *They Stand Together: The Letters of C. S. Lewis to Arthur Greeves 1914–1963*. Edited by Walter Hooper. London: Collins, 1979.
> Arthur Greeves was a lifelong friend of Lewis's. They shared much together, from a love of Wagner, to matters of faith.

1985

——. *C. S. Lewis: Letters to Children*. Edited by Lyle W. Dorsett and Marjorie Lamp Mead; Foreword, Douglas Gresham. New York: Touchstone, 1985.
> Lewis's correspondence with children—often about Narnia—but also on matters of schools, pets, etc. Lewis respected children and did not talk down to them.

1988

——. *Letters of C. S. Lewis*. 2nd edition. Revised and enlarged. Edited by Walter Hooper. London: Fount, 1988.

——. Don Giovanna Calabria and Martin Moynihan. *The Latin Letters of C. S. Lewis*. Edited and translated by Martin Moynihan. South Bend: St Augustine's Press, 1998.
> Lewis corresponded with two Italian readers of his work from 1947-1963. Neither knew any English so the correspondence was conducted in Latin.

2004

——. *Collected Letters, Vol. I: Family Letters 1905-1931*. Edited by Walter Hooper. San Francisco: Harper San Francisco, 2004.

——. *Collected Letters, Vol. II: Books, Broadcasts and War 1931-1949*. Edited by Walter Hooper. San Francisco: Harper San Francisco, 2004.

2007

——. *Collected Letters, Vol. III: Narnia, Cambridge and Joy 1950-1963*. Edited by Walter Hooper. San Francisco: Harper San Francisco, 2007.

2011

——. *Yours, Jack: The Inspirational Letters of C. S. Lewis*. Edited by Paul F. Ford. San Francisco, CA: Harper Collins, 2011.
> A selection of relevant and distinct passages from the three main volumes 2004–2007.

4

Helen Joy Davidman: An Annotated Historical Bibliography

1. PRIMARY SOURCES

1938
Books

Davidman, Joy, *Letter to a Comrade*. New Haven, CT: Yale University Press, 1938.

1940
Books

Davidman, Joy, *Anya*. New York: Macmillan, 1940.

1943
Books

Davidman, Joy, editor, *War Poems of the United Nations: The Songs and Battle Cries of a World at War, Three Hundred Poems, One Hundred and Fifty Poets from Twenty Countries*. New York: Dial Press, 1943.

1944
Books

Alexander F. Bergman and Joy Davidman, *They Look Like Men*. New York: B. Ackerman, 1944.

Essays, Academic Papers, and Short Stories

Thomas Yoseloff, editor, *Seven Poets in Search of an Answer: Maxwell Bodenheim, Joy Davidman, Langston Hughes, Aaron Kramer, Alfred Kreymborg, Martha Millet, Norman Rosten. Introduction by Shaemas O'Sheel*. New York: B. Ackerman, 1944.

1949
Essays, Academic Papers, and Short Stories

"Theatre Party." *Blue Book Magazine* (Feb. 1949). New York: McCall Corporation.
    A short story in a women's magazine, an issue on the theme of, Early Days of Virginia the Mother of States.

1950
Books

Weeping Bay. New York: Macmillan, 1950.

1951
Essays, Academic Papers, and Short Stories

"The Longest Way Round." In *These Found the Way: Thirteen Converts to Protestant Christianity*, edited by David Soper. Philadelphia: Westminster Press, 1951, 13–26.

1954
Books

Smoke on the Mountain: An Interpretation of the Ten Commandments in Terms of Today. Foreword by C. S. Lewis; Philadelphia: The Westminster Press, 1954.

2. SECONDARY SOURCES

Allego, Donna M. "The Construction and Role of Community in Political Long Poems by Twentieth-Century American Women Poets: Lola Ridge, Genevieve Taggard, Joy Davidman, Margaret Walker, and Muriel Rukeyser." PhD thesis, Southern Illinois University at Carbondale, 1997.

Dorsett, Lyle W. *Eine andere Art von Hunger: Joy Davidman—ihr Leben u. ihre Ehe mit C. S. Lewis*. Basel: Brunnen-Verlag, 1985.

———. *And God Came In: The Extraordinary Story of Joy Davidman, her Life and Marriage to C. S. Lewis*. New York: Macmillan, 1983.

———. *A Love Observed: Joy Davidman's Life and Marriage to C. S. Lewis.* 2nd ed. Reprint. North Wind Books. Colorado Springs, CO: Harold Shaw Publishers, 1998.

Fleischer, Leonore, and William Nicholson. *Shadowlands: A Novel.* New York: Signet, 1993.

Gresham, Douglas H. *Lenten Lands: My Childhood with Joy Davidman and C. S. Lewis.* London: HarperCollins, 1998.

Harwood, Laurence. *C. S. Lewis, My Godfather: Letters, Photos, and Recollections.* Downers Grove, IL: InterVarsity Press, 2007.

Hatfield, Jamie Elisa. S"uppressed by Jack: The Discovery of Lewis's Views on Women." Milligan College, TN: Milligan College, 1996.

King, Don. "Joy Davidman and the New Masses: Communist Poet and Reviewer." *The Chronicle of the Oxford University C. S. Lewis Society*, 4.1 (2007) 18–44.

Nelson, Cary. *Anthology of Modern American Poetry.* London: Oxford University Press, 2000.

Pilat, Oliver. "Girl Communist: An Intimate Story of Eight Years in the Party." Serialized in *The New York Post*, 1949.

Salzman, Jack and Leo Zanderer. *Social Poetry of the 1930s: A Selection.* New York: Burt Franklin, 1978.

Sibley, Brian. *Shadowlands: The True Story of C. S. Lewis and Joy Davidman.* London: Hodder & Stoughton, 1985.

———. *Shadowlands—eine späte Liebe: die Geschichte von C. S. Lewis und Joy Davidman.* Basel: Brunnen-Verlag, 1987.

Storm, Hans Otto. *American Writing.* Prairie City, IL: J. A. Decker, 1940.

Yoseloff, Thomas, *Seven Poets in Search of an Answer: A Poetic Symposium.* Miami: Granger Books, 1976.

5

C. S. Lewis: Revelation And The Christ: Secondary Sources—Books

The following is a brief a comprehensive, though not definitive, bibliography of works about Lewis. This relates to his Christology and understanding of revelation specifically, and to Lewis's *corpus* generally. In compiling it became clear that the traditional pattern of book production and publishing has changed. Some works are self-published through websites such as www.lulu.com. Others are publishing houses that only exist and sell through the World Wide Web (and hence being part of multinational companies have no geographic address).

All sources can be accessed through one of three websites: Amazon;[1] ABE (Advanced Book Exchange: a website that collates the databases of tens of thousands of second-hand bookshops and resellers worldwide);[2] and WorldCat (OCLC: an academic site that collates the library catalogues from thousands of universities, colleges and public libraries).[3]

Adey, Lionel. *C. S. Lewis: Writer, Dreamer and Mentor*. Grand Rapids: Eerdmans, 1998.

Aeschliman, Michael D. *The Restitution of Man: C. S. Lewis and the Case against Scientism*. Grand Rapids: Eerdmans, 1998.

Almodovar, Nancy A. *The Problem of Pain: A Brief History and Account and Critique of C. S. Lewis's Work*. Seattle, WA: Create Space, 2012.

Arnott, Anne. *The Secret Country of C. S. Lewis*. London: Hodder and Stoughton, 1974.

---

1 Amazon: www.amazon.com; www.amazon.co.uk; www.amazon.de; www.amazon.fr; etc.
2 ABE: www.abebooks.com; www.abebooks.co.uk.
3 WorldCat: www.worldcat.org.

Athanasius. *The Incarnation of the Word: Being the Treatise of St Athanasius, De incarnatione Verbi Dei.* Translated by Sr Penelope CSMV, "Introduction" by C. S. Lewis. London: Centenary, 1944.

Balfour, Arthur James, and, Michael W. Perry. *Theism and Humanism: The Book That Influenced C. S. Lewis.* www.inklingsbooks.com: Inkling Books, 2000.

Barfield Owen. *Owen Barfield on C. S. Lewis.* www.barfieldsociety.org: Barfield Press, 2011.

Bassham, Gregory and Jerry L. Walls. *The Chronicles of Narnia and Philosophy : The Lion, The Witch, and The Worldview.* Chicago, IL: Carus, 2005.

Bendicks, Christina. *Die Apologie des Christentums bei C. S. Lewis und ihre möglichen Auswirkungen auf die religionspädagogische Praxis.* München, Germany: Grin, 2011.

Benge, Janet, and Geoff Benge. *C. S. Lewis: Master Storyteller. Christian Heroes: Then and Now.* Seattle: YWAM, 2007.

Berman, Jeffrey. *Companionship in Grief: Love and Loss in the Memoirs of C. S. Lewis, John Bayley, Donald Hall, Joan Didion, and Calvin Trillin.* Amherst, MA: University of Massachusetts Press, 2010.

Beversluis, John. *C. S. Lewis and the Search for Rational Religion.* Grand Rapids: Eerdmans, 1985.

Billy, Dennis J. *C. S. Lewis on the Fullness of Life: Longing for Deep Heaven.* Boston: Paulist, 2009.

Bleakley, David. *C. S. Lewis at Home in Ireland: a Centenary Biograph.* Foreword by Walter Hooper. Bangor, N. Ireland: Strandtown, 1998.

Boenig, Robert. *C. S. Lewis and the Middle Ages.* Kent, OH: Kent State University Press, 2012.

Brand, Hilary. *Not a Tame Lion: A Lent Course Based on the Writings of C. S. Lewis.* London: Darton, Longman and Todd, 2008.

Bray, Suzanne, and, Kathryn Feldman. *A travers l'Armoire magique: C-S Lewis et l'univers de Narnia.* Montréal, Québec: Farel, 2005.

Brown, Devin. *Inside Narnia. A Guide to Exploring The Lion, the Witch and the Wardrobe.* Grand Rapids: Baker, 2005.

5. C. S. Lewis: Revelation and The Christ: Secondary Sources—Books

Brunner, Kurt, and, Jim Ware. *Finding God in the Land of Narnia*. Carol Stream, IL: Saltriver, 2005.

Burson, Scott R., and Jerry L. Walls. *C. S. Lewis and Francis Schaeffer: Lessons for a New Century from the Most Influential Apologists of Our Time*. Downers Grove, IL: InterVarsity, 1998.

Carnell, Corbin S. *Bright Shadow of Reality: C. S. Lewis and the Feeling Intellect*. Grand Rapids: Eerdmans, 1974.

———. *Bright Shadow of Reality: Spiritual Longing in C. S. Lewis*. Grand Rapids: Eerdmans, 1999.

Carpenter, Humphrey. *The Inklings: C. S. Lewis, J. R. R. Tolkien, Charles Williams and Their Friends*. London: George Allen and Unwin, 1997.

Caughey, Shanna. *Revisiting Narnia. Fantasy, Myth and Religion in C. S. Lewis' Chronicles*. Dallas, TX: Bella, 2005.

Christensen, Michael J. *C. S. Lewis on Scripture*. London: Hodder and Stoughton, 1980.

Clark, David George. *C. S. Lewis: A Guide to his Theology*. Blackwell Brief Histories of Religion. Oxford: Wiley-Blackwell, 2007.

———. *C. S. Lewis Goes to Heaven: A Reader's Guide to The Great Divorce*. wingedlionpress.com: Winged Lion, 2012.

Como, James. *Remembering C. S. Lewis: Recollections of Those Who Knew Him*. San Francisco: Ignatius, 1994.

Conn, Marie A. *C. S. Lewis and Human Suffering: Light Among the Shadows*. Bel Air, CA: HiddenSpring, 2008.

Connolly, Sean. *Inklings of Heaven: C. S. Lewis and Eschatology*. Leominster, UK: Gracewing, 2007.

Coren, Michael. *C. S. Lewis: The Man Who Created Narnia*. San Francisco: Ignatius, 1994.

———. *C. S. Lewis: The Man Who Created Narnia*. San Francisco: Ignatius, 2006.

———. *The Man Who Created Narnia: Story of C. S. Lewis*. Grand Rapids: Eerdmans, 1997.

Cunningham, Richard Bryan. *C. S. Lewis: Defender of the Faith*. 1967. Reprint. C. S. Lewis Secondary Studies. Eugene, OR: Wipf and Stock, 2008.

De Segovia, José. *El Principe Caspian Y La Fe De C. S. Lewis*. Barcelona, España: Publicaciones Andamio, 2010.

Derrick, Christopher. *C. S. Lewis and the Church of Rome*. San Francisco: Ignatius, 1981.

Dickerson, Matthew, and, David A. O'Hara. *Narnia and the Fields of Arbol: The Environmental Vision of C. S. Lewis. Culture of the Land*. Lexington, KY: The University Press of Kentucky, 2009.

Doris, T. M. *C. S. Lewis in Context*. Kent, OH: Kent State University Press, 1998.

Dorman, Susan C. *Fantastic Travelogue: Mark Twain and C. S. Lewis Talk Things Over in The Hereafter*. Raleigh, N.C: www.lulu.com, 2010.

Dorsett, Lyle W. *Seeking the Secret Place: The Spiritual Formation of C. S. Lewis*. Ada, MI: Baker, 2004.

Downing, David C. *Into the Wardrobe: C. S. Lewis and the Narnia Chronicles*. Hoboken, NJ: Wiley and Sons, 2005.

———. *Planets in Peril: A Critical Study of C. S. Lewis's Ransom Trilogy*. Amherst, MA: University of Massachusetts Press, 1992.

Draper, Sarah. *A Theological Journey into Narnia: An Analysis of the Message Beneath the Text of the Lion, the Witch and the Wardrobe*. Göttingen: Vandenhoeck and Ruprecht, 2005.

Duriez, Colin. *The C. S. Lewis Chronicles. The Indispensable Biography of the Creator of Narnia Full of Little-Known Facts, Events and Miscellany*. London, Darton, Longman and Todd, 2005.

———. *C. S. Lewis Handbook*. Eastbourne, UK: Monarch, 1990.

———. *The C. S. Lewis Encyclopedia. A Complete Guide to his Life, Thought and Writings*. Wheaton, IL : Crossway, 2000.

———. *J. R. R. Tolkien and C. S. Lewis: The Story of Their Friendship.* Stroud, UK: History, 2005.

Edwards, Bruce L. (editor). *C. S. Lewis: Life, Works, and Legacy. 4 Vols.* Santa Barbara, CA: Praeger, 2007.

———. *Further Up and Further In: Understanding C. S. Lewis's the Lion, the Witch and the Wardrobe.* Nashville, TN: Broadman and Holman, 2005.

Elst, Philip Vander. *Thinkers of our Time: C. S. Lewis.* London: Claridge, 1996.

Feddes, David. *Missional Apologetics: Cultural Diagnosis and Gospel Plausibility in C. S. Lewis and Lesslie Newbigin.* www.missionalapologetics.com: Missional Apologetics, 2012.

Fernandez, Irène. *Mythe, raison ardente: Imagination et réalité selon C. S. Lewis.* Genève Switzerland: AD Solem, 2005.

Fernández, Pablo de Felipe. *C. S. Lewis. Biografía De Bolsillo.* Barcelona: Andamio, 2008.

Ferrier, Jordan. *Calvin and C. S. Lewis Solving the Riddle of the Reformation.* Allendale, MI: Jordan Ferrier, 2010.

Filmer, Kath. *The Fiction of C. S. Lewis: Mask and Mirror.* New York: St. Martin's, 1993.

Ford, Paul F. *Companion to Narnia: A Complete Guide to the Magical World of C. S. Lewis's the Chronicles of Narnia.* Grand Rapids: ZonderKidz, 2005.

Fredrick, Candice and Sam McBride. *Women among the Inklings: Gender, C. S. Lewis, J. R. R. Tolkien and Charles Williams.* Contributions in Women's Studies. Westport, CT: Greenwood, 2001.

Friskney, Paul. *Sharing the Narnia Experience: A Family Guide to C. S. Lewis's the Lion, the Witch, and the Wardrobe.* Peabody, MA: Standard, 2005.

Gibb, Jocelyn, editor. *Light on C. S. Lewis.* London: Bles, 1965.

Gibson, Evan K. *C. S. Lewis, Spinner of Tales: a Guide to his Fiction.* Washington, DC: Christian University Press, 1980.

Gilbert, Douglas R. *C. S. Lewis: Images of his World*. London: Hodder and Stoughton, 1973.

Glaspey, Terry, and, George Grant, editors. *Not a Tame Lion: The Spiritual Legacy of C. S. Lewis. Leaders in Action*. Nashville, TN: Cumberland House, 2008.

Glyer, Diana Pavlac. *The Company They Keep: C. S. Lewis and J. R. R. Tolkien as Writers in Community*. Kent, OH: Kent State University Press, 2008.

Goffar, Jane, editor and compiler. *C. S. Lewis Index. Rumours from the Sculptor's Shop*. Carlisle, UK: Paternoster, 1995.

Gray, William. *C. S. Lewis*. Tabor City, NC: Atlantic, 2010.

Green, Roger Lancelyn, and Walter Hooper. *C. S. Lewis: a Biography*. 1st ed. London: Harper Collins, 1974.

Green, Roger Lancelyn, and Walter Hooper. *C. S. Lewis: a Biography*. 2nd ed., revised and expanded. London: Harper Collins, 2002.

Griffin, William. *C. S. Lewis, The Authentic Voice*. Oxford: Lion, 1988.

———. *C. S. Lewis: Spirituality for Mere Christians*. 1st ed. New York: Crossroads, 1998.

———. *C. S. Lewis: Spirituality for Mere Christians*. 2nd ed. Eugene, OR: Wipf and Stock, 2007.

———. *Clive Staples Lewis: A Dramatic Life*. San Francisco: Harper and Row, 1986.

Gulisano, Paolo. *C. S. Lewis. Tra fantasy e Vangelo*. Milano, Italy: Ancora, 2005.

Hannay, Margaret P. *C. S. Lewis*. New York: Ungar, 1981.

Hardy, Elizabeth Baird. *Milton, Spenser and the Chronicles of Narnia: Literary Sources for the C. S. Lewis Novels*. Jefferson, NC: McFarland, 2007.

Harries, Richard. *C. S. Lewis: the Man and his God*. London: Fount, 1987.

Hart, Dabney Adams. "C. S. Lewis's Defense of Poesie." Thesis. Madison, WI: University of Wisconsin, 1959.

———. *Through the Open Door: A New Look at C. S. Lewis.* Tuscaloosa, AL: The University of Alabama Press, 2011.

Hiley, Margaret. *The Loss and the Silence. Aspects of Modernism in the Works of C. S. Lewis, J. R. R. Tolkien and Charles Williams.* Zollikofen, Switzerland: Walking Tree, 2011.

Hill, Richard, and, Lyle Smith. *Teaching C. S. Lewis: A Handbook for Professors, Church Leaders, and Lewis Enthusiasts.* Cambridge: Cambridge Scholars, 2007.

Holbrook, David. *The Skeleton in the Wardrobe: C. S. Lewis's Fantasies—A Phenomenological Study.* Lewisburg, PA: Bucknell University Press, 1991.

Hooper, Walter. *C. S. Lewis A Companion and Guide.* London: Harper Collins, 1996.

———, editor. *Mark vs. Tristram: Correspondence between C. S. Lewis and Owen Barfield.* Cambridge, MA: Lowell House, 1967.

———. *Past Watchful Dragons: The Origin, Interpretation, and Appreciation of the Chronicles of Narnia.* C. S. Lewis Secondary Studies. Eugene, OR: Wipf and Stock, 2007.

Howard, Thomas. *C. S. Lewis: Man of Letters—A Reading of his Fiction.* San Francisco: Ignatius, 1987.

———. *Narnia and Beyond: A Guide to the Fiction of C. S. Lewis.* Foreword, Peter Kreeft. San Francisco: Ignatius, 2006.

Hübscher, Susanne, editor. *Es leuchtet die Welt der Weihnacht entgegen: Mit Geschichten von Adrian Plass, C. S. Lewis, Dorothy L. Sayers.* www.brendow-verlag.de: Moers, Germany: Brendow, 2011.

Huttar, Charles A., and Peter J. Shakel, editors. *Word and Story in C. S. Lewis.* Columbia, MO: University of Missouri Press, 1991.

Jebb, Sharon. *Writing God and the Self: Samuel Beckett and C. S. Lewis.* Distinguished Dissertations in Christian Theology. Eugene, OR: Pickwick, 2011.

Keefe, Carolyn, editor. *C. S. Lewis, Speaker and Teacher.* Grand Rapids: Zondervan, 1971.

Kilby, Clyde S. *The Christian World of C. S. Lewis.* Grand Rapids: Eerdmans, 1964.

———. *Images of Salvation in the Fiction of C. S. Lewis*. Wheaton, IL: Shaw, 1978.

King, Don W. *C. S. Lewis, Poet: The Legacy of his Poetic Impulse*. Kent, OH: Kent State University Press, 2001.

Knight, Gareth. *The Magical World of the Inklings: J. R. R. Tolkien, C. S. Lewis, Charles Williams, Owen Barfield*. Shaftesbury, UK: Element, 1990.

Kort, Wesley A. *C. S. Lewis Then and Now*. Oxford: Oxford University Press, 2004.

Kranz, Gisbert. *C. S. Lewis: Studien zu Leben und Werk*. Bonn: Claren, 1974.

———. *Studien zu C. S. Lewis*. Claren-Taschenbuch. Bonn: Claren, 1983.

Kreeft, Peter, editor. *Between Heaven and Hell: A Dialog Somewhere Beyond Death with John F. Kennedy, C. S. Lewis and Aldous Huxley*. 1982. 2nd ed. Downers Grove, IL: InterVarsity, 2008.

———, editor. *C. S. Lewis for the Third Millenium*. San Francisco: Ignatius, 1994.

———. *Narnia and Beyond: A Guide to the Fiction of C. S. Lewis*. San Francisco: Ignatius, 2006.

———, editor. *The Shadowlands of C. S. Lewis: the Man Behind the Movie*. San Francisco: Ignatius, 1994.

Latta, Corey. *Functioning Fantasies: Theology, Ideology, and Social Conception in the Fantasies of C. S. Lewis and J. R. R. Tolkien*. Saarbrücken, Germany: VDM Dr. Müller, 2010.

Lee Poe, Harry, and Rebecca Whitten Poe, editors. *C. S. Lewis Remembered. Collected Recollections of Students and Friends*. Grand Rapids: Zondervan, 2006.

Lee, Ernest George. *C. S. Lewis and Some Modern Theologians. Religion in a Changing World II*. London: Lindsey, 1944.

Lindskoog, Kathryn Ann. *The Lion of Judah in Never-Never Land: The Theology of C. S. Lewis Expressed in his Fantasies for Children*. Grand Rapids: Eerdmans, 1976.

———. *Sleuthing C. S. Lewis*. Macon, GA: Mercer University Press, 2001.

Lindsley, Art. *C. S. Lewis's Case for Christ. Insights from Reason, Imagination and Faith*. Downers Grove, IL: InterVarsity, 2005.

Lindvall, Terry. *Surprised by Laughter: The Comic World of C. S. Lewis.* 1996. Reprint. Nashville, TN: Thomas Nelson, 2012.

Lobdell, Jared. *The Scientifiction Novels of C. S. Lewis: Space and Time in the Ransom Stories.* London: McFarland, 2004.

Loomis, Steven and Jacob Rodriguez. *C. S. Lewis: A Philosophy of Education.* Basingstoke, UK: Palgrave Macmillan, 2009.

Lovell, Steven. "Philosophical themes from C. S. Lewis." PhD Thesis, University of Sheffield, 2003.

Macdonald, Michael H. and Andrew A. Tadie, editors. *G. K. Chesterton and C. S. Lewis: The Riddle of Joy. Conference papers of the Seattle Pacific University Intercollegiate Studies Institute 1987.* London: Collins, 1989.

MacSwain, Robert, and Michael Ward, editors. *Cambridge Companion to C.S. Lewis.* Cambridge: Cambridge University Press, 2010.

Maia, Andrea. *Colazione con un centauro. Cibo e cucina in «Le cronache di Narnia» di C. S. Lewis.* Torino, Italy: Il Leone Verde, 2009.

Markos, Louis. *Lewis Agonistes: How C. S. Lewis Can Train Us to Wrestle with the Modern and Postmodern World.* Nashville, TN: Broadman and Holman, 2003.

Marshall, Cynthia, editor. *Essays on C. S. Lewis and George MacDonald: Truth, Fiction and the Power of Imagination.* Studies in British Literature 11. Lewiston, NY: Mellen, 1991.

Martindale, Wayne. *Beyond the Shadowlands: C. S. Lewis on Heaven and Hell.* Wheaton IL: Crossway Books, 2005.

McCarthy, Daryl, Bob VanderVennen, and Joy McBride. *Surprised by Faith: Conversion and the Academy. A Collection of Papers Commemorating the 75th Anniversary of the Conversion of C. S. Lewis.* Cambridge: Cambridge Scholars, 2007.

McColman, Carl. *The Lion, the Mouse, and the Dawn Treader: Spiritual Lessons from C. S. Lewis's Narnia.* Brewster, MA: Paraclete, 2011.

McDowell, Josh. *A Ready Defence.* Nashville, TN: Thomas Nelson, 1990.

McInnis, Jeff. *Shadows and Chivalry: Pain, Suffering, Evil and Goodness in the Works of George MacDonald and C. S. Lewis*. Studies in Christian History and Thought. Milton Keynes, UK: Paternoster, 2007.

Menuge, Angus J. L., editor. *C. S. Lewis Lightbearer in the Shadowlands*. Wheaton, IL: Crossway, 1997.

Miethe, Terry L. *Shepherd's Notes: C. S. Lewis's Miracles*. Nashville, TN: Broadman and Holman, 2000.

Mills, David. *The Pilgrim's Guide: C. S. Lewis and the Art of Witness*. Grand Rapids: Eerdmans, 1998.

Mochel-Caballero, Anne-Frédérique. *L'Evangile selon C. S. Lewis: Le dépassement du masculin/féminin dans la quête de Dieu*. Nord-Pas de Calais, France: Presses Universitaires du Septentrion, 2011.

Montgomery, John Warwick, editor. *Myth, Allegory, and Gospel: an Interpretation of J. R. R. Tolkien, C. S. Lewis, G. K. Chesterton, Charles Williams*. Minneapolis, MN: Bethany Fellowship, 1974.

Morris, Tom. *Discuss Grief: A Discussion Guide for A Grief Observed by C. S. Lewis*. Raleigh, N.C: www.lulu.com, 2010.

Mueller, Stephen P. *Not a Tame God. Christ in the Writings of C. S. Lewis*. St Louis, MO: Concordia, 2002.

Muhling, Markus. *Gott Und Die Welt in Narnia: Eine Theologische Orientierung Zu C. S. Lewis's Der Konig Von Narnia. Philosophie Und Psychologie Im Dialog*. Göttingen, Germany: Vandenhoeck and Ruprecht, 2005.

Myers, Doris T. *Bareface: A Guide to C. S. Lewis's Last Novel*. Columbia, MO: University of Missouri Press, 2004.

Myers, Doris T. *C. S. Lewis in Context*. Kent, OH: Kent State University Press, 1994.

Newell, Roger J. *The Feeling Intellect: Reading the Bible with C. S. Lewis*. Eugene, OR: Wipf and Stock, 2010.

Nicholi, Armand. *The Question of God: C. S. Lewis and Sigmund Freud Debate God, Love, Sex and the Meaning of Life*. New York: Free, 2002.

5. C. S. Lewis: Revelation and The Christ: Secondary Sources—Books

Nichols Gillespie, Natalie. *Believing in Narnia: A Kid's Guide to Unlocking the Secret Symbols of Faith in C. S. Lewis's The Chronicles of Narnia.* Nashville, TN: Thomas Nelson, 2010.

Odero, Mari a Dolores, and Jose Miguel Odero, *C. S. Lewis y la imagen del hombre. Nt. Lengua y literatura.* Pamplona, Spain: Eunsa, 1993.

Patterson Hannay, Margaret. *C. S. Lewis: A Map of His Worlds.* C. S. Lewis Secondary Studies. Eugene, OR: Wipf and Stock, 2009.

Payne, Leanne. *Real Presence: The Holy Spirit in the Works of C. S. Lewis.* Oxford: Monarch, 1989

Pearce, Joseph. *C. S. Lewis and the Catholic Church.* San Francisco: Ignatius, 2003.

Pérez Díez, María del Carmen. *Por siempre jamás: C. S. Lewis y la tierra de Narnia.* Universidad De León, Leon, Spain: Secretariado De Publicaciones Y Medios Audiovisuales, 2004.

Phillips, Justin. *C. S. Lewis at the BBC: Messages of Hope in the Darkness of War.* London: Harper Collins, 2002.

———. *C. S. Lewis in a Time of War.* Grand Rapids: Zondervan, 2006.

Purtill, Richard L. *C. S. Lewis' Case for the Christian Faith.* San Francisco: Ignatius, 2004.

Rendel, Christian. *Ganz fantastisch!: C. S. Lewis—wie Narnia aus Geschichten geboren wurde.* Moers, Germany: Brendow, 2008.

Reppert, Victor. *C. S. Lewis's Dangerous Idea: a Philosophical Defence of Lewis's Argument from Reason.* Downers Grove, IL: InterVarsity, 2003.

Rogers, Jonathan. *The World According to Narnia: Christian Meaning in C. S. Lewis's Beloved Chronicles.* Brentwood TN: Warner Faith, 2005

Root, Gerald R. "C. S. Lewis and a Problem of Evil: An Investigation of a Pervasive Theme." PhD Thesis, Oxford Centre for Mission Studies, 2003.

Sayer, George. *Jack: A Life of C. S. Lewis.* London: Hodder and Stoughton, 1997.

Sayers, Dorothy, J. R. R. Tolkien, C. S. Lewis, A. O. Barfield, Gervase Mathew, and W. H. Lewis, contributors. *Essays presented to Charles Williams*. Oxford: Oxford University Press, 1947.

Schakel, Peter J., editor. *Imagination and the Arts in C. S. Lewis: Journeying to Narnia and Other Worlds*. Columbia, MO: University of Missouri Press, 2011.

———. *Longing for a Form: Essays on the Fiction of C. S. Lewis. 1977*. Reprint. C. S. Lewis Secondary Studies. Eugene, OR: Wipf and Stock, 2008

———. *Reason and Imagination in C. S. Lewis: A Study of Till We Have Faces*. Grand Rapids: Eerdmans, 1984.

Sellars, J. T. *Reasoning beyond Reason: Imagination as a Theological Source in the Work of C. S. Lewis*. Eugene, OR: Pickwick, 2010.

Seper, Charles. *C. S. Lewis Called Him Master*. Belleville, IL: Broadstreet and Johnson, 2007.

Sibley, Brian. *Shadowlands: The True Story of C. S. Lewis and Joy Davidman*. London: Hodder and Stoughton, 1985.

Simmons, Martha C. *A Guide through Narnia*. London: Hodder, 1979.

Simpson, Paul. *A Brief Guide to C. S. Lewis: The Man Who Created Narnia*. London: Robinson, 2012.

Slack, Anna. *Doors in the Air: C. S. Lewis and the Imaginative World*. Basingstoke UK: Portal, 2010.

Starr, Charlie W. and Walter Hooper. *Light: C. S. Lewis's First and Final Short Story*. wingedlionpress.com: Winged Lion, 2012

Stiefel, Elisabeth. *Kleine Chronik großer Paare: Aus dem Leben von Ida und Friedrich von Bodelschwingh, Anna Rebekka und Matthias Claudius, Coretta Scott King und Martin . . . Joy Davidman und C. S. Lewis und anderen*. www.francke-buch.de: Francke Buchhandlung Gmbh, 2009.

Stone, Elaine Murray. *C. S. Lewis: Creator of Narnia*. Boston, MA: Paulist, 2000.

Sturch, Richard. *Four Christian Fantasists. A Study of the Fantastic Writings of George MacDonald, Charles Williams, C. S. Lewis and J. R. R. Tolkien*. Zollikofen, Switzerland: Walking Tree, 2007.

Svensson, Manfred. *Etica y Politica: Una Mirada desde C. S. Lewis*. Galvani, España: Editorial Clie, 2009.

Tischler, Nancy M. *Encyclopedia of Contemporary Christian Fiction: From C. S. Lewis to Left Behind*. Westport, CT: Greenwood, 2009

Toropov, Brandon. *Beyond Mere Christianity: C. S. Lewis and the Betrayal of Christianity*. Riyadh, Saudi Arabia: Darussalam, 2005.

Urang, Gunnar. *Shadows of Heaven. Religion and Fantasy in the Fiction of C. S. Lewis, Charles Williams and J. R. R. Tolkien*. London: SCM, 1971.

Van Zee, Amy. *How to Analyze the Works of C. S. Lewis*. Essential Critiques Set 3. Minneapolis, MN: Abdo, 2012.

Vanauken, Sheldon. *A Severe Mercy. C. S. Lewis and a Pagan Love invaded by Christ as Told by One of the Lovers*. London: Hodder and Stoughton, 1977.

Vander Elst, Philip. *C. S. Lewis: A Short Introduction*. Continuum Icons. London: Continuum, 2005.

Vaus, Will, and Anne Waller Jenkins. *The Hidden Story of Narnia: A Book-By-Book Guide to C. S. Lewis' Spiritual Themes*. wingedlionpress.com: Winged Lion, 2010.

———. *Mere Theology: A Guide to the Thought of C. S. Lewis*. Downers Grove, IL: InterVarsity, 2004.

———. *The Professor of Narnia: The C. S. Lewis Story*. www.believebooks.com: Believe, 2008.

Wald, Berthold, and Thomas Möllenbeck, editors. *Wahrheit und Selbstüberschreitung: C. S. Lewis und Josef Pieper über den Menschen*. Paderborn, Germany: Schoeningh Ferdinand, 2011.

Walker, Andrew. *Different Gospels: Christian Orthodoxy and Modern Theologies*. London: Hodder and Stoughton Religious, 1988.

Walker, Andrew, and James Patrick, editors. *A Christian for All Christians: Essays in Honour of C. S. Lewis*. London: Hodder and Stoughton, 1990.

Walker, Andrew, and Luke Bretherton, editors. *Remembering Our Future: Explorations in Deep Church*. Milton Keynes, UK: Paternoster, 2007.

Walsh, Chad. *C. S. Lewis: Apostle to the Skeptics*. New York: Macmillan, 1949.

———. *The Literary Legacy of C. S. Lewis*. C. S. Lewis Secondary Studies. Eugene, OR: Wipf and Stock, 2008.

Walsh, Milton T. *Second Friends: C. S. Lewis and Ronald Knox in Conversation*. San Francisco: Ignatius, 2008.

Ward, Michael. *The Narnia Code: C. S. Lewis and the Secret of the Seven Heavens*. Milton Keynes, UK: Paternoster, 2010.

———. *Planet Narnia: The Seven Heavens in the Imagination of C. S. Lewis*. Oxford: Oxford University Press, 2008.

Weichselmann, Sonja. *Einer trage des andern Last: Der Topos der Stellvertretung bei C. S. Lewis*. Berlin: Lit, 2011.

Wellman, Sam. *C. S. Lewis: Heroes of the Faith*. Uhrichsville, OH: Barbour, 1997.

Wheeler, Andrew. *C. S. Lewis: Clarity and Confusion: A Balanced Introduction to His Writings*. Leominster, UK: Day One, 2006.

White, William Luther. *The Image of Man in C. S. Lewis*. Nashville, TN: Abingdon, 1969.

Wilson, A. N. *C. S. Lewis: A Biography*. London: Collins, 1990.

Wolfe, Judith E., and Brendan N. Wolfe, editors. *C. S. Lewis and the Church*. London: Continuum, 2011.

Zorn, Otto. *Analyse Der Filmischen Umsetzung Des Romans Von C. S. Lewis: Narnia. Der K Nig Von Narnia*. La Vergne, TN: Lightning Source, 2008.

6

C. S. Lewis: Revelation and the Christ: Secondary Sources—Articles and Essays

This is a large section listing articles and essays, secondary material, that relate directly to Lewis, or indirectly to his Christology and topics within that Christology and doctrine of revelation. For example: the question of Jesus, merely human or God incarnate; revelation and reason; christological prefigurement; narrative as theology; the question of multiple incarnations; purgation and hell; the Pittenger-Lewis debate; Jesus's self-understanding; Lewis's conversion; a baptized imagination; Platonism and pre-Kantian philosophy; the Inklings; myth, illumination and truth; extra-terrestrial life and the gospel; and so forth.

1. CHRISTOLOGY AND ESCHATOLOGY

Brazier, P. H. "C. S. Lewis & Christological Prefigurement." *The Heythrop Journal*, 48.5 (Sept. 2007) 742–75.

———. "C. S. Lewis: A Doctrine of Transposition." *The Heythrop Journal*, 50.4 (July 2009) 669–88.

———. "'God . . . or a Bad, or Mad, Man': C. S. Lewis's Argument for Christ—A Systematic Theological, Historical and Philosophical Analysis of *aut Deus aut malus homo*." *The Heythrop Journal*. Published online early, free access, Wiley-Blackwell Online Library website 29 November 2010: http://onlinelibrary.wiley.com/doi/10.1111/j.1468-2265.2010.00625.x/full.

———. "The Pittenger–Lewis Debate: Fundamentals of an Ontological Christology." *The Chronicle of the Oxford University C. S. Lewis Society* 6.1 (Jan. 2009) 7–23.

Davis, Stephen T. "Was Jesus Mad, Bad or God?" In *Christian Philosophical Theology*, 149–71. Oxford: Oxford University Press, 2006.

Evans, C. Stephen. "The Incarnational Narrative as Myth and History." *Christian Scholar's Review* 23.4 (1994) 387–407.

Ferry, Patrick T. "Mere Christianity Because There Are No Mere Mortals: Reaching Beyond the Inner Ring." In *Translated Theology: C. S. Lewis Light Bearer in the Shadowlands*, edited by Arthur J. L. Menuge, 169–90. Wheaton, IL: Crossway, 1997.

Harmon, Kendall S. "Nothingness and Human Destiny: Hell in the Thought of C. S. Lewis." In *The Pilgrim's Guide: C. S. Lewis and the Art of Witness*, edited by D. Mills, 236–54. Grand Rapids: Eerdmans, 1998.

Hebblethwaite, Brian. "Impossibility of Multiple Incarnations." *Theology* 104 (Sept–Oct 2001) 323–34.

Keeble, Neil H. "C. S. Lewis, Richard Baxter, and 'Mere Christianity.'" *Christianity and Literature* 30.3 (Spring 1981) 27–44.

Kevern, Peter. "Limping Principles: A Reply to Brian Hebblewaite on the Impossibility of Multiple Incarnations." *Theology* 105 (Sept–Oct 2002) 342–47.

Lacoste, Jean-Yves. "Anonymous Theology and Pseudonymous Christology: C. S. Lewis and The Chronicles of Narnia." *The Chronicle of the Oxford University C. S. Lewis Society* 4.1 (2007) 4–17.

Madigan, Patrick SJ. Review of Bad, Mad or God? Proving the Divinity of Christ from John's Gospel by John Redford. *The Heythrop Journal* 47.4 (Oct 2006) 631–33.

Norris, Jr, Richard A. "Memorial Eucharist for W. Norman Pittenger, Chapel of the Good Shepherd, The General Theological Seminary, The Feast of Lancelot Andrewes, 1997." In *The Anglican Theological Review* (Winter 1998). Online: http://findarticles.com/p/articles/mi_qa3818/is_199801/ai_n8791642/.

Pevear, Richard. "Aslan: The Image of Christ in C. S. Lewis's Chronicles of Narnia." *Sourozh* 76 (May 1999) 44–47.

Pittenger, W. Norman. "Apologist versus Apologist: a Critique of C. S. Lewis as 'Defender of the Faith.'" *Christian Century* (1 Oct 1958) 1104–7.

Root, Jerry. "C. S. Lewis and the Problem of Evil." In *Translated Theology: C. S. Lewis Light Bearer in the Shadowlands*, edited by Arthur J. L. Menuge, 353–66. Wheaton, IL: Crossway, 1997.

Startzman, Eugene. "Christ the Lover in the Works of Flannery O'Connor and C. S. Lewis." *Christianity and the Arts* 6 (Spring 1999) 32–36.

Stock, Robert Douglas. "Dionysus, Christ, and C. S. Lewis." *Christianity and Literature* 34.2 (Winter 1985) 7–13.

Wall, Robert W. "The Problem of Observed Pain: a Study of C. S. Lewis on Suffering." *Journal of the Evangelical Theological Society* 26 (1983) 443–51.

Walsh, Chad. "Last Things First Things: the Eschatology of C. S. Lewis." *Theology Today* 6 (1949) 25–30.

Ward, Michael. "On Suffering." In *The Cambridge Companion to C. S. Lewis*, edited by Robert MacSwain and Michael Ward, 203–19. Cambridge: Cambridge University Press, 2010.

Wolterstorff, Nicholas. "C. S. Lewis on the Problem of Suffering." *The Chronicle of the Oxford University C. S. Lewis Society* 7.3 (2010) 3–20.

Wright, N. T. "Jesus and the Identity of God." *Ex Auditu* 14 (1998) 42–56.

———. "Jesus' Self-Understanding." In *The Incarnation. An Interdisciplinary Symposium on the Incarnation of the Son of God*, edited by Stephen T. Davis, David Kendall SJ, and Gerald O'Collins, 47–61. Oxford: Oxford University Press, 2002.

2. CONVERSION AND THE CHRISTIAN LIFE

Abraham, William J. "C. S. Lewis and the Conversion of the West." *Perspectives* 10 (1995) 12–17.

Beversluis, John. "Surprised by Freud: A Critical Appraisal of A. N. Wilson's Biography of C. S. Lewis." *Christianity and Literature* 41 (Winter 1992) 179–95.

Bramlett, Perry C. "Lewis the Reluctant Convert: Surprised by Faith." In *C. S. Lewis Life, Works, and Legacy, Vol. 1: An Examined Life*, edited by Bruce L. Edwards, 103–26. Santa Barbara, CA: Praeger, 2007.

Bratman, David. "'Gifted Amateurs': C. S. Lewis and the Inklings." In *C. S. Lewis Life, Works, and Legacy, Vol. 3: Apologist Philosopher and Theologian*, edited by Bruce L. Edwards, 279–320. Santa Barbara, CA: Praeger, 2007.

Cook, Alice H. "A Grief Observed: C. S. Lewis Meets the Great Iconoclast." In *C. S. Lewis Life, Works, and Legacy, Vol. 1: An Examined Life*, edited by Bruce L. Edwards, 295–313. Santa Barbara, CA: Praeger, 2007.

Dunckel, Mona, and Karen Rowe. "Understanding C. S. Lewis's Surprised by Joy: 'A Most Reluctant' Autobiography." In *C. S. Lewis Life, Works, and Legacy, Vol. 3: Apologist Philosopher and Theologian*, edited by Bruce L. Edwards, 257–78. Santa Barbara, CA: Praeger, 2007.

Duriez, Colin. "Lewis and Military Service: War and Remembrance (1917–1918)." In *C. S. Lewis Life, Works, and Legacy, Vol. 1: An Examined Life*, edited by Bruce L. Edwards, 79–102. Santa Barbara, CA: Praeger, 2007.

Edwards, Bruce L. "A Thoroughly Converted Man: C. S. Lewis in the Public Square" In *The Pilgrim's Guide: C. S. Lewis and the Art of Witness*, edited by D. Mills, 27–40. Grand Rapids: Eerdmans, 1998.

———. "Valediction from the Shadowlands: C. S. Lewis and the Gospel of Homesickness." In *C. S. Lewis Life, Works, and Legacy, Vol. 4: Scholar, Teacher and Public Intellectual*, edited by Bruce L. Edwards, 303–14. Santa Barbara, CA: Praeger, 2007.

Fernandez, Irène. "C. S. Lewis on Joy." *Communio* 9 (1982) 247–57.

Hipolito, Jane. "C. S. Lewis and Owen Barfield: Adversaries and Confidantes." In *C. S. Lewis Life, Works, and Legacy, Vol. 1: An Examined Life*, edited by Bruce L. Edwards, 219–48. Santa Barbara, CA: Praeger, 2007.

Holmer, Paul L. "C. S. Lewis: the Rules of the Game." *Journal of Faith and Thought* 3.10 (1985) 11–21.

Hooper, Walter. "C. S. Lewis and C. S. Lewises." In *G. K. Chesterton and C. S. Lewis: The Riddle of Joy, Conference Papers of the Seattle Pacific University Intercollegiate Studies Institute 1987*, edited by Michael H. Macdonald and Andrew A. Tadie, 33–52. London: Collins, 1989.

Houston, James M. "The Prayer-Life of C. S. Lewis." *Crux* 24 (Mar 1988) 2–10.

Howe, Rex. "C. S. Lewis: Surprised by Joy." *Expository Times* 101 (Sept. 1990) 356–59.

Hyatt, Douglas T. "Joy, the Call of God in Man: A Critical Appraisal of Lewis's Argument from Desire." In *Translated Theology: C. S. Lewis Light Bearer in the Shadowlands*, edited by Arthur J. L. Menuge, 305–28. Wheaton, IL: Crossway, 1997.

Leig, D. "The Psychology of Conversion in Chesterton's and Lewis's Autobiographies." In *G. K. Chesterton and C. S. Lewis: The Riddle of Joy, Conference Papers of the Seattle Pacific University Intercollegiate Studies Institute 1987*, edited by Michael H. Macdonald and Andrew A. Tadie, 290–304. London: Collins, 1989.

Lindskoog, Kathryn. "Bright Shoots of Everlastingness: C. S. Lewis's Search for Joy." *Perspectives* 8 (Sept 1993) 17–21.

———. "Getting it Together: C. S. Lewis and the Two Hemispheres of Knowing." *Journal of Psychology and Theology* 3 (1975) 290–93.

———, and Gracia F. Ellwood. "C. S. Lewis: Natural Law, the Law in our Hearts." *Christian Century* 101 (1984) 1059–62.

Loades, Ann. "C. S. Lewis: Grief Observed, Rationality Abandoned, Faith Regained." *Literature and Theology* 3 (Mar. 1989) 107–21.

McTavish, John. "The Most Reluctant Convert in all England." *Touchstone* 7 (Spring 1989) 42–47.

Mead, Marjorie Lamp. "Letters to Malcolm: C. S. Lewis on Prayer." In *C. S. Lewis Life, Works, and Legacy, Vol. 3: Apologist Philosopher and Theologian*, edited by Bruce L. Edwards, 209–36. Santa Barbara, CA: Praeger, 2007.

Meilaender, Gilbert. "Psychoanalyzing C. S. Lewis." *Christian Century* 107 (1990) 525–29.

Purtill, Richard L. "Did C. S. Lewis Lose his Faith?" In *A Christian for all Christians: Essays in Honour of C. S. Lewis*, edited by Andrew Walker and James Patrick, 27–62. London: Hodder & Stoughton, 1990.

Ward, Michael. "Escape to Wallaby Wood: Lewis's Depictions of Conversion." In *Translated Theology: C. S. Lewis Light Bearer in the Shadowlands*, edited by Arthur J. L. Menuge, 143–68. Wheaton, IL: Crossway, 1997.

Williams, Donald T. "An Apologist's Evening Prayer: Reflecting on C. S. Lewis's Reflections on the Psalms." In *C. S. Lewis Life, Works, and Legacy, Vol. 3: Apologist Philosopher and Theologian*, edited by Bruce L. Edwards, 237–56. Santa Barbara, CA: Praeger, 2007.

Wirt, Sherwood E., and C. S. Lewis. "Heaven, Earth and Outer Space." *Decision* II (October, 1963) 4.

———. "I was Decided Upon." *Decision* II (September, 1963) 3.

3. ECCLESIOLOGY

Baxter, Richard. "What History is Credible, and What Not." In *Church-History of the Government of Bishops and their Councils*. London: Thomas Simmons, 1680.

Como, James. "C. S. Lewis's Quantum Church: an Uneasy Meditation." In *C. S. Lewis and the Church: Essays in Honour of Walter Hooper*, edited by Judith E. Wolfe and Brendan N. Wolfe, 90–102. London: Continuum, 2011.

Gibbs, Lee W. "C. S. Lewis and the Anglican *via media*." *Restoration Quarterly* 32.2 (1990) 105–19. Online: http://www.religion-online.org/showarticle.asp?title=77.

Herapath, Jonathan. "'You Must Throw Yourself In': C. S. Lewis and the Victorian Literary Church." In *C. S. Lewis and the Church: Essays in Honour of Walter Hooper*, edited by Judith E. Wolfe and Brendan N. Wolfe, 40–51. London: Continuum, 2011.

Kantra, Robert A. "Undenominational Satire: Chesterton and Lewis Revisited." *Religion and Literature* 24 (Spring 1992) 33–57.

Ker, Ian, "'Mere Christianity' and Catholicism." In *C. S. Lewis and the Church: Essays in Honour of Walter Hooper*, edited by Judith E. Wolfe and Brendan N. Wolfe, 129–34. London: Continuum, 2011.

Macdonald, M., and M. Shea. "Saving Sinners and Reconciling Churches: an Ecumenical Meditation on Mere Christianity." In *The Pilgrim's Guide: C. S. Lewis and the Art of Witness*, edited by D. Mills, 43–52. Grand Rapids: Eerdmans, 1998.

Myers, D. "Growing in Grace: the Anglican Spiritual Style in the Chronicles of Narnia." In *The Pilgrim's Guide: C. S. Lewis and the Art of Witness*, edited by D. Mills, 185–202. Grand Rapids: Eerdmans, 1998.

Walker, Andrew. "Under the Russian Cross: a Research note on C. S. Lewis and the Eastern Orthodox Church." In *A Christian for All Christians: Essays in Honour of C. S. Lewis*, edited by Andrew Walker and James Patrick, 63–67. London: Hodder & Stoughton, 1990.

Ward, Michael. "The Church in C. S. Lewis's Fiction." In *C. S. Lewis and the Church: Essays in Honour of Walter Hooper*, edited by Judith E. Wolfe and Brendan N. Wolfe, 67–89. London: Continuum, 2011.

Ware, Bishop Kallistos. "God of the Fathers: C. S. Lewis and Eastern Christianity." In *The Pilgrim's Guide: C. S. Lewis and the Art of Witness*, edited by D. Mills, 53–69. Grand Rapids: Eerdmans, 1998.

———. "C. S. Lewis, an 'Anonymous Orthodox'?" In *C. S. Lewis and the Church: Essays in Honour of Walter Hooper*, edited by Judith E. Wolfe and Brendan N. Wolfe, 135–53. London: Continuum, 2011.

Warner, Francis. "Lewis' Involvement in the Revision of the Psalter." In *C. S. Lewis and the Church: Essays in Honour of Walter Hooper*, edited by Judith E. Wolfe and Brendan N. Wolfe, 52–63. London: Continuum, 2011.

Wolfe, Brendan. "C. S. Lewis on Relations between the Churches." In *C. S. Lewis and the Church: Essays in Honour of Walter Hooper*, edited by Judith E. Wolfe and Brendan N. Wolfe, 117–25. London: Continuum, 2011.

Wolfe, Judith. "C. S. Lewis and the Eschatological Church." In *C. S. Lewis and the Church: Essays in Honour of Walter Hooper*, edited by Judith E. Wolfe and Brendan N. Wolfe, 103–16. London: Continuum, 2011.

4. LITERATURE AND ANALOGICAL NARRATIVE

Campbell, Joseph. "Mythological Themes in Creative Literature and Art." In *Myths, Dreams and Religion*, 138–75. New York: Dutton, 1970.

Carretero-González, Margarita. "Cartography and Fantasy: Hidden Treasures in the Maps of The Chronicles of Narnia." In *C. S. Lewis Life, Works, and Legacy, Vol. 2: Fantasist, Mythmaker and Poet*, edited by Bruce L. Edwards, 115–34. Santa Barbara, CA: Praeger, 2007.

———. "Sons of Adam, Daughters of Eve, and Children of Aslan: An Environmentalist Perspective on The Chronicles of Narnia." In *C. S. Lewis Life, Works, and Legacy, Vol. 2: Fantasist, Mythmaker and Poet*, edited by Bruce L. Edwards, 93–114. Santa Barbara, CA: Praeger, 2007.

Cassidy, Joseph P. "On Discernment." In *The Cambridge Companion to C. S. Lewis*, edited by Robert MacSwain and Michael Ward, 132–45. Cambridge: Cambridge University Press, 2010.

Christopher, Joe R. "Archetypal Patterns in Till We Have Faces." In *Longing for a Form: Essays on the Fiction of C. S. Lewis*, edited by Peter J. Schakel, 193–212. Kent, OH: Kent State University Press, 1977.

Clark, James Andrew. "The Idea of the Good, Duality and Unity: a Study of C. S. Lewis, J. R. R. Tolkien, and Charles Williams." *Ashland Theological Journal* 19 (Fall 1987) 1–34.

Collings, Michael R. "Of Lions and Lamp-Posts: C. S. Lewis's The Lion, the Witch, and the Wardrobe as Response to Olaf Stapledon's Sirius." *Christianity and Literature* 32.4 (1983) 33–38.

Cox, John D. "Epistemological Release in The Silver Chair." In *Longing for a Form: Essays on the Fiction of C. S. Lewis*, edited by Peter J. Schakel, 159–68. Kent, OH: Kent State University Press, 1977.

Douglas, J. D. "Legacy of C. S. Lewis." *Christianity Today* 8 (Dec. 20, 1963) 27.

Downing, David C. "From Pillar to Postmodernism: C. S. Lewis and Current Critical Discourse." *Christianity and Literature* 46 (Winter 1997) 169–78.

———. "Perelandra: A Tale of Paradise Retained." In *C. S. Lewis Life, Works, and Legacy, Vol. 2: Fantasist, Mythmaker and Poet*, edited by Bruce L. Edwards, 35–52. Santa Barbara, CA: Praeger, 2007.

———. "Rehabilitating H. G. Wells: C. S. Lewis's *Out of the Silent Planet*." In *C. S. Lewis Life, Works, and Legacy, Vol. 2: Fantasist, Mythmaker and Poet*, edited by Bruce L. Edwards, 13–34. Santa Barbara, CA: Praeger, 2007.

———. "Sub-Creation or Smuggled Theology: Tolkien contra Lewis on Christian Fantasy." Online, *The C. S. Lewis Institute*: http://www.cslewisinstitute.org/cslewis/downing_theology.htm.

———. "That Hideous Strength: Spiritual Wickedness in High Places." In *C. S. Lewis Life, Works, and Legacy, Vol. 2: Fantasist, Mythmaker and Poet*, edited by Bruce L. Edwards, 53–70. Santa Barbara, CA: Praeger, 2007.

Duriez, C. "The Romantic Writer: Lewis's Theology of Fantasy." In *The Pilgrim's Guide: C. S. Lewis and the Art of Witness*, edited by D. Mills, 98–110. Grand Rapids: Eerdmans, 1998.

Edwards, Bruce L. "'Patches of Godlight': C. S. Lewis as Imaginative Writer." In *C. S. Lewis Life, Works, and Legacy, Vol. 2: Fantasist, Mythmaker and Poet*, edited by Bruce L. Edwards, 1–12. Santa Barbara, CA: Praeger, 2007.

Edwards, Mark. "C. S. Lewis and Early Christian Literature." In *C. S. Lewis and the Church: Essays in Honour of Walter Hooper*, edited by Judith E. Wolfe and Brendan N. Wolfe, 23–39. London: Continuum, 2011.

6. C. S. Lewis: Revelation and the Christ: Secondary Sources—Articles and Essays

Edwards, Mark. "Classicist." In *The Cambridge Companion to C. S. Lewis*, edited by Robert MacSwain and Michael Ward, 58–71. Cambridge: Cambridge University Press, 2010.

Fairfield, L. "Fragmentation and Hope: the Healing of the Modern Schisms in *That Hideous Strength*." In *The Pilgrim's Guide: C. S. Lewis and the Art of Witness*, edited by D. Mills, 145–60. Grand Rapids: Eerdmans, 1998.

Fleming, John V. "Literary Critic." In *The Cambridge Companion to C. S. Lewis*, edited by Robert MacSwain and Michael Ward, 15–28. Cambridge: Cambridge University Press, 2010.

Forbes, Cheryl. "Narnia: Fantasy, but." *Christianity Today* 20 (Apr 23 1976) 6–10.

Fuller, E. "After the Moon Landings: A Further Report on the Christian Spaceman C. S. Lewis." In *Myth, Allegory, and Gospel: an Interpretation of J. R. R. Tolkien, C. S. Lewis, G. K. Chesterton, Charles Williams*, edited by John Warwick Montgomery, 79–96. Minneapolis: Bethany Fellowship, 1974.

Gibson, E. "The Centrality of Perelandra to Lewis's Theology." In *G. K. Chesterton and C. S. Lewis: The Riddle of Joy, Conference Papers of the Seattle Pacific University Intercollegiate Studies Institute 1987*, edited by Michael H. Macdonald and Andrew A. Tadie, 125–38. London: Collins, 1989.

Guite, Malcolm. "Poet." In *The Cambridge Companion to C. S. Lewis*, edited by Robert MacSwain and Michael Ward, 294–310. Cambridge: Cambridge University Press, 2010.

Hannay, Margaret P. "A Preface to Perelandra." In *Longing for a Form: Essays on the Fiction of C. S. Lewis*, edited by Peter J. Schakel, 73–90. Kent, OH: Kent State University Press, 1977.

Harper, Katherine. "C. S. Lewis's Short Fiction and Unpublished Works." In *C. S. Lewis Life, Works, and Legacy, Vol. 2: Fantasist, Mythmaker and Poet*, edited by Bruce L. Edwards, 157–74. Santa Barbara, CA: Praeger, 2007.

Harrold, Philip. "Stealing Past the Watchful Dragons: C. S. Lewis's Incarnational Aesthetics and Today's Emerging Imagination." In *C. S. Lewis Life, Works, and Legacy, Vol. 3: Apologist Philosopher and Theologian*, edited by Bruce L. Edwards, 183–208. Santa Barbara, CA: Praeger, 2007.

Hedley, Douglas. "C. S. Lewis on Stories and Religion." *The Chronicle of the Oxford University C. S. Lewis Society*, 3.3 (2006) 6–21.

Hinten, Marvin D. "The World of Narnia: Medieval Magic and Morality." In *C. S. Lewis Life, Works, and Legacy, Vol. 2: Fantasist, Mythmaker and Poet*, edited by Bruce L. Edwards, 71–92. Santa Barbara, CA: Praeger, 2007.

Holyer, Robert. "C. S. Lewis on the Epistemic Significance of the Imagination." *Soundings* 74 (Spr-Sum, 1991) 215–41.

Hooper, Walter. "Narnia: The Author, the Critics, and the Tale." In *Longing for a Form: Essays on the Fiction of C. S. Lewis*, edited by Peter J. Schakel, 105–18. Kent, OH: Kent State University Press, 1977.

———. "Past Watchful Dragons: the Fairy Tales of C. S. Lewis." In *Imagination and the Spirit: Essays in Literature and the Christian Faith Presented to Clyde S. Kilby*, edited by Charles A. Huttar, 277–339. Grand Rapids: Eerdmans, 1971.

Howard, T. "Looking Backward: C. S. Lewis's Literary Achievement at Forty Years' Perspective." In *G. K. Chesterton and C. S. Lewis: The Riddle of Joy, Conference Papers of the Seattle Pacific University Intercollegiate Studies Institute 1987*, edited by Michael H. Macdonald and Andrew A. Tadie, 89–99. London: Collins, 1989.

Howard, T. "The Triumphant Vindication of the Body: the End of Gnosticism in *That Hideous Strength*." In *The Pilgrim's Guide: C. S. Lewis and the Art of Witness*, edited by D. Mills, 133–44. Grand Rapids: Eerdmans, 1998.

Huttar, Charles A. "C. S. Lewis, T. S. Eliot, and the Milton Legacy: The Nativity Ode Revisited." *Texas Studies in Literature and Language* 44.3 (2002) 324–48.

———. "C. S. Lewis's Narnia and the 'Grand Design.'" In *Longing for a Form: Essays on the Fiction of C. S. Lewis*, edited by Peter J. Schakel, 119–35. Kent, OH: Kent State University Press, 1977.

Jacobs, Alan. "The Chronicles of Narnia." In *The Cambridge Companion to C. S. Lewis*, edited by Robert MacSwain and Michael Ward, 265–80. Cambridge: Cambridge University Press, 2010.

Jasper, David. "The Pilgrim's Regress and Surprised by Joy." In *The Cambridge Companion to C. S. Lewis*, edited by Robert MacSwain and Michael Ward, 223–36. Cambridge: Cambridge University Press, 2010.

Johnston, Robert K. "Image and Content: the Tension in C. S. Lewis' Chronicles of Narnia." *Journal of the Evangelical Theological Society* 20 (1977) 253–64.

6. C. S. Lewis: Revelation and the Christ: Secondary Sources—Articles and Essays

Keating, Daniel. "Subcreation in J. R. R. Tolkien and Dorothy Sayers." *The Chronicle of the Oxford University C. S. Lewis Society*, 3.2 (2006) 11–20.

Kilby, Clyde S. "Mythic and Christian Elements in Tolkien." In *Myth, Allegory, and Gospel: An Interpretation of J. R. R. Tolkien, C. S. Lewis, G. K. Chesterton, Charles Williams*, edited by John Warwick Montgomery, 119–43. Minneapolis: Bethany Fellowship, 1974.

———. "Till We Have Faces: An Interpretation." In *Longing for a Form: Essays on the Fiction of C. S. Lewis*, edited by Peter J. Schakel, 171–81. Kent, OH: Kent State University Press, 1977.

King, Don W. "Columns of Light: The Preconversion Narrative Poetry of C. S. Lewis." In *C. S. Lewis Life, Works, and Legacy, Vol. 2: Fantasist, Mythmaker and Poet*, edited by Bruce L. Edwards, 209–32. Santa Barbara, CA: Praeger, 2007.

———. "Early Lyric Poetry: Spirits in Bondage (1919) and 'Joy' (1924)." In *C. S. Lewis Life, Works, and Legacy, Vol. 2: Fantasist, Mythmaker and Poet*, edited by Bruce L. Edwards, 233–58. Santa Barbara, CA: Praeger, 2007.

———. "Topical Poems: C. S. Lewis's Postconversion Poetry." In *C. S. Lewis Life, Works, and Legacy, Vol. 2: Fantasist, Mythmaker and Poet*, edited by Bruce L. Edwards, 259–311. Santa Barbara, CA: Praeger, 2007.

King, James R. "Christian Fantasy in the Novels of C. S. Lewis and Charles Williams." *Journal of Religious Thought* 11.1 (1953–54) 46–60.

Kuhn, Daniel K. "The Joy of the Absolute: A Comparative Study of the Romantic Visions of William Wordsworth and C. S. Lewis." In *Imagination and the Spirit: Essays in Literature and the Christian Faith presented to Clyde S. Kilby*, edited by Charles A. Huttar, 189–214. Grand Rapids: Eerdmans, 1971.

Logan, Stephen. "Literary Theorist." In *The Cambridge Companion to C. S. Lewis*, edited by Robert MacSwain and Michael Ward, 29–42. Cambridge: Cambridge University Press, 2010.

MacDonald, George. "The Fantastic Imagination." In *A Dish of Orts: Chiefly Papers on the Imagination, and on Shakespeare*, 203–8. London: Sampson, Low, Marston & Co., 1867.

———. "The Imagination: Its Functions and Its Culture." In *A Dish of Orts: Chiefly Papers on the Imagination, and on Shakespeare*, 1–28. London: Sampson, Low, Marston & Co., 1867.

Mackey, A. "The Christian Influence of G. K. Chesterton on C. S. Lewis." In *A Christian For All Christians: Essays in Honour of C. S. Lewis*, edited by Andrew Walker and James Patrick, 68–82. London: Hodder & Stoughton, 1990.

Martindale, Wayne. "The Great Divorce: Journey to Heaven and Hell." In *C. S. Lewis Life, Works, and Legacy, Vol. 3: Apologist Philosopher and Theologian*, edited by Bruce L. Edwards, 133–52. Santa Barbara, CA: Praeger, 2007.

Meacham, Steve. "The Shed where God Died." *Sydney Morning Herald Online* (Dec. 13, 2003) Section: "Spectrum," 8. Online: http://www.smh.com.au/articles/2003/12/12/1071125644900.html.

Mills, David. "To See Truly through a Glass Darkly: C. S. Lewis, George Orwell, and the Corruption of Language." *Touchstone: A Journal of Ecumenical Orthodoxy* 11 (July–Aug 1998) 36–43.

Milward, Peter. "Wise Fools in Shakespeare." *Christianity and Literature* 33.2 (1984) 21–27.

Montgomery, John Warwick. "The Chronicles of Narnia and the Adolescent Reader." In *Myth, Allegory, and Gospel: An Interpretation of J. R. R. Tolkien, C. S. Lewis, G. K. Chesterton, Charles Williams*, edited by John Warwick Montgomery, 97–118. Minneapolis: Bethany Fellowship, 1974.

Pearson, Brooke. "Opinion Piece: Ethnocentricity in the Chronicles of Narnia." *The Chronicle of the Oxford University C. S. Lewis Society*, 3.1 (2006) 9–10.

Peterson, Eugene H. "Writers and Angels: Witnesses to Transcendence." *Theology Today* 51 (Oct 1994) 394–404.

Purtill, Richard L. "*That Hideous Strength*: A Double Story." In *Longing for a Form: Essays on the Fiction of C. S. Lewis*, edited by Peter J. Schakel, 91–102. Kent, OH: Kent State University Press, 1977.

Pyles, Franklin A. "The Language Theory of C. S. Lewis." *Trinity Journal* 4 (Autumn 1983) 82–91.

Quinn, Dermot. "Chesterton, Lewis, and the Uses of Enchantment." *The Chronicle of the Oxford University C. S. Lewis Society*, 3.2 (2006) 4–10.

Roberts, J. "Wordsworth's Apocalypse." *Literature and Theology* 20.4 (2006) 361–78.

6. C. S. Lewis: Revelation and the Christ: Secondary Sources—Articles and Essays

Robinson, John. "Faerie in J. R. R. Tolkien and C. S. Lewis: Escape vs. Recovery." *The Chronicle of the Oxford University C. S. Lewis Society*, 5.2 (2008) 4–21.

Rowe, Karen. "Till We Have Faces: A Study of the Soul and the Self." In *C. S. Lewis Life, Works, and Legacy, Vol. 2: Fantasist, Mythmaker and Poet*, edited by Bruce L. Edwards, 135–56. Santa Barbara, CA: Praeger, 2007.

Schakel, P. "Elusive Birds and Narrative Nets: the Appeal of Story in C. S. Lewis' Chronicles of Narnia." In *A Christian for All Christians: Essays in Honour of C. S. Lewis*, edited by Andrew Walker and James Patrick, 116–31. London: Hodder & Stoughton, 1990.

Schakel, Peter J. "Till We Have Faces." In *The Cambridge Companion to C. S. Lewis*, edited by Robert MacSwain and Michael Ward, 281–93. Cambridge: Cambridge University Press, 2010.

Seerveld, Calvin. "Imagination in Theology." In *IVP New Dictionary of Theology*, edited by Sinclair B. Ferguson and David F. Wright, 330–31. Leicester, UK: Inter-Varsity, 1989.

———. "Imaginativity." *Faith and Philosophy* 4 (Jan 1987) 43–58.

Sellin, B. "Journeys into Fantasy: The Fiction of David Lindsay and C. S. Lewis." In *A Christian for all Christians: Essays in Honour of C. S. Lewis*, edited by Andrew Walker and James Patrick, 98–115. London: Hodder & Stoughton, 1990.

Shippey, T. A. "The Ransom Trilogy." In *The Cambridge Companion to C. S. Lewis*, edited by Robert MacSwain and Michael Ward, 237–50. Cambridge: Cambridge University Press, 2010.

Shumaker, Wayne. "Cosmic Trilogy of C. S. Lewis." In *Longing for a Form: Essays on the Fiction of C. S. Lewis*, edited by Peter J. Schakel, 51–63. Kent, OH: Kent State University Press, 1977.

Smith, S. "Awakening from the Enchantment of Worldliness: *The Chronicles of Narnia* as Pre–Apologetics." In *The Pilgrim's Guide: C. S. Lewis and the Art of Witness*, edited by D. Mills, 168–81. Grand Rapids: Eerdmans, 1998.

Stahl, John T. "Nature and Function of Myth in the Christian Thought of C. S. Lewis." *Christian Scholar's Review* 7.4 (1978) 330–36.

Storey, Ian. "Classical Allusion in C. S. Lewis's *Till We Have Faces*." *The Chronicle of the Oxford University C. S. Lewis Society*, 4.2 (2007) 5–20.

Taliaferro, Charles A. "A Narnian Theory of the Atonement: Ransom Theory in C. S. Lewis, *The Lion, the Witch, and the Wardrobe*." *Scottish Journal of Theology* 41.1 (1988) 75–92.

Tegnér, Esaias. "Drapa." In *The Seaside and the Fireside by Henry Wadsworth Longfellow*. Boston, MA: Ticknor, Reed, and Fields 1849. Online: http://www.thehypertexts.com/Tegner's%20Drapa%20Translation.htm.

Timmerman, John H. "The Epistemology of C. S. Lewis: Reason and Belief in Till We Have Faces." *Religion in Life* 46 (1977) 497–508.

Tixier, Eliane. "Imagination Baptized, or, 'Holiness' in The Chronicles of Narnia." In *Longing for a Form: Essays on the Fiction of C. S. Lewis*, edited by Peter J. Schakel, 136–58. Kent, OH: Kent State University Press, 1977.

Tolkien, J. R. R. "Mythopoeia." In *Tree and Leaf*, edited by Christopher Tolkien, 85–90. London: Allen and Unwin, 1978.

———. "On Fairy Stories." In *Essays Presented to Charles Williams*, edited by C. S. Lewis, 38–89. Oxford: Oxford University Press, 1947.

Toynbee, Polly. "Narnia Represents Everything That Is Most Hateful about Religion." *The Guardian* (5th Dec. 2005). Online: http://www.guardian.co.uk/books/2005/dec/05/cslewis.booksforchildrenandteenagers.

Travers, Michael. "The Letters of C. S. Lewis: C. S. Lewis as Correspondent." In *C. S. Lewis Life, Works, and Legacy, Vol. 4: Scholar, Teacher and Public Intellectual*, edited by Bruce L. Edwards, 19–49. Santa Barbara, CA: Praeger, 2007.

Walls, Jerry L. "*The Great Divorce*." In *The Cambridge Companion to C. S. Lewis*, edited by Robert MacSwain and Michael Ward, 251–64. Cambridge: Cambridge University Press, 2010.

Walsh, Chad. "Charles Williams' Novels and the Contemporary Mutation of Consciousness." In *Myth, Allegory, and Gospel: an Interpretation of J. R. R. Tolkien, C. S. Lewis, G. K. Chesterton, Charles Williams*, edited by John Warwick Montgomery, 53–78. Minneapolis: Bethany Fellowship, 1974.

Watkin, Julia. "Fighting for Narnia: Søren Kierkegaard and C. S. Lewis." In *Kierkegaard on Art and Communication*, edited by George Pattison, 137–49. New York: St Martin's, 1992.

6. C. S. Lewis: Revelation and the Christ: Secondary Sources—Articles and Essays

Weele, Steve J van der. "From Mt. Olympus to Glome: C. S. Lewis's Dislocation of Apuleius's 'Cupid and Psyche' in *Till We Have Faces*." In *Longing for a Form: Essays on the Fiction of C. S. Lewis*, edited by Peter J. Schakel, 182–92. Kent, OH: Kent State University Press, 1977.

Williams, Donald T. "*English Literature in the Sixteenth Century*: C. S. Lewis as a Literary Historian." In *C. S. Lewis Life, Works, and Legacy, Vol. 4: Scholar, Teacher and Public Intellectual*, edited by Bruce L. Edwards, 143–62. Santa Barbara, CA: Praeger, 2007.

Witherspoon, Janice Neuleib. "The Creative Act: Lewis on God and Art." In *Longing for a Form: Essays on the Fiction of C .S. Lewis*, edited by Peter J. Schakel, 40–47. Kent, OH: Kent State University Press, 1977.

Wood, Ralph C. "The Baptized Imagination: C. S. Lewis's Fictional Apologetics." *Christian Century* 112 (30 Aug–6 Sept, 1995) 812–15.

Yandell, Stephen. "*The Allegory of Love* and *The Discarded Image*: C. S. Lewis as Medievalist." In *C. S. Lewis Life, Works, and Legacy, Vol. 4: Scholar, Teacher and Public Intellectual*, edited by Bruce L. Edwards, 117–42. Santa Barbara, CA: Praeger, 2007.

5. PHILOSOPHY AND NATURALISM, SCIENTISM AND RATIONALITY

Aeschliman, M. D. "C. S. Lewis on Mere Science." *First Things* 86 (Oct. 1998) 16–18.

Anscombe, G. E. M. "Introduction." In *Collected Philosophical Papers, Vol. II Metaphysics and the Philosophy of Mind*, vii–x. Oxford: Blackwell, 1981.

———. "A Reply to Mr C. S. Lewis's Argument that 'Naturalism is Self-Refuting.'" In *Collected Philosophical Papers, Vol. II Metaphysics and the Philosophy of Mind*, 224–32. Oxford: Blackwell, 1981.

Blamires, Harry. "Teaching the Universal Truth: C. S. Lewis Among the Intellectuals." In *The Pilgrim's Guide: C. S. Lewis and the Art of Witness*, edited by D. Mills, 15–26. Grand Rapids: Eerdmans, 1998.

Editor. "Notes of C. S. Lewis's Reply to G. E. M. Anscombe, from The Oxford Socratic Club minute-book for 2 February 1948." The Socratic Digest 4 (1948) 15. Reprinted at the conclusion of C. S. Lewis. "Religion Without Dogma?" In *Undeceptions: Essays on Theology and Ethics*, 113–14. London: Bles, 1971.

Ferngren, Gary B., and Numbers, Ronald L. "C. S. Lewis on Creation and Evolution: The Acworth Letters 1944–1960." *Perspectives on Science and Christian Faith* 48 (Mar 1996) 28–33.

Haldene, J. B. S. "Auld Hornie, FRS." *Modern Quarterly* 1.4 (Autumn 1946). Online: http://www.marxists.org/archive/haldane/works/1940s/oncslewis.htm.

Holyer, Robert. "C. S. Lewis: The Rationalist?" *Christian Scholar's Review* 18.2 (1988) 148–67.

Hooper, Walter. "Oxford's Bonny Fighter." In *Remembering C. S. Lewis. Recollections of Those Who Knew Him*, edited by James T. Como, 241–308. San Francisco, CA: Ignatius, 2005.

Inwagen, Peter van. "C. S. Lewis' Argument against Naturalism." *The Chronicle of the Oxford University C. S. Lewis Society* 7.1 (Hilary Term, Jan 2010) 2–12.

Jeffery, Richard. "C. S. Lewis and the Scientists." *The Chronicle of the Oxford University C. S. Lewis Society*, 2.2 (2005) 3–7.

Mitchell, Basil. "Reflections on C. S. Lewis, Apologetics, and the Moral Tradition, Basil Mitchell in Conversation with Andrew Walker." In *A Christian for All Christians: Essays in Honour of C. S. Lewis*, edited by Andrew Walker and James Patrick, 7–26. London: Hodder & Stoughton, 1990.

Morris, Thomas V. "C. S. Lewis and the Search for Rational Religion." *Faith and Philosophy* 5.3 (1988) 319–22.

Patrick, James. "C. S. Lewis and Idealism." In *A Christian for all Christians: Essays in Honour of C. S. Lewis*, edited by Andrew Walker and James Patrick, 156–73. London: Hodder & Stoughton, 1990.

Peters, Thomas C. "The War of the Worldviews: H. G. Wells and Scientism versus C. S. Lewis and Christianity." In *The Pilgrim's Guide: C. S. Lewis and the Art of Witness*, edited by D. Mills, 203–20. Grand Rapids: Eerdmans, 1998.

Reichenbach, Bruce R. "C. S. Lewis on the Desolation of De-Valued Science." *Christian Scholar's Review* 11.2 (1982) 99–111.

Reppert, Victor. "Defending the Dangerous Idea: An Update on C. S. Lewis's Argument from Reason." *Sehnsucht*, 1.1 (2007) 43–56.

———. "Miracles: C. S. Lewis's Critique of Naturalism." In *C. S. Lewis Life, Works, and Legacy, Vol. 3: Apologist Philosopher and Theologian*, edited by Bruce L. Edwards, 153–82. Santa Barbara, CA: Praeger, 2007.

———. "The Ecumenical Apologist: Understanding C. S. Lewis's Defence of Christianity." In *C. S. Lewis Life, Works, and Legacy, Vol. 3: Apologist Philosopher and Theologian*, edited by Bruce L. Edwards, 1–28. Santa Barbara, CA: Praeger, 2007.

———. "The Green Witch and the Great Debate: Freeing Narnia from the Spell of the Lewis–Anscombe Legend." In *The Chronicles of Narnia and Philosophy: The Lion, the Witch and the Worldview*, edited by Gregory Bassam and Jerry L. Wallis, 260–72. La Salle, IL: Open Court, 2005.

———. "The Lewis–Anscombe Controversy: A Discussion of the Issues." *Christian Scholar's Review* 19 (Sept. 1989) 32–48.

Rose, Mary C. "The Christian Platonism of C. S. Lewis, J. R. R. Tolkien and Charles Williams." In *Neoplatonism and Christian Thought*, edited by D. O'Meara, 203–212, Studies In Neoplatonism 3. Albany, NY: State University of New York Press, 1982.

Sarot, Marcel. "Lewis on Naturalism: A Reply to Peter van Inwagen." *The Chronicle of the Oxford University C. S. Lewis Society* 7.3 (Oct. 2010) 21–27.

Taliaferro, Charles. "On Naturalism." In *The Cambridge Companion to C. S. Lewis*, edited by Robert MacSwain and Michael Ward, 105–18. Cambridge: Cambridge University Press, 2010.

Tonning, Judith E. "A Romantic in the Republic: A Few Critical Comments on The Abolition of Man." *The Chronicle of the Oxford University C. S. Lewis Society*, 5.1 (2008) 27–39.

Travers, Michael. "*The Abolition of Man*: C. S. Lewis's Philosophy of History." In *C. S. Lewis Life, Works, and Legacy, Vol. 3: Apologist Philosopher and Theologian*, edited by Bruce L. Edwards, 107–32. Santa Barbara, CA: Praeger, 2007.

Wolterstorff, Nicholas. "Is it Possible and Desirable for Theologians to Recover from Kant?" *Modern Theology* 14.1 (1998) 1–18.

6. PREACHER AND APOLOGIST, TEACHER AND PROFESSIONAL

Anderson, Greg M. "A Most Potent Rhetoric: C. S. Lewis, 'Congenital Rhetorician.'" In *C. S. Lewis Life, Works, and Legacy, Vol. 4: Scholar, Teacher and Public Intellectual*, edited by Bruce L. Edwards, 195–228. Santa Barbara, CA: Praeger, 2007.

———. "The Sermons of C. S. Lewis: The Oxford Don as Preacher." In *C. S. Lewis Life, Works, and Legacy, Vol. 3: Apologist Philosopher and Theologian*, edited by Bruce L. Edwards, 75–106. Santa Barbara, CA: Praeger, 2007.

Brumley, Mark. "The Relevance and Challenge of C. S. Lewis," Nov. 29, 2005. Online: http://www.ignatiusinsight.com/features2005/print2005/mbrumley_relcslewis_nov05.html.

Burton, J. "G. K. Chesterton and C. S. Lewis: the Men and their Times." In *G. K. Chesterton and C. S. Lewis: The Riddle of Joy, Conference Papers of the Seattle Pacific University Intercollegiate Studies Institute 1987*, edited by Michael H. Macdonald and Andrew A. Tadie, 160–72. London: Collins, 1989.

Calhoun, Scott. "C. S. Lewis and J. R. R. Tolkien: Friends and Mutual Mentors." In *C. S. Lewis Life, Works, and Legacy, Vol. 1: An Examined Life*, edited by Bruce L. Edwards, 249–74. Santa Barbara, CA: Praeger, 2007.

———. "C. S. Lewis as Philologist: *Studies in Words*." In *C. S. Lewis Life, Works, and Legacy, Vol. 4: Scholar, Teacher and Public Intellectual*, edited by Bruce L. Edwards, 81–98. Santa Barbara, CA: Praeger, 2007.

Colson, Charles W, and Nancy R. Pearcey. "The Oxford Prophet." *Christianity Today* 42 (June 15, 1998) 72.

Danielson, Dennis. "Intellectual Historian." In *The Cambridge Companion to C. S. Lewis,* edited by Robert MacSwain and Michael Ward, 43–57. Cambridge: Cambridge University Press, 2010.

Davies, Horton. "C. S. Lewis and B. L. Manning: Lay Champions of Christianity." *Religion in Life* 31 (Autumn, 1952) 598–609.

Derrick, C. "Some Personal Angles on Chesterton and Lewis." In *G. K. Chesterton and C. S. Lewis: The Riddle of Joy, Conference Papers of the Seattle Pacific University Intercollegiate Studies Institute 1987*, edited by Michael H. Macdonald and Andrew A. Tadie, 3–19. London: Collins, 1989.

6. C. S. Lewis: Revelation and the Christ: Secondary Sources—Articles and Essays

Dorsett, Lyle W., and Jake Hanson. "C. S. Lewis and Joy Davidman: Severe Mercies, Late Romance." In *C. S. Lewis Life, Works, and Legacy, Vol. 1: An Examined Life, Conference Papers of the Seattle Pacific University Intercollegiate Studies Institute 1987*, edited by Bruce L. Edwards, 275–94. Santa Barbara, CA: Praeger, 2007.

———. "C. S. Lewis: some Keys to his Effectiveness." In *G. K. Chesterton and C. S. Lewis: The Riddle of Joy*, edited by Michael H. Macdonald and Andrew A. Tadie, 215-25. London: Collins, 1989.

Downing, David. "C. S. Lewis: Apostle to the Imagination." *Christianity Today* 16 (Oct 8, 1971) 10–12.

Dunckel, Mona. "C. S. Lewis as Allegorist: The Pilgrim's Regress." In *C. S. Lewis Life, Works, and Legacy, Vol. 3: Apologist Philosopher and Theologian*, edited by Bruce L. Edwards, 29–50. Santa Barbara, CA: Praeger, 2007.

———. "The Christian Intellectual in the Public Square: C. S. Lewis's Enduring American Reception." In *C. S. Lewis Life, Works, and Legacy, Vol. 4: Scholar, Teacher and Public Intellectual*, edited by Bruce L. Edwards, 1–18. Santa Barbara, CA: Praeger, 2007.

———. "An Examined Life: Introducing C. S. Lewis." In *C. S. Lewis Life, Works, and Legacy, Vol. 1: An Examined Life*, edited by Bruce L. Edwards, 1–16. Santa Barbara, CA: Praeger, 2007.

Edwards, Michael I., and, Bruce L. Edwards. " 'Everyman's Tutor': C. S. Lewis on Reading and Criticism." In *C. S. Lewis Life, Works, and Legacy, Vol. 4: Scholar, Teacher and Public Intellectual*, edited by Bruce L. Edwards, 163–194. Santa Barbara, CA: Praeger, 2007.

Fiddes, P. "C. S. Lewis the Myth-Maker." In *A Christian for all Christians: Essays in Honour of C. S. Lewis*, edited by Andrew Walker and James Patrick, 132–55. London: Hodder & Stoughton, 1990.

George Musacchio. "Exorcising the Zeitgeist: Lewis as Evangelist to the Modernists." In *Translated Theology: C. S. Lewis Light Bearer in the Shadowlands*, edited by Arthur J. L. Menuge, 213–34. Wheaton, IL: Crossway, 1997.

Heck, Joel D. "Praeparatio Evangelica." In *C. S. Lewis Light Bearer in the Shadowlands*, edited by Angus J. L. Menuge, 235–57. Wheaton, IL: Crossway, 1997.

Horne, Brian. "A Peculiar Debt: The Influence of Charles Williams on C. S. Lewis." In *A Christian for all Christians: Essays in Honour of C. S. Lewis*, edited by Andrew Walker and James Patrick, 83–97. London: Hodder & Stoughton, 1990.

———. "The Two Faces of C. S. Lewis." *Expository Times* 110.7 (Apr 1999) 210–13.

Huttar, Charles A. "Apostle to Twentieth Century Skeptics." *Eternity* 15 (Feb 1964) 35–37.

Jacobs, Alan. "The Second Coming of C. S. Lewis." *First Things* 47 (Nov 1994) 27–30.

James, Richard V. "C. S. Lewis's Belfast Childhood." In *C. S. Lewis Life, Works, and Legacy, Vol. 1: An Examined Life*, edited by Bruce L. Edwards, 17–44. Santa Barbara, CA: Praeger, 2007.

———. "Lewis's Early Schooling: Trials and Tribulations." In *C. S. Lewis Life, Works, and Legacy, Vol. 1: An Examined Life*, edited by Bruce L. Edwards, 45–78. Santa Barbara, CA: Praeger, 2007.

Kilby, Clyde S. "C. S. Lewis and his Critics." *Christianity Today* 3 (Dec 8, 1958) 13–15.

———. "C. S. Lewis: Everyman's Theologian." *Christianity Today* 8 (Jan 3, 1964) 11–13.

———, and Linda J. Evans. "C. S. Lewis and Music." *Christian Scholar's Review* 4.1 (1974) 1–15.

Kirk, Russell. "Chesterton, Madmen, and Madhouses." In *Myth, Allegory, and Gospel: An Interpretation of J. R. R. Tolkien, C. S. Lewis, G. K. Chesterton, Charles Williams*, edited by John Warwick Montgomery, 33–52. Minneapolis: Bethany Fellowship, 1974.

Kranz, Gisbert. "C. S. Lewis." *Hochland*, 60 (1968) 772–79.

———. "C. S. Lewis." In *Europas christliche Literatur 1500–1960*, edited by Gisbert Kranz, 425–32. Aschaffenburg: Pattloch, 1961.

———. "Die Oxforder Inklings-Autoren: Anmerkungen zu C. S. Lewis, J. R. R. Tolkien, Charles Williams." *Internationale Katholische Zeitschrift Communio*, 15.1 (1986) 70–78.

———. "Die Stillbare Sehnsucht: Der Dichter und Essayist, C. S. Lewis." *Stimmen Der Zeit* 85 (July 1960) 286–301.

———. "Neue Scönheit und neue Tragik: C. S. Lewis nach 1954." *Wort Und Warheit* 24 (Jan–Feb 1969) 55–63.

———. "The Reception of C. S. Lewis in Germany." *The Bulletin of the New York C. S. Lewis Society*, 18 (Apr 1971)1–3.

Kreeft, Peter. "How to Save Western Civilization: C. S. Lewis as Prophet." In *A Christian for All Christians: Essays in Honour of C. S. Lewis*, edited by Andrew Walker and James Patrick, 190–212. London: Hodder & Stoughton, 1990.

Masterman, Margaret. "C. S. Lewis: The Author and the Hero." *Twentieth Century* 158 (1955) 539–48.

Meynell, Hugo A. "An Attack on C. S. Lewis." *Faith and Philosophy* 8 (1991) 305–16.

Michael, Mary. "Our Love Affair with C. S. Lewis: Why Does This Bookish, Beer-Drinking Anglican Grip the American Imagination?" *Christianity Today* 37 (25 Oct 1993) 34–36.

Mitchell, Christopher W. "Bearing the Weight of Glory: the Cost of C. S. Lewis's Witness." In *The Pilgrim's Guide: C. S. Lewis and the Art of Witness*, edited by D. Mills, 3–14. Grand Rapids: Eerdmans, 1998.

———. "University Battles: C. S. Lewis and the Oxford University Socratic Club." In *C. S. Lewis Light Bearer in the Shadowlands*, edited by Angus J. L. Menuge, 329–51. Wheaton, IL: Crossway, 1997.

Neuhaus, Richard John. "C. S. Lewis in the Public Square." *First Things* 88 (Dec. 1998) 30–35.

Pippert, Wesley G. "A Home for C. S. Lewis." *Christianity Today* 18 (24 May 1994) 49–50.

Puerta, Marta Garcia de la. "The Inklings Abroad: Reading C. S. Lewis and J. R. R. Tolkien Outside the United Kingdom and North America." In *C. S. Lewis Life, Works, and Legacy*, edited by Bruce L. Edwards, Vol. 4: Scholar, Teacher and Public Intellectual, 99–116. Santa Barbara, CA: Praeger, 2007.

Uszynski, Edward. "C. S. Lewis as Scholar of Metaphor, Narrative, and Myth." In *C. S. Lewis Life, Works, and Legacy, Vol. 4: Scholar, Teacher and Public Intellectual*, edited by Bruce L. Edwards, 229–56. Santa Barbara, CA: Praeger, 2007.

Van Nattan, Steve and Mary. "C. S. Lewis: An Heretic Reviewed." *The Chronicle of the Oxford University C. S. Lewis Society* 1.1 (2004) 5–9.

Vaus, Will. "Lewis in Cambridge: The Professorial Years (1954–1963)." In *C. S. Lewis Life, Works, and Legacy, Vol. 1: An Examined Life*, edited by Bruce L. Edwards, 197–218. Santa Barbara, CA: Praeger, 2007.

———. "Lewis in Oxford: The Early Tutorial Years (1924–1939)." In *C. S. Lewis Life, Works, and Legacy, Vol. 1: An Examined Life*, edited by Bruce L. Edwards, 149–72. Santa Barbara, CA: Praeger, 2007.

———. "Lewis in Oxford: The Later Tutorial Years (1939–1953)." In *C. S. Lewis Life, Works, and Legacy, Vol. 1: An Examined Life*, edited by Bruce L. Edwards, 173–96. Santa Barbara, CA: Praeger, 2007.

———. "Lewis in Oxford: The Student Years (1917–1923)." In *C. S. Lewis Life, Works, and Legacy, Vol. 1: An Examined Life*, edited by Bruce L. Edwards, 127–48. Santa Barbara, CA: Praeger, 2007.

Veith, Gene Edward. "A Vision, Within a Dream, Within the Truth: C. S. Lewis as Evangelist to the Postmodernists." In *Translated Theology: C. S. Lewis Light Bearer in the Shadowlands*, edited by Arthur J. L. Menuge, 367–87. Wheaton, IL: Crossway, 1997.

Walsh, Chad "The Re-Education of the Fearful Pilgrim." In *Longing for a Form: Essays on the Fiction of C. S. Lewis*, edited by Peter J. Schakel, 64–72. Kent, OH: Kent State University Press, 1977.

Wilson, John. "An Appraisal of C. S. Lewis and His Influence on Modern Evangelicalism." *Scottish Bulletin of Evangelical Theology* 9.1 (1991) 22–39.

Wolfe, Judith. "On Power." In The Cambridge Companion to C. S. Lewis, edited by Robert MacSwain and Michael Ward, 174–88. Cambridge: Cambridge University Press, 2010.

Wright, Greg and Jenn. "C. S. Lewis and the Media: Cinematic and Stage Treatments of C. S. Lewis's Life and Works." In *C. S. Lewis Life, Works, and Legacy, Vol. 4: Scholar, Teacher and Public Intellectual*, edited by Bruce L. Edwards, 257–82. Santa Barbara, CA: Praeger, 2007.

Wright, N. T. "Simply Lewis: Reflections on a Master Apologist After 60 Years." *Touchstone Magazine* 20.2 (Mar 2007) 39–40.

Zogby, Edward G. "Triadic Patterns in Lewis's Life and Thought." In *Longing for a Form: Essays on the Fiction of C. S. Lewis*, edited by Peter J. Schakel, 20–39. Kent, OH: Kent State University Press, 1977.

7. RELIGION AND CULTURE, LIBERALISM AND HUMANISM, SECULARITY

Anderson, George C. "C. S. Lewis: Foe of Humanism." *Christian Century* 63 (1946) 1562–63.

Babbage, Stuart Barton. "C. S. Lewis and the Humanist Dilemma." *Reformed Theological Review* 32 (Sept–Oct, 1973) 73–81.

———. "C. S. Lewis and the Humanitarian Theory of Punishment." *Christian Scholar's Review* 2.3 (1972) 224–35.

Balsbaugh, John. "The Pagan and the Post-Christian: Lewis's Understanding of Diversity outside the Faith." In *Translated Theology: C. S. Lewis Light Bearer in the Shadowlands*, edited by Arthur J.L. Menuge, 191–210. Wheaton, IL: Crossway, 1997.

Barnard, Justin D. "The Hangman's Duty: C. S. Lewis on Christian Citizenship in Wartime." *The Chronicle of the Oxford University C. S. Lewis Society*, 4.3 (2007) 15–29.

Bramlett, Perry. "The Weight of Glory: C. S. Lewis as a Preacher." *Preaching* 10 (Sept–Oct, 1994) 45–48.

Root, J. "Tools Inadequate and Incomplete: C. S. Lewis and the Great Religions." In *The Pilgrim's Guide: C. S. Lewis and the Art of Witness*, edited by D. Mills, 221–35. Grand Rapids: Eerdmans, 1998.

8. REVELATION AND REASON

Armstrong, Charles I. "The Absolute Implied: Coleridge on Wordsworth and the Bible." *Literature and Theology* 14.4 (2000) 363–72.

Bartel, T. W. "What C. S. Lewis Didn't Tell You About Divine Providence, Human Freedom and the Problem of Evil." *The Chronicle of the Oxford University C. S. Lewis Society*, 2.1 (2005) 7–12.

Brazier, P. H. "C. S. Lewis on Revelation & Second Meanings: A Philosophical & Pneumatological Justification." *The Chronicle of the Oxford University C. S. Lewis Society* 7.1 (2010) 18–35.

———. "C. S. Lewis on Scripture and the Christ, the Word of God: Convergence and Divergence with Karl Barth." *Sehnsucht* 4 (2010) 89–109.

———. "Why Father Christmas Appears in Narnia." *Sehnsucht* 3 (2009) 61–77.

Bruce L. McCormack. "Divine Revelation and Human Imagination." *Scottish Journal of Theology* 37 (1984) 431–55.

Caldecott, Stratford. "Speaking the Truths Only the Imagination May Grasp: An Essay on Myth and 'Real Life.'" In *Touchstone: A Journal of Ecumenical Orthodoxy* 11(Sept–Oct, 1998) 44–48.

———. "The Reflection of Christian Truth in the Mythopoetic Imagination." *Epiphany* 14.4 (1994) 74–86.

———. "Speaking the Truths only the Imagination may Grasp." In *The Pilgrim's Guide: C. S. Lewis and the Art of Witness*, edited by D. Mills, 86–97. Grand Rapids: Eerdmans, 1998.

Carnell, Corbin Scott. "Longing, Reason, and the Moral Law in C. S. Lewis's Search." In *Translated Theology: C. S. Lewis Light Bearer in the Shadowlands*, edited by Arthur J. L. Menuge, 103–14. Wheaton, IL: Crossway, 1997.

Oury, Scott. "The Thing Itself: C. S. Lewis and the Value of Something Other." In *Longing for a Form: Essays on the Fiction of C. S. Lewis*, edited by Peter J. Schakel, 1–19. Kent, OH: Kent State University Press, 1977.

Packer, James. "Living Truth for a Dying World: The Message of C. S. Lewis." *Crux* 34 (Dec 1998) 3–12.

Pasnau, Robert. "Divine Illumination." *The Stanford Encyclopedia of Philosophy*. Online edition: http://www.science.uva.nl/~seop/entries/illumination/.

Shaw, Luci. "A Chiaroscoro God: Light, Darkness, and Desire in C. S. Lewis." *Crux* 30 (Mar 1994) 6–18.

Torrance, T. F. "The Deposit of Faith." *Scottish Journal of Theology* 36.1 (1983) 1–28.

6. C. S. Lewis: Revelation and the Christ: Secondary Sources—Articles and Essays

Walker, Andrew. "Scripture, Revelation and Platonism in C. S. Lewis." *Scottish Journal of Theology* 55.1 (2002) 19–35.

9. THEOLOGY AND BIBLICAL STUDIES

Anderson, Gary, editor. "The Sense of the Holy." *Epiphany* 2.2 (1981) 2–116.

Bonting S. L. "Theological Implications of Possible Extraterrestrial Life." *Zygon* 38.3 (2003) 587–602.

Brown, Devin. "The Screwtape Letters: Telling the Truth Upside Down." In *C. S. Lewis Life, Works, and Legacy, Vol. 2: Fantasist, Mythmaker and Poet*, edited by Bruce L. Edwards, 175–208. Santa Barbara, CA: Praeger, 2007.

Bruce, F. F. "Marius Victorinus and His Works." *The Evangelical Quarterly* 18 (1946) 132–53.

Carnell, Corbin S. "C. S. Lewis on Eros as a Means of Grace." In *Imagination and the Spirit: Essays in Literature and the Christian Faith Presented to Clyde S. Kilby*, edited by Charles A. Huttar, 341–51. Grand Rapids: Eerdmans, 1971.

Clasper, Paul. "C. S. Lewis's Contribution to a 'Missionary Theology': An Asian Perspective." *Ching Feng* 24.4 (1981) 203–14.

Cole, Graham A. "C. S. Lewis: An Evangelical Appreciation." *Reformed Theological Review* 53 (Sept–Dec, 1994) 101–14.

Edwards, Michael. "C. S. Lewis: Imagining Heaven." *Literature and Theology* 6 (June 1992) 107–24.

Fiddes, Paul S. "On Theology." In *The Cambridge Companion to C. S. Lewis*, edited by Robert MacSwain and Michael Ward, 89–104. Cambridge: Cambridge University Press, 2010.

Fisher, Christopher L., and David Fergusson. "Karl Rahner and the Extra-Terrestrial Intelligence Question." *The Heythrop Journal* 47.2 (2006) 275–90.

Glasson, Thomas Francis. "C. S. Lewis on St John's Gospel." *Theology* 71 (June 1968) 267–69.

Hauerwas, Stanley. "On Violence." In *The Cambridge Companion to C. S. Lewis*, edited by Robert MacSwain and Michael Ward, 189–202. Cambridge: Cambridge University Press, 2010.

Heck, Joel D. "Mere Christianity: Uncommon Truth in Common Language." In *C. S. Lewis Life, Works, and Legacy, Vol. 3: Apologist Philosopher and Theologian*, edited by Bruce L. Edwards, 51–74. Santa Barbara, CA: Praeger, 2007.

Holt, Torbjørn. "Sketches of a Narnian Theology (Part I)." *The Chronicle of the Oxford University C. S. Lewis Society* 2.3 (2005) 1–4.

———. "Sketches of a Narnian Theology (Part II)." *The Chronicle of the Oxford University C. S. Lewis Society* 3.1 (2006) 5–8.

Huttar, Charles A. "Angels in the Thought of C. S. Lewis." *Perspectives* 9 (Feb. 1994) 12–15.

Jolley, Reed. "Apostle to Generation X: C. S. Lewis and the Future of Evangelism." In *Translated Theology: C. S. Lewis Light Bearer in the Shadowlands*, edited by Arthur J. L. Menuge, 79–100. Wheaton, IL: Crossway, 1997.

———. "C. S. Lewis and the Case for Christianity." In *The Intellectuals Speak out About God*, edited by R. Varghese, 223–29. Chicago: Regnery Gateway, 1984.

———. "C. S. Lewis's Argument from Desire." In *G. K. Chesterton and C. S. Lewis: The Riddle of Joy, Conference Papers of the Seattle Pacific University Intercollegiate Studies Institute 1987*, edited by Michael H. Macdonald and Andrew A. Tadie, 249–72. London: Collins, 1989.

Loades, Ann. "On Gender." In *The Cambridge Companion to C. S. Lewis*, edited by Robert MacSwain and Michael Ward, 160–73. Cambridge: Cambridge University Press, 2010.

Macky, Peter W. "The Role of Metaphor in Christian Thought and Experience as Understood by Gordon Clark and C. S. Lewis." *Journal of the Evangelical Theological Society* 24 (Sept 1981) 239–50.

Malanga, Michael. "*The Four Loves*: C. S. Lewis's Theology of Love." In *C. S. Lewis Life, Works, and Legacy, Vol. 4: Scholar, Teacher and Public Intellectual*, edited by Bruce L. Edwards, 49–80. Santa Barbara, CA: Praeger, 2007.

Martindale, Wayne. "C. S. Lewis on Gender Language in the Bible: A Caution." *Touchstone: A Journal of Ecumenical Orthodoxy* 4 (Summer, 1990) 5–8.

———. "*Shadowlands*: Inadvertent Evangelism." In *Translated Theology: C. S. Lewis Light Bearer in the Shadowlands*, edited by Arthur J. L. Menuge, 31–54. Wheaton, IL: Crossway, 1997.

6. C. S. Lewis: Revelation and the Christ: Secondary Sources—Articles and Essays

Meilaender, Gilbert "On Moral Knowledge." In *The Cambridge Companion to C. S. Lewis*, edited by Robert MacSwain and Michael Ward, 119–31. Cambridge: Cambridge University Press, 2010.

Menuge, Angus J. L. "God's Chosen Instrument: The Temper of an Apostle." In *Translated Theology: C. S. Lewis Light Bearer in the Shadowlands*, edited by Arthur J. L. Menuge, 115–42. Wheaton, IL: Crossway, 1997.

——. "Fellow Patients in the Same Hospital: Law and Gospel in the Works of C. S. Lewis." *Concordia Journal* 25 (Apr 1999) 151–63.

Mitchell, Christopher W. "Lewis and Historic Evangelicalism." In *C. S. Lewis and the Church: Essays in Honour of Walter Hooper*, edited by Judith E. Wolfe and Brendan N. Wolfe, 154–73. London: Continuum, 2011.

Montgomery, John Warwick. "Revue Critique: *The Christian World of C. S. Lewis* par Clyde S. Kilby." In *Myth, Allegory, and Gospel: an Interpretation of J. R. R. Tolkien, C. S. Lewis, G. K. Chesterton, Charles Williams*, edited by John Warwick Montgomery, 148–50. Minneapolis: Bethany Fellowship, 1974.

Morris, Francis J., and Ronald C. Wendling. "Coleridge and 'the Great Divide,' in Between C. S. Lewis and Owen Barfield." *Studies in the Literary Imagination* 12.2 (1989) 149–59.

Mueller, Stephen P. "C. S. Lewis and the Atonement." *Concordia Journal* 25 (Apr 1999) 164–78.

——. "Translated Theology: Christology in the Writings of C. S. Lewis." In *Translated Theology: C. S. Lewis Light Bearer in the Shadowlands*, edited by Arthur J. L. Menuge, 279–302. Wheaton, IL: Crossway, 1997.

Odero, Jose Miguel. "El problema del dolor humano: Reflexiones al hilo del pensamiento de C. S. Lewis." *Revista Española De Teologia* 51.2–3 (1991) 377–85.

——. "La 'experiencia', in como lugar antropológico en C. S. Lewis." *Scripta Theologica* 26 (May–Aug 1994) 403–82.

——, and Jose Miguel Odero. "C. S. Lewis y las imagin del hombre." *Scripta Theologica* 26 (May–Aug 1994) 857–58.

Olli-Pekka Vainio. "The Aporia of Arguments from 'Love': A Meditation on C. S. Lewis' *Four Loves*." *The Chronicle of the Oxford University C. S. Lewis Society*, 4.2 (2007) 21–30.

Patrick, James M. "The Heart's Desire and the Landlord's Rules: C. S. Lewis as a Moral Philosopher." In *The Pilgrim's Guide: C. S. Lewis and the Art of Witness*, edited by D. Mills, 70–85. Grand Rapids: Eerdmans, 1998.

———. "In Defense of C. S. Lewis's Analysis of God's Goodness." *International Journal for Philosophy of Religion* 36 (Aug 1994) 45–56.

Rossow, Francis C. "Giving Christian Doctrine a New Translation: Selected Examples from the Novels of C. S. Lewis." *Concordia Journal* 21 (July 1995) 281–97.

———. "Old Wine in New Wineskins." In *Translated Theology: C. S. Lewis Light Bearer in the Shadowlands*, edited by Arthur J. L. Menuge, 259–78. Wheaton, IL: Crossway, 1997.

———. "Problems in Prayer and Their Gospel Solutions in Four Poems by C. S. Lewis." *Concordia Journal* 20 (Apr 1994) 106–14.

Ryken, Philip G. "Winsome Evangelist: The Influence of C. S. Lewis." In *Translated Theology: C. S. Lewis Light Bearer in the Shadowlands*, edited by Arthur J. L. Menuge, 55–78. Wheaton, IL: Crossway, 1997.

———. "Lewis as the Patron Saint of American Evangelicalism." In *C. S. Lewis and the Church: Essays in Honour of Walter Hooper*, edited by Judith E. Wolfe and Brendan N. Wolfe, 174–85. London: Continuum, 2011.

Simon, Caroline J. "On Love." In *The Cambridge Companion to C. S. Lewis*, edited by Robert MacSwain and Michael Ward, 146–59. Cambridge: Cambridge University Press, 2010.

Sprague, Duncan. "The Unfundamental C. S. Lewis: Key Components of Lewis's View of Scripture." *Mars Hill Review* 2 (Summer 1995) 53–63.

Swift, Jennifer. "A More Fundamental Reality than Sex: C. S. Lewis and the Hierarchy of Gender." *The Chronicle of the Oxford University C. S. Lewis Society* 5.1 (2008) 5–26.

Sys, J. "'Look Out! It's Alive!': C. S. Lewis on Doctrine." In *A Christian for All Christians: Essays in Honour of C. S. Lewis*, edited by Andrew Walker and James Patrick, 174–89. London: Hodder & Stoughton, 1990.

Talbott, Thomas. "C. S. Lewis and the Problem of Evil." *Christian Scholar's Review* 17.1 (1987) 36–51.

6. C. S. Lewis: Revelation and the Christ: Secondary Sources—Articles and Essays

Terrasa Messuti, Eduardo. "Imagen y mysterio: Sobre el conocimiento metafórico en C. S. Lewis." *Scripta Theologica* 25 (Jan–Apr 1993) 95–132.

Vanhoozer, Kevin J. "On Scripture." In *The Cambridge Companion to C. S. Lewis*, edited by Robert MacSwain and Michael Ward, 75–88. Cambridge: Cambridge University Press, 2010.

Watkins, Duff. "The Screwtape Letters and Process Theism." *Process Studies* 8 (Summer 1978) 114–18.

7

Secondary Sources—Related to Lewis's Development

1. BOOKS CITED BY LEWIS

These are works mentioned explicitly by Lewis in acknowledgement to the profound developmental effect they had on him from his teenage years through his early years at Oxford and into the intense period of post-conversion Christian reading in the 1930s.

Alexander, Samuel. *Space, Time and Deity*. The Gifford Lectures 1910–1918. Volumes I and II. London: Macmillan, 1920.

> Lewis cites Alexander's *Space, Time and Deity* as crucial in the final stages of his conversion, where he came across the distinction between "enjoyment" and "contemplation"—it was this in part that enabled him to see how he had mistaken the mystical pang of Sehnsucht/"Joy" for an end in itself (Lewis, *Surprised by Joy*, 210).

Aquinas, Thomas, *Summa Theologiae*. The complete paperback set: 60 volumes, plus one index volume; dual language, Latin–English. 1962–76. Reprint. Cambridge: Cambridge University Press, 2006.

> Lewis read and studied Aquinas's great unfinished tome on a daily basis in the 1940s (even only for 15 minutes, but usually longer) in its original Latin, which gave his apologetics and philosophical theology a distinctively sharp logical edge.

Augustine, *Confessions*. Translated by Henry Chadwick. Oxford World's Classics. Oxford: Oxford University Press, 1991.

———. *The City of God*. Edited by David Knowles, translated by Henry Bettenson. Harmondsworth, UK: Pelican Classics, 1972.

> Much of Lewis's doctrine of the fall is derived from his reading of patristic theologians and philosophers—specifically Augustine's *de civitate Dei* (*The City of God*). Lewis's reading is essentially from five years after his final conversion. Lewis read in depth Augustine's *Confessiones* (*Confessions*) in

1936, and *de civitate Dei* (*The City of God*) in 1937, both in the original Latin, returning to them regularly over the next decade, as well as translating *de civitate Dei* himself. See, Lewis writing to Dom Bede Griffiths, April 24, 1936; and, Lewis writing to Dom Bede Griffiths, May 23 1936. Lewis, *Collected Letters Vol. II*, 187–90 and 191–95.

Aulén, Gustaf, *Christus Victor: An Historical Study of the Three Main Types of the Idea of the Atonement*. London: SPCK, 1931.
> Lewis laid out his theological masters, and the education he received from them, in a letter in response to an enquiry from a reader, in 1958 (Lewis writing to Corbin Scott Carnell, Oct. 13, 1958. Lewis, *Collected Letters*, Vol. III, 978–98). When the correspondent questions the complexity of the debts Lewis owes to modern theologians, he comments that his debt to the "moderns" is hardly anything at all, that he knows not the "moderns" and what they stand for. He admits his ignorance on many modern theologians and philosophers, with the exception of two orthodox and traditional Protestant-Reformed works: Anders Nygren's *Agape and Eros* (on the nature of Christian love) and Gustaf Aulén's seminal work on Christ's sacrifice, *Christus Victor*: both works drew heavily on the patristic tradition, but also on the Reformation tradition from the sixteenth and seventeenth centuries.

Baxter, Richard, *Church–History of the Government of Bishops and their Councils*. London: Thomas Simmons, 1680.
> From his reading of Baxter, Lewis gleaned the term, "Mere Christianity," but importantly what it represented (Lewis writing to *The Church Times*, Feb. 8, 1952. Lewis, *Collected Letters* Vol. III, 164) Baxter commented, page xvii, that, "You know not of what Party I am of; nor what to call me; I am sorrier for you in this than for myself; if you know not, I will tell you, I am a Christian, a Meer[1] Christian, of no other Religion; and the Church that I am of is the Christian Church, and hath been visible where ever the Christian Religion and Church hath been visible."

Berkeley, George, *A Treatise concerning the Principles of Human Knowledge*. Hackett, 1982.
> Published by the Platonist Bishop George Berkeley in 1710, *A Treatise concerning the Principles of Human Knowledge*, along with the work of other pre-Kantian philosophers, gave Lewis a sound philosophical basis for his faith. Berkeley's philosophy, along with the seventeenth-century Cambridge Platonist Henry More, was formative, though as the Anscombe-Lewis debate demonstrated, it also proved to be an Achilles' heel.

---

1   *Meer*: the word Meer is correct spelling for seventeenth century early modern English. Meer is from medieval English, and means *pure, sheer*, even, *simply*, rather than the *solely, no more than, only*, or *less than*, as is often the case in modern English.

7. Secondary Sources—Related to Lewis's Developmen

Chesterton, G. K., *The Everlasting Man*. London: Hodder & Stoughton, 1925.
> Lewis regarded Chesterton's *Everlasting Man*, as the soundest account of the human condition ever written (see, Lewis, "Christian Apologetics" 1954). Chesterton's work had a profound impact on him which he acknowledged on many occasions.

Frazer, Sir James George, *The Golden Bough: A Study in Magic and Religion*. 12 volumes. London: Macmillan, 1911–15.

———. *The Golden Bough: A Study in Magic and Religion*. Abridged edition. Introduction by George W. Stocking Jn. 1922. Reprint. Harmondsworth, UK: Penguin, 1996.
> Initially published in two volumes in 1890, the work then grew to the final 12 volume 3rd edition published 1911–15: Vol. 1–2, part I, *The Magic Art*; Vol. 3, part II, *Taboo and the Perils of the Soul*; Vol. 4, part III, *The Dying God*; Vol. 5–6, part IV, *Adonis, Attis, Osiris Studies in the History of Oriental Religion*; Vol. 7–8, part V, *Spirits of the Corn and of the Wild*; Vol. 9, part VI, *The Scapegoat*; Vol. 10–11, part VII, *Balder the Beautiful the Fire-Festivals of Europe and the Doctrine of the External Soul*; Vol. 12, *Bibliography and General Index*.
>
> Lewis read Frazer's massive work as a young man. When he became a Christian he could not dismiss Frazer's atheistic suppositions but had to find some way of accommodating and "Christianizing" Frazer's conclusions. He did this in his doctrine of christological prefigurement, whereby the evidence of the gospel story in pagan myths and religions was not explained psychologically (as Frazer had done invoking Feuerbach and Freud) but as intimations of the one true myth that was to become an actuality.

Hooker, Richard, *Of the Lawes of Ecclesiastical Politie* (1593–1662) Vols. 1–4 published in 1594; Vol. 5 in 1597; Vols. 6–9 published posthumously.
> Lewis valued Hooker's Anglican *via media*—the middle way between the Catholic and Puritan—immensely, and wrote his own complementary critique (*English Literature in the Sixteenth Century*, 451–63). Although Lewis's doctrine of the Church was Augustinian (invoking a distinction between the visible church we see as flawed and compromised, as compared to the true church, invisible, but stretched out in eternity), Hooker's *via media* complemented this position. Therefore, for Lewis, none of the churches since the Reformation can claim the authority the church once had.
>
> Modern edition: Richard Hooker, *Of the Laws of Ecclesiastical Polity*. Edited by A. S. McGrade. Cambridge: Cambridge University Press, 1989.

MacDonald, George, *Phantastes, a Faerie Romance*. 1858. Reprint. Grand Rapids: Eerdmans, 2000.
> Lewis declared MacDonald as his master on many occasions. Lewis was visited by a profound mystical experience that effectively scattered and annihilated his atheism, briefly, as a teenager when he discovered McDonald's,

Phantastes, on a station bookstall on a profoundly beautiful autumn evening, shrouded in mist in the heart of the Surrey countryside. (Lewis, *Surprised by Joy*, 172–73.)

Nygren, Anders, *Agape & Eros* (Part 1: *A Study of the Christian Idea of Love* and Part II: *The History of the Christian Idea of Love*, in one volume). Translated by Philip S. Watson. London: SPCK, 1957.

 See annotation above, on Gustaf Aulén's, *Christus Victor*.

Plato, *Complete Works*. Edited by John M. Cooper, translated by M. J. Levett, revised by Myles Burnyeat. Indianapolis, IN: Hackett, 1997.

 Lewis's Platonism informs and shapes all of his writings. He was particularly influenced by Plato's *Republic* and *Theaetetus*. A doctrine of transposition is the key to all of Lewis's works, which is itself platonically framed, including what he describes as the philosophy of the incarnation. (See: *Transposition and Other Addresses* (1949) 9–20).

Thompson, Francis, *The Hound of Heaven*. London: Burns Oates & Washbourne, 1900.

 Cited as of profound importance by Lewis's wife, Joy Davidman, in coming to understand what had happened in her conversion.

Vincentius of Lérins, *The Commonitory of Vincent of Lérins, for the Antiquity and Universality of the Catholic Faith against the Profane Novelties of all Heresies*. Translated by C. A. Heurtley, edited by Philip Schaff and Henry Wace. In *The Nicene and Post-Nicene Fathers, Second Series, Volume 11, Sulpitius Severus, Vincent of Lerins, John Cassian*. Grand Rapids: Eerdmans, 2002.

 Lewis's method was defined by content: the content was derived from the patristic theologian Vincentius of Lérins and the seventeenth-century Puritan Richard Baxter (above). Lewis's content-led method in his apologetics is two-fold: one element is broadly Catholic, the other broadly Evangelical (Baxter—more pertinently, Puritan). First, was an appeal to the basic core of the faith established in the centuries after Christ's resurrection, a basic core that was essentially complete by the mid-fifth century, but with much of the detail worked out by the mid-eighth century, this common core to the faith was endorsed by Scripture and by the developing church tradition. ("The Commonitory of Vincent of Lérins," 207–60.)

2. WORKS RELATING TO LEWIS'S PATRISTIC AND PHILOSOPHICAL DEVELOPMENT

Anselm of Canterbury. *The Proslogion*. In *Anselm of Canterbury: The Major Works*, edited by Brian Davies and G. R. Evans. Oxford: Oxford University Press, 1998.

Berkeley, George. *Three Dialogues between Hylas and Philonous, in Opposition to Sceptics and Atheists* (1713). London: Dent, 1910.

Bettenson, Henry, translator and editor. *The Early Christian Fathers. A Selection from the Writings of the Fathers from St Clement of Rome to St Athanasius*. Oxford: Oxford University Press, 1956.

———, translator and editor. *The Later Christian Fathers. A Selection from the Writings of the Fathers from St Cyril of Jerusalem to St Leo the Great*. Oxford: Oxford University Press, 1970.

Chesterton, G. K. *St Thomas Aquinas*. Garden City, NY: Image, 1956.

———. *Orthodoxy*. 1908. Reprint. New York: Doubleday, 2001.

Coleridge, Samuel Taylor. *Biographia literaria: or, Biographical Sketches of My Literary Life and Opinions*. Edited and introduced by George Watson, Everyman's library 11. 1817. Reprint. London: Dent, 1997.

———. *Collected Letters of Samuel Taylor Coleridge*, Vol. II: 1801–1806. Edited by E. L. Griggs. Oxford: Clarendon, 1956.

———. *Confessions of an Inquiring Spirit*. 1840. Reprint. Stanford, CA: Stanford University Press, 1957.

———. *The Complete Works of Samuel Taylor Coleridge*. Ann Arbor, MI: Scholarly Publishing Office, University of Michigan Library, 2006.

———. *The Table Talk of S. T. Coleridge*. Introduction, H. Morley. London: Routledge, 1884.

MacDonald, George. *George MacDonald: An Anthology*. Edited by C. S. Lewis. London: Bless, 1946.

———. *Unspoken Sermons Series I, II and III*. Charleston, SC: Biblio Bazar, 2007.

Roberts, Alexander, James Donaldson, Philip Schaff, and Henry Wace, editors and translators. *The Early Church Fathers: Ante-Nicene Fathers—Translations of the Writings of the Fathers Down to A.D. 325; The Nicene and Post-Nicene Fathers of the Christian Church, First and Second Series*. 38 Volume Set. Grand Rapids: Eerdmans, 1979.

Stevenson, J., editor. *Creeds, Councils and Controversies. Documents Illustrating the History of the Church, AD 337–461*. Revised by W. H. C. Frend, SPCK Church History. London: SPCK, 1966.

3. WORKS RELATING TO LEWIS'S DEFENCE OF PAGAN MYTHOLOGY

Markos, Louis. *From Achilles to Christ: Why Christians Should Read the Pagan Classics*. Downers Grove, IL: InterVarsity, 2007.

O'Donaghue, Heather, *From Asgard to Valhalla. The Remarkable History of the Norse Myths*. New York, I. B. Tauris, 2007.

4. INKLINGS RELATED

Bassham, Gregory and Eric Bronson. *The Lord of the Rings and Philosophy: One Book to Rule Them All*. Chicago: Carus, 2003.

Burns, Marjorie. *Perilous Realms. Celtic & Norse in Tolkien's Middle Earth*. Toronto: University of Toronto Press, 2005.

Carpenter, Humphrey, editor. *The Letters of J. R. R. Tolkien*. Boston: Houghton Mifflin, 1981.

———. *J. R. R. Tolkien: A Biography*. London: George Allen & Unwin, 1977.

———. *The Inklings: C. S. Lewis, J. R. R. Tolkien, Charles Williams and their Friends*. London: George Allen & Unwin, 1978.

Dearborn, Kerry. *Baptized Imagination: The Theology of George MacDonald*. Ashgate Studies in Theology, Imagination and the Arts. Aldershot UK: Ashgate, 2006.

Hammond, Wayne G., and Christina Scull, editors. *The Lord of the Rings: Scholarship in Honor of Richard E. Blackwelder*. Milwaukee, WI, Marquette University Press, 2006.

Simmons, Laura K., *Creed Without Chaos. Exploring Theology in the Writings of Dorothy L Sayers*. Grand Rapids, Baker Academic, 2005.

Wood, Ralph C., *The Gospel According to Tolkien: Visions of the Kingdom of Middle Earth*. Louisville, KY: Westminster John Knox, 2003.

8

Web Resources

The World Wide Web is now a resource that anyone wanting to research Lewis cannot ignore; however, as with Wikipedia, the free-access online encyclopedia, caution must be exercised. Many sites may contain inaccurate information. Wikipedia is generally trustworthy but it must be remembered that anyone can logon, and change, edit, alter a page within Wikipedia. The Wikipedia foundation does employ people to check pages, but this does not remove the risk of inaccurate or erroneous information. This notwithstanding, there are many websites that will help develop an understanding of Lewis generally, his understanding of the Christ specifically.

In general terms two websites standout for authority, accuracy, and relevance (one has Reformed Church roots, the other, Roman Catholic, and thus complement Lewis's assertion that he was a Catholic Evangelical!):

Christian Classics Ethereal Library (CCEL) is a volunteer-based project founded and directed by Harry Plantinga, a professor of computer science at Calvin College. It was started at Wheaton College in 1993, and currently maintained by Calvin College. CCEL provides online texts of many important theological works

www.ccel.org/

New Advent is a Roman Catholic website likewise providing online texts of many important theological works:

The Catholic Encyclopedia

www.newadvent.org/cathen/

The Patristic Tradition— the Writings of the Early Fathers
http://www.newadvent.org/fathers/index.html

C. S. LEWIS—AN ANNOTATED BIBLIOGRAPHY AND RESOURCE

1. C. S. LEWIS ON THE WEB

Wikipedia—C.S. Lewis
en.wikipedia.org/wiki/C._S._Lewis

The Marion E. Wade Centre, Wheaton College
www.wheaton.edu/wadecenter/

The Oxford University C. S. Lewis Society
sites.google.com/site/lewisinoxford/

The New York C. S. Lewis Society
www.nycslsociety.com/

The C. S. Lewis Society of California
www.lewissociety.org/

The Arizona C. S. Lewis Society
www.azcslewissociety.org/

The C. S. Lewis Society
www.apologetics.org/

The C. S. Lewis Society Blog
apologeticsorg.blogspot.com/

The Taylor C. S. Lewis Society
www.taylor.edu/academics/supportservices/cslewis/society.shtml

The C. S. Lewis Society of Chattanooga
cslewischattanooga.org/

The C. S. Lewis Foundation
www.cslewis.org/

Narnia.com (official web site for the films)
www.narnia.com/

Narnia Fans
www.narniafans.com/

Narnia Web
www.narniaweb.com/

The Aslan Society
www.aslansociety.org/

The C. S. Lewis & Inklings Society
www.okcu.edu/english/cslis/home.html

The C. S. Lewis Festival
www.cslewisfestival.org/

The C. S. Lewis Institute
www.cslewisinstitute.org/

The C. S. Lewis Reading Group (St George's Episcopal Church, Dayton Ohio)
www.stgeorgeohio.org/Education/lewisgroup.htm

The C. S. Lewis Society at Rudgers University
episcopal.rutgers.edu/episcopal/C._S._Lewis.html

The C. S. Lewis Society of Frederick, Maryland
frederickcslewissociety.blogspot.com/

The C. S. Lewis Society of Idaho
www.daystarlife.org/cslewissociety.htm

The C. S. Lewis Society, Mississippi
www.facebook.com/group.php?gid=41578687092

The C. S. Lewis Society, Harrisonburg, Pennsylvania
www.willvaus.com/c__s__lewis_society

Memphis C. S. Lewis Society
www.narnia.org/

Toronto C. S. Lewis Society
cslewis.oceandigital.ca/

C. S. Lewis News
www.topix.net/who/c-s-lewis

The Cumberland River Lamp Post
www.crlamppost.org/cslewis.htm

"Dangerous Idea"—Victor Reppert Blog
www.dangerousidea.blogspot.com/

"Into the Wardrobe"—A C. S. Lewis Web Site
cslewis.drzeus.net/

"C. S. Lewis & Public Life" Discovery Institute
www.discovery.org/cslewis/

"Planet Narnia"—Michael Ward
www.planetnarnia.com/

Will Vaus
www.willvaus.com/c__s__lewis

Will Vaus, Blog
willvaus.blogspot.com/

"The Question of God"—Lewis & Freud
www.pbs.org/wgbh/questionofgod/

The Stone Table
www.thestonetable.com/landing_pages/1,3.html

Lewisiana—Arend Smilde, Utrecht, The Netherlands
www.lewisiana.nl/essayquotes/

"Never Enough Tea"—Reflections on all Things Lewis
www.afcmin.org/merelewis/

Mere C. S. Lewis
www.merecslewis.blogspot.com/

C. S. Lewis Today
www.cslewistoday.com/

C. S. Lewis Chronicles
www.scriptoriumnovum.com/l.html

C. S. Lewis & Narnia (Kroniikai Hungary)
www.narniakronikai.ro/index.php

Narnia Films (Netherlands)
narniafilms.nl/

Narnia Faith
www.narniafaith.com/

The Narnia Academy
www.thenarniaacademy.org/

The Lion's Call
www.thelionscall.com/

"Aslan Alive"—Explore the Magic of Mystical Narnia
www.explorefaith.org/lewis/narnia.html

The One-Ring Visits Narnia
www.theonelion.net/

Narnia (Italy)
www.narnia.it/

Narnia Editions & Translations
inklingsfocus.com/index.html

2. THE INKLINGS

C. S. Lewis was a member of the Inklings, who were an informal gathering of like-minded writers, academics, and literati. Essentially a discussion group, and a critical base for sharing developing work, members of the circle were associated with the University of Oxford, meeting on average twice a week during term time (Tuesday mornings usually at the Eagle and Child pub on St Giles, and on Thursday evenings in C. S. Lewis's rooms at Magdalen College). The Inklings were not a formal society or club and had no rules, officers, or formal meetings. The members were all men who met to discuss literature and Christian doctrine and ethics (however, not all were Christian). The aim of the group was discussion—and the reading of works-in-progress. J. R. R. Tolkien's shared *The Lord of the Rings* with the group as it developed; likewise Lewis and Charles Williams shared work as they wrote.

The Inklings met from 1939 to 1962. Many writers passed through; however, the core consisted of C. S. Lewis and his brother Warren (or "Warnie"), J. R. R. Tolkien (later joined by his son Christopher), Owen Barfield, Charles Williams, Nevill Coghill, Hugo Dyson, Roger Lancelyn Green, Adam Fox, R. A. Havard, J. A. W. Bennett, and Lord David Cecil.

Presented here is a comprehensive list of links to websites about the Inklings, and individual members.

i. The Inklings

The Eagle and Child—
www.headington.org.uk/oxon/stgiles/tour/west/48_49_eagle.htm

The Inklings: The Other Oxford Movement—
www.catholiceducation.org/articles/arts/al0142.html

Wikipedia—The Inklings—
en.wikipedia.org/wiki/Inklings

Facebook - Inklings—
www.facebook.com/pages/Inklings/108132979214642

Inklings-Gesellschaft(German based site)—
www.inklings-gesellschaft.de/

The Inklings – Blog—
oxfordinklings.blogspot.com/

The Inklings (page on a Tolkien site)—
www.tolkien-online.com/inklings.html

Inkling Resources—
personal.bgsu.edu/~edwards/inklings.html

The Oxford Dictionary of National Biography—
www.oxforddnb.com/public/themes/92/92544.html

The Mythopoeic Society—
www.mythsoc.org/

The C. S. Lewis & The Inklings Society—
www.oru.edu/academics/resources/cs_lewis/index.php

ii. J. R. R. Tolkien

Wikipedia—J. R. R. Tolkien.
en.wikipedia.org/wiki/Tolkien

Tolkien-Online
www.tolkien-online.com/

The Tolkien Society
www.tolkiensociety.org/index.html

The American Tolkien Society
www.americantolkiensociety.org/

The Brazilian Tolkien Society
jrrtolkien.com.br/

Cambridge Tolkien Society
tolkien.soc.ucam.org/

"Taruithorn"—The Oxford C.S. Lewis Society
users.ox.ac.uk/~tolksoc/

The North-East Tolkien Society
herenistarionnets.blogspot.com/

"Forodrim"—The Tolkien Society (Sweden)
www.forodrim.org/index_en.html

The University of Wisconsin Tolkien Society
homepages.cae.wisc.edu/~rcwest/

"Skies of Rohan"—the Idaho & Montana Tolkien Society
www.skiesofrohan.com/

The Tolkien Gateway
tolkiengateway.net/wiki/The_Tolkien_Society

Finnish Tolkien Society
www.suomentolkienseura.fi/e_general.html

Sociedad Tolkien Espanola
www.sociedadtolkien.org/texto.php?id=11

"Arthedain"—The Tolkien Society of Norway
www.arthedain.org/english.html

Minnesota Tolkien Society
www.tc.umn.edu/~d-lena/MinnesotaTolkienSociety.html

The Philippine Tolkien Society
www.flickr.com/photos/ulan25/collections/72157612091721937/

"Endorion"—The Bulgarian Tolkien Society
www.endorion.org/eng.html

The Toronto Tolkien Society
wellinghallsmial.blogspot.com/

"Rohirrim"—The Tolkien Society, Italy
www.rohirrim.it/

"Falas"—Website of the Falathrim, Scottish Smial of the Tolkien Society
homepage.mac.com/anneforbes/index.html

Spanish Tolkien Society
www.musicoflotr.com/2010/11/spanish-tolkien-society.html

iii. Charles Williams

Wikipedia—Charles Williams
en.wikipedia.org/wiki/Charles_Williams_(British_writer)

The Charles Williams Society
www.charleswilliamssociety.org.uk/

"Web of Exchange", an internet group on Williams
www.coinherence.faithweb.com/

"What About Charles Williams" Touchstone, a Journal of Mere Christianity
www.touchstonemag.com/archives/article.php?id=17-10-033-f

"The Lost Club Journal" The Novels of Charles Williams
freepages.pavilion.net/tartarus/williams.html

iv. Owen Barfield

Owen Barfield Literary Estate, for copyright and permissions
www.owenbarfield.org/

Owen Barfield Society. A community of scholars, for news and announcements of interest to Barfieldians
barfieldsociety.org/

The Barfield Bibliography. The definitive list of published works by Owen Barfield
barfieldsociety.org/Bibliography.htm

Archive of Owen Barfield Papers (Opened 2010). Main repository of all original manuscripts and papers, including unpublished material, Bodleian Library, University of Oxford, England
www.bodley.ox.ac.uk/dept/scwmss/wmss/online/modern/barfield/barfield.html

Owen Barfield University Collection. Printed-papers, artifacts, and OB library books in German: Marion E. Wade Center, Wheaton College, IL, USA
www.wheaton.edu/wadecenter/authors/authors_OB.html

Owen Barfield/S. T. Coleridge Collection With manuscript of Barfield's edition of Coleridge's "Lectures 1818–1819. On the History of Philosophy". University of Toronto, E. J. Pratt Library of Victoria College Library, Canada
library.vicu.utoronto.ca/special/index.htm

Owen Barfield Family Collection. Early book library and file papers. Azusa Pacific University, Special Collections Library, CA, USA
www.apu.edu/library/specialcollections/

Owen Barfield: Understanding Equity
www.secondspring.co.uk/articles/Barfield%20on%20Equity.pdf

Owen Barfield/C. S. Lewis Estate Collection Approximately 300 letters by Barfield dealing with Lewis's literary matters, dated circa 1970–1980. University of North Carolina, Special Collections Library, NC, USA
www.lib.unc.edu/wilson/

Encyclopedia Barfieldiana. Reference source
davidlavery.net/Barfield/Encyclopedia_Barfieldiana/Encyclopedia%20Barfieldiana2.html

Rocky Mountains Modern Language Association (RMMLA) Permanent session on Owen Barfield at the annual convention
rmmla.wsu.edu/default.asp

Owen Barfield: The Evolution of Consciousness
www.natureinstitute.org/about/who/barfield.htm

Owen Barfield and the Technological Society
www.natureinstitute.org/txt/st/barfield.htm

Owen Barfield on Wikipedia
en.wikipedia.org/wiki/Owen_Barfield

Lucy Barfield (1935–2003) Daughter of Owen Barfield and Godchild of C. S. Lewis. "The Lion, the Witch and the Wardrobe" was written for her and dedicated to her. She wrote two collections of poems.
en.wikipedia.org/wiki/Lucy_Barfield

"Saving the Appearances: A Study in Idolatry" (first published 1957, 3rd ed. Barfield Press 2011) The seminal text.
en.wikipedia.org/wiki/Saving_the_Appearances:_A_Study_in_Idolatry

Review of the Owen Barfield fictional novellas "Night Operation" and "Eager Spring", (2009)
www.mythsoc.org/reviews/night.operation.eager.spring/

Owen Barfield Literary Estate on Facebook
www.facebook.com/home.php?#!/pages/Owen-Barfield-Literary-Estate/128584977175154

v. Warren "Warnie" Hamilton Lewis

Wikipedia—Warren Lewis
en.wikipedia.org/wiki/Warren_Lewis

Warren Lewis
www.hedweb.com/bgcharlton/warren-lewis.html

C. S. Lewis Institute: Profile of Warren Lewis
www.cslewisinstitute.org/files/webfm/knowing_doing/ProfileWarrenLewis.pdf

vi. Nevill Coghill

Wikipedia—Nevill Coghill
en.wikipedia.org/wiki/Nevill_Coghill

Archive Hub: Nevill Coghill
archiveshub.ac.uk/features/0612coghill.html

Nevill Coghill
www.curtisbrown.co.uk/nevill-coghill/

vii. Roger Lancelyn Green

Wikipedia—Roger Lancelyn Green
en.wikipedia.org/wiki/Roger_Lancelyn_Green

Wikipedia—Roger Lancelyn Green
en.wikipedia.org/wiki/Roger_Lancelyn_Green

Roger Lancelyn Green
www.goodreads.com/author/show/13867.Roger_Lancelyn_Green

Tolkien Gateway—Roger Lancelyn Green
tolkiengateway.net/wiki/Roger_Lancelyn_Green

Facebook—Roger Lancelyn Green
www.facebook.com/pages/Roger-Lancelyn-Green/112257402118855

Roger Lancelyn Green – Bibliography
www.librarything.com/author/greenrogerlancelyn

viii. Hugo Dyson

Wikipedia—Hugo Dyson
en.wikipedia.org/wiki/Hugo_Dyson

"World Lingo"
www.worldlingo.com/ma/enwiki/en/Hugo_Dyson

Tolkien Gateway—Hugo Dyson
tolkiengateway.net/wiki/Hugo_Dyson

Facebook—Hugo Dyson
www.facebook.com/pages/Hugo-Dyson/112449362105400

The Cumberland River Lamp Post: Hugo Dyson
www.crlamppost.org/dyson.htm

ix. Lord David Cecil

Wikipedia—Lord David Cecil
en.wikipedia.org/wiki/Lord_David_Cecil

xi. J.A.W. Bennett

Wikipedia—J. A. W. Bennett
en.wikipedia.org/wiki/J._A._W._Bennett

x. R.A. "Humphrey" Havard

Wikipedia—R. A. Harvard
en.wikipedia.org/wiki/Robert_Havard

xii. Adam Fox

Wikipedia—Adam Fox
en.wikipedia.org/wiki/Adam_Fox

3. A YOUNGER GENERATION

i. Christopher Tolkien

Wikipedia—Christopher Tolkien
en.wikipedia.org/wiki/Christopher_Tolkien

Facebook—Christopher Tolkien
www.facebook.com/pages/Christopher-Tolkien/112781172069187

Tolkien Gateway—Christopher Tolkien
tolkiengateway.net/wiki/Christopher_Tolkien

The Tolkien Society: Christopher Tolkien – Publications
www.tolkiensociety.org/tolkien/bibl4.html

Wikia: Christopher Tolkien
lotr.wikia.com/wiki/Christopher_Tolkien

Christopher Tolkien: Bibliography
www.tolkienbooks.net/html/cjrt_bibliography.htm

ii. Douglas Gresham

In Lenten Lands
www.mrrena.com/2001/Lewis.shtml

IMBD Database
www.imdb.com/name/nm1007130/

Narnia.web Interview with Douglas Gresham
www.narniaweb.com/2005/04/narniaweb-exclusive-interview-with-douglas-gresham/

The Sydney Morning Herald—"In the Name of the Father"
www.smh.com.au/news/film/in-the-name-of-the-father-/2005/12/04/1133631142936.html

Christianity Today—"Narnia Comes to Life"
www.christianitytoday.com/ct/movies/interviews/2005/douglasgresham2.html

The Guardian—"My Step-Dad C. S. Lewis"
www.guardian.co.uk/books/2007/oct/04/cslewis.fiction

"Accurate Objective Accountable"
www.duncanentertainment.com/interview_gresham.php

C. S. Lewis Today—"Meet Douglas Gresham"
www.cslewistoday.com/conference-2006/meet-douglas-gresham

Academic Dictionaries & Encyclopedias
en.academic.ru/dic.nsf/enwiki/234391

CBN.com: Douglas Gresham—the Man Behind Narnia
www.cbn.com/spirituallife/InspirationalTeaching/vonBuseck_DouglasGresham_studio10.aspx

Facebook: Douglas Gresham
www.facebook.com/pages/Douglas-Gresham/112116908801194

4. OTHER MEMBERS & GUESTS

i. John Barrington Wain

Wikipedia—John Wain
en.wikipedia.org/wiki/John_Wain

The Observer – Obituary
www.independent.co.uk/news/people/obituary-john-wain-1438370.html

The Independent – Obituary
www.independent.co.uk/news/people/obituary-john-wain-1438370.html

John Wain – Bibliography
www.fantasticfiction.co.uk/w/john-wain/

John Wain Profile & Works
www3.shropshire-cc.gov.uk/wain.htm

Tolkien Gateway—John Wain
tolkiengateway.net/wiki/John_Wain

ii. Percy Bates

Wikipedia—Percy Bates
en.wikipedia.org/wiki/Percy_Bates

iii. John David Arnett & Jon Fromke

As yet, no web presence.

iv. Courteney Edward Stevens

Tolkien Gateway—C. E. Stephens
tolkiengateway.net/wiki/C.E._Stevens

v. Colin Hardie

Oxford Dictionary of National Biography—Colin Hardie
www.oxforddnb.com/index/101071117/Colin-Hardie

Tolkien Gateway—Colin Hardie
tolkiengateway.net/wiki/Colin_Hardie

vi. R. B. McCallum

Wikipedia—R. B. McCallum
en.wikipedia.org/wiki/R._B._McCallum

Tolkien Gateway—R. B. McAllum
tolkiengateway.net/wiki/R.B._McCallum

vii. Gervase Mathew

Tolkien Gateway—Gervase Mathew
tolkiengateway.net/wiki/Gervase_Mathew

viii. Roy Campbell

Wikipedia—Roy Campbell
en.wikipedia.org/wiki/Roy_Campbell_(poet)

ix. James Dundas-Grant

Tolkien Gateway—James Dundas Grant
tolkiengateway.net/wiki/James_Dundas-Grant

x. Eric Rucker Eddison

Wikipedia—Eric Rucker Eddison
en.wikipedia.org/wiki/Eric_R%C3%BCcker_Eddison

Eric Rucker Eddison Works
ebooks.adelaide.edu.au/e/eddison/er/

xi. Charles Leslie Wrenn

Wikipedia—Charles Leslie Wrenn
en.wikipedia.org/wiki/Charles_Leslie_Wrenn

"Library Thing"—Charles Leslie Wrenn
www.librarything.com/author/wrenncl

Tolkien Gateway—Charles Leslie Wrenn
tolkiengateway.net/wiki/Charles_Leslie_Wrenn

5. WRITERS VALUED BY THE INKLINGS AND ASSOCIATED WITH THEIR WORK

i. Joy Davidman

Wikipedia—Joy Davidman
en.wikipedia.org/wiki/Joy_Davidman

The San Francisco Chronicle: "Lost in the Shadow of C. S. Lewis's Fame"
www.sfgate.com/cgi-bin/article.cgi?file=/c/a/2006/01/01/RVGQFGC5DO1.DTL

Modern American Poetry
www.english.illinois.edu/MAPS/poets/a_f/davidman/davidman.htm

Smoke on the Mountain—online text
www.worldinvisible.com/library/davidman/smoke/smoke.c.htm

C. S. Lewis Institute—Joy Davidman
www.cslewisinstitute.org/cslewis/JDavidmanProfile.htm

"Boundless Webzine"—Joy Davidman
www.boundless.org/2005/articles/a0001188.cfm

The Joy Davidman [Gresham Lewis] Project
www.montreat.edu/dking/Joy%20Davidman/JoyDavidmanProject.htm

"Researching Joy Davidman"
quazen.com/reference/biography/researching-joy-davidman/

Helen Joy Davidman Lewis
www.findagrave.com/cgi-bin/fg.cgi?page=gr&GRid=8026820

Awesome Stories
www.awesomestories.com/religion/cs-lewis/cs-lewis-and-joy-gresham

Joy Davidman—Biography
www.english.illinois.edu/maps/poets/a_f/davidman/bio.htm

WorldCat Bibliography
www.worldcat.org/identities/lccn-n82-214737

Will Vaus's Bog—Joy Davidman
willvaus.blogspot.com/2009/07/joy-davidman.html

HBNet—A Joy Observed
findarticles.com/p/articles/mi_m1252/is_n6_v121/ai_14960794/

"And God Came In"
www.mrshields.com/and-god-came-in-the-extraordinary-story-of-joy-davidman-by-lyle-w-dorsett/

ii. Dorothy Sayers

Wikipedia—Dorothy Sayers
en.wikipedia.org/wiki/Dorothy_Sayers

The Dorothy Sayers Society
www.sayers.org.uk/

"Fantastic Fiction"
www.fantasticfiction.co.uk/s/dorothy-l-sayers/

Books & Writers—Dorothy Sayers
kirjasto.sci.fi/dlsayers.htm

Dorothy L. Sayers: A Christian Humanist for Today
www.religion-online.org/showarticle.asp?title=1267

Catholic Education Resource Centre
www.catholiceducation.org/articles/arts/al0138.html

Mystery.net
www.mysterynet.com/sayers/

"The Lost Tools of Learning"
www.gbt.org/text/sayers.html

Dorothy Sayers: Writer & Theologian
justus.anglican.org/resources/bio/19.html

iii. G. E. M. Anscombe

The Anscombe Society
blogs.princeton.edu/anscombe/

Wikipedia—G. E. M. Anscombe
en.wikipedia.org/wiki/G._E._M._Anscombe

Wikiquotes—G. E. M. Anscombe
en.wikiquote.org/wiki/G._E._M._Anscombe

Stanford Encyclopedia of Philosophy
plato.stanford.edu/entries/anscombe/

G. E. M. Anscombe - Bibliography
www.unav.es/filosofia/jmtorralba/anscombe_bibliography.htm

Orthodoxy Today—Anscombe on Contraception & Chastity
www.orthodoxytoday.org/articles/AnscombeChastity.php

The Daily Telegraph—Professor G. E. M. Anscombe
www.telegraph.co.uk/news/obituaries/1313382/Professor-G-E-M-Anscombe.html

The Information Philosopher
www.informationphilosopher.com/solutions/philosophers/anscombe/

Philosophy - Obituary
old.nationalreview.com/weekend/philosophy/philosophy-george020301.shtml

Philosophy on the Internet—
www.trincoll.edu/depts/phil/philo/phils/anscombe.html

PhilPapers—
philpapers.org/browse/g-e-m-anscombe

iv. George MacDonald

Wikipedia—George MacDonald
en.wikipedia.org/wiki/George_Macdonald

The George MacDonald Informational Web
georgemacdonald.info/

The Golden Key: George MacDonald
george-macdonald.com/

George MacDonald
www.victorianweb.org/authors/gm/index.html

The Literature Network. George MacDonald
www.online-literature.com/george-macdonald/

Brainy Quotes: George MacDonald
www.brainyquote.com/quotes/authors/g/george_macdonald.html

Christian Classics Ethereal Library: Biography of George MacDonald
www.ccel.org/m/macdonald

v. G. K. Chesterton

Wikipedia—G. K. Chesterton
en.wikipedia.org/wiki/Gk_chesterton

The American Chesterton Society
www.chesterton.org/

Christian Classics Ethereal Library: Biography of G. K. Chesterton
www.ccel.org/c/chesterton

A Starter Course on G. K. Chesterton
www.river.org/~dhawk/chesterton.html

Books & Writers: G. K. Chesterton
www.kirjasto.sci.fi/gkchest.htm

Literature Network
www.online-literature.com/chesterton/

G. K. Chesterton
www.gkc.org.uk/gkc/index.html

Quotations by Author: G. K. Chesterton
www.quotationspage.com/quotes/G._K._Chesterton/

Wikiquote: G. K. Chesterton
en.wikiquote.org/wiki/G._K._Chesterton

Biblical Evidence for Catholicism: G. K. Chesterton
socrates58.blogspot.com/2006/04/gk-chesterton-colossal-genius-links.html

Fantastic Fiction: G. K. Chesterton—Bibliography
www.fantasticfiction.co.uk/c/g-k-chesterton/

9

Glossary

A brief select glossary of terms that some readers of the three main volumes in this series may not be familiar with (terms that relate to Lewis's apologetics and philosophical theology and therefore to his understanding of the Christ) is to be considered of value. Much more detailed definitions can be found in standard volumes, encyclopaedias, or dictionaries, of Christianity. All of these terms are used by Lewis, or referred to synonymously, and are used in the three main books in this series.

Although often classified as an amateur, Lewis was a highly educated man. Despite the astute sharpness and strength of his intellect, Lewis tried to avoid specialized theological language (jargon).[1] However, some terms do need to be explained for readers unfamiliar with them. Some readers familiar with Lewis's books may not appreciate the full meaning and use of the terms used in the three main books. Professionals familiar with these terms may still gain some understanding of the context in which they are used in this series. Many Catholics and Evangelicals are familiar with these terms derived from New Testament Greek, and from *ecclesial* (i.e., church) Latin—ironically it is often Lewis's Anglicans who are ignorant of them. Lewis's apologetics, philosophical theology, and narratives are orthodox, traditional. This is confirmed by his invocation of "the Creation, Fall, Incarnation, Resurrection, Second Coming, and the Four Last Things."[2] The heart of the Christian faith, the basics, are in some ways summarized by the creation and the fall into original sin set out in the book of Genesis; by the incarnation, crucifixion, resurrection, and second coming of God in Christ, in the New Testament; but also the four "last things" (death, judgement, heaven, and hell) from the book of Revelation as well as the Gospels. This is Lewis's basic summary of the faith. Lewis believed in the traditional faith, set out by the apostles, and the early church fathers, which was biblical. At the centre of the Bible story is, as Lewis asserted the creation, the fall, the incarnation, the resurrection, the second coming, and the four last things.[3] First, whatever we may learn about evolution and the origin of the world and the universe, God created everything out of nothing and sustains it. Second,

---

1 See, Lewis, *Screwtape Letters*, Letter 1, for Lewis on the dangers of "jargon." 11–12.
2 Lewis writing to *The Church Times*, Feb. 8, 1952. Lewis, *Collected Letters Vol. III*, 164.
3 Ibid.

that humanity, through its own fault, disobeyed God and was infected by original sin; furthermore we brought this on ourselves, and the predicament we find ourselves in is perilous. Third, God became incarnated as a human being, Jesus Christ, who was crucified for our sins and was resurrected, all to atone for our fall into original sin and restore us to a right relationship with God. Fourth, that this same Jesus Christ will return to judge all at the end of the world, which will be, as Lewis terms it, the four last things: death, judgment, heaven, and hell. This is the *eschaton* (from the Greek for last or final things). This glossary in essence explains the detail of Lewis's understanding of Christ—who is at the centre of the human play that is the creation, the fall, the incarnation, the resurrection, the second coming, and the four last things.

AGE OF REASON, THE, AND THE ENLIGHTENMENT

The Age of Reason often seen as synonymous with the Enlightenment grew out of, in many ways, the friction and dislocation within the churches issuing from the Reformation in Europe that had led to religious wars. Religious dogma and the power and authority of the churches came in for question. In the Age of Reason many leading intellectuals and opinion formers placed an almost religious trust in the power of reason to solve humanity's problems. In Britain, the philosopher John Locke represents what is considered the beginning of the reason led Enlightenment. Although the early protagonists were prepared to be "religious," this led, amongst other approaches, to the religion of Deism, which explicitly denied Christ's divinity. The apparent universality of science, human thought, and reasoning was all important. However, despite its long-term influence still on the West (many of today's New Atheist see the power of reason through the Western Enlightenment as the foundation of all that they believe and disbelieve), the Age of Reason and the Enlightenment began to wane and dissipate into Romanticism by the end of the eighteenth century. France had been the key centre in the eighteenth century, and though its revolution was warmly welcomed by Enlightened thinkers the chaos and brutality, the fear and retribution, along with the dictatorial empire-building pretensions of Napoleon soon caused disillusionment.

ANALOGIA ENTIS AND *ANALOGIA FIDEI*

Do we know and understand about God through the world, through nature, does revelation come to us through creation, do we draw conclusions by analogy from our sense perception, from the world? Or does our knowledge and understanding come primarily from faith. If it is the latter, then we must accept God as revealed in Jesus Christ as the basis for our theology? Grounding our theology in creation, the world, is termed the *analogia entis* (the analogy of being); the latter, where the primary link between God and humanity is in and through the Christ, is the *analogia fidei* (the analogy of faith). Scientists and Naturalists will assert that we can know from the world—the accident of evolution which is claimed to be the universe. Theologians and philosophers who work from the *analogia entis* claim we can know of a God from the world. If the ground of revelation is in the *analogia fidei*, our starting point must be in Christ?

Our knowledge of God is by analogy. In both instances, whether through "being" or through "faith," analogy is the mode of knowledge and understanding: both the *analogia fidei* and the *analogia entis* are knowledge and understanding by analogy. The *analogia fidei* is derived from the fourth century patristic theologian and philosopher Augustine; the *analogia entis* is derived from the medieval theologian and philosopher Thomas Aquinas. Revelation in Christ—the *analogia fidei*—informs us that God is Triune, that we are corrupted by original sin, that Christ's sacrifice is necessary to save us. This cannot be derived from the *analogia entis*. The *analogia fidei* relates closely to the rule of faith (*regula fidei*). The *analogia entis* and *analogia fidei* is at the heart of the development of Lewis's theological method following on from the famous debate between the young don, G. E. M. Anscombe and C. S. Lewis in 1948. See: Naturalism/Scientism; New Atheists, The; and, *regula fidei*.

Apollinarianism

Apollinarius (c.310–390 CE) was trained under his father in Beirut. Like Eutyches he became a defender of orthodoxy against the Arians. Although Apollinarius was orthodox in that he saw that it was the unchangeable divine nature, the λόγος (*Logos* the *Word* of God, John 1), that could save humanity (that human nature on its own was lost because of the inherently fallible and wilful, the *fallen* and changeable nature of humanity) he began to believe that the divine nature—God—alone could save humanity without our full humanity in the incarnation. This led him to question the presence of a human mind in Jesus Christ; therefore he was arguing that Christ was not fully human: if Christ's human nature—specifically his mind—is not complete, the same as us, then Christ did not redeem the whole of human nature, the human person, but only the physical body, which imperils our salvation. The heterodox concept of Apollinarianism was invoked in the Pittenger-Lewis debate. See: Arianism; Docetism; and, Eutychianism. See also: Deism; and Theism.

Apologetics

As reasoned argument attempting to justify a belief system, a theory or doctrine, in the face of contradictory belief systems, apologists will argue and confront the apparent disagreements and divergences that are evident between competing belief systems. The term comes from the Greek word ἀπολογία, *apologia*, meaning to speak in defence. Christian apologetics are considered different to theology, *per se*, because in apologetics the truth of the gospel is represented in such a way as possibly to change the content in reaction to a perceived threat, indeed the apologetic content may be defined by the threat. Academic theology is considered to be impartial, disinterested, and neutral—in theory—therefore in some ways superior, yet if the gospel is true we cannot hold to an impartial multi-faith position that regards all religions and philosophies as equal, more pertinently that regards the content of all world religions as equally valid. Lewis did not; he understood that the gospel stands in contrast to the world, was against the world in many ways. Most of the theological writings in the early church are considered to be apologetics because they were written against the background of pagan Roman religion and politics, and were often written under persecution. The nature and weakness of apologetics is perhaps best illustrated by the often acrimonious debate between biblical theologians and Darwinian evolutionists. The Bible states that the universe was created, it had a beginning. An apologetic countering leads to the problem of dilution, at the very least the emphasis is skewed. Lewis's arguments and emphasis in "The World's Last Night" illustrate this fundamental weakness in the method and nature of apologetics. Lewis's rebuttal of Sir Fred Hoyle's Steady-State Theory in this essay is an example; much of the "The World's Last Night," argues against a Steady-State Theory when nowadays scientists and cosmologists no longer accept Hoyle's theory that the universe always existed, they dismiss Hoyle's argument against creation, that nature has no beginning and no end. Scientists now accept as fact that the universe had a beginning: the so-called "big-bang." A transitory, illusory, and wrong scientific theory forced Lewis to provide an unbalanced apologetic defence.

Arianism

Arianism was probably one of the most widespread and insidious of christological heresies, characterized by an imbalance between Christ as fully God and fully man: thus Christ's divinity was compromised. Arius (c.256–336), a priest in Alexandria, argued that the Son *was not* consubstantial (that is, not of the same substance or essence) as the Father; but he also argued that the Son was not coeternal with the Father (that is, that *he* had not always been). Arius and his supporters claimed that the Son was *created*, not *eternally begotten* (created, yes, before the universe, created before anything that exists: therefore, there was when the Son was not). This contradicted the orthodoxy that the relation of the Son to the Father had no beginning, was coeternal (John 1:1–3). Arianism effectively made Christ less than fully divine, not fully God. See: Apollinarianism; Docetism; and, Eutychianism. See also: Deism; and Theism.

Arminian(ism)

Though he does not explicitly align his atonement theory and understanding of salvation with Arminianism, Lewis's position is widely, though often implicitly, seen as Arminian: that is, concurring with that defined by the teaching of Jacobus Arminius, 1560–1609, professor of theology, University of Leiden, whose views became known as Arminianism. This accords with the early church and the patristic era in the sense that it was widely understood that we must actualize our salvation through faith (though in the end God in Christ judges whether our faith was genuine and sufficient a response to the cross), but then we may also throw away our salvation through our beliefs and actions: a central principle of Arminianism is therefore that grace is *resistible*, salvation cannot be universal. Lewis's account of the Christ, and the theology we can read from it, invokes an important distinction between *prelapsarian* humanity, *postlapsarian* humanity,[4] and redeemed humanity, defined by the centrality of the corrupting influence of original sin, but also the concept of the unfallen, that is, humanity before the *fall* (but also the speculation with regard to other sentient species, other rational creatures, God may have created in the universe or other worlds, who have not *fallen*: paradise retained. Lewis critically deconstructs a doctrine of total depravity, applying his

---

4 *Prelapsarian*: before, *pre*, the fall, *lapse* or *lapsarian*. *Postlapsarian*: after, *post*, the fall.

training in logic, concluding that it cannot be so, or we would not be able to perceive it. There is therefore still, for Lewis, some goodness left in humanity, corrupt in manifold ways though the human is through the *fall*, this goodness, in relation to, indeed initiated by, prevenient grace, will give us some perception of what God has done for us on the cross: Christ has done all: all we need to do is turn—but can we? Can humanity still hold out against God? Lewis's neo-Arminian doctrine of atonement would affirm the possibility of eternal damnation, still, for some. God's grace is resistible precisely because of humanity's willfulness.

The Holy Spirit will act on us all, but people respond in different ways, in differing degrees. Lewis's atonement theory is inherently Arminian—humanity can hold out against God. If humanity could not hold out against God, we would never have *fallen* in the first place! According to Classical Arminianism depravity is total, but atonement is intended for all because Jesus's death was for all people. Jesus draws all to him, through the Holy Spirit; the opportunity for salvation through faith is open to all because Jesus's death satisfies God's justice, however, again, grace is resistible: God takes the initiative in salvation, his grace then is open to all, but God respects human free will to respond or resist, election is therefore conditional: election justifies believers, *in potential*, This contrasts with a Calvinistic doctrine of election. Calvinism is often characterized by an *election independent of faith*; Arminians believe that election is "in Christ" (i.e., anyone who is "in Christ" is elect, but faith is essential to become united with Christ: election is conditional upon faith). Salvation is (to use modern terminology) universal, *in potentia*, in its potency, or its potential, because it has the capability or openness of actualizing the salvation of all, but is not yet in existence, actualized. And there is the reality attested to by Jesus of Nazareth, the Christ, in his sayings and parables, that points to the reality of damnation—of heaven and hell. All are invited; not all come into the kingdom. All are included; many choose to stay outside. All are invited; not all accept salvation. Lewis noted often in *The Chronicles of Narnia*, that all get what they want, not all like what they get.[5] See: Atonement; and, Prevenient Grace.

Atheism

Atheism at its simplest is a declaration that God, or the "gods," do not exist; however, it has often been used to indicate a lack of belief in the God of Judaism and Christianity. An accusation of atheism must always be backed up by a simple declaration by the atheist. Then it is a case of which g/God the atheist does not believe in, which complicates matters, especially given how the Holy Spirit may be pressing on an atheist's mind. In C. S. Lewis' view, atheism is corrupting—one only has to think of the beliefs, politics, and morality of many who reject the gospel to realize this. Lewis claimed atheism as a young man, though reading his spiritual autobiography,[6] illustrates how God still pressed on him and influenced him. Atheism, thought Lewis, is dangerous, but very difficult to quantify and define outside of a simple declaration by the protagonist.

Atonement

Invented in the sixteenth century by the Bible scholar and translator William

---

5 Lewis, *The Chronicles of Narnia: The Magician's Nephew*, Ch. 14, 162.
6 *Surprised by Joy* (1955),

Tyndale the word atonement ("at" "onement") was coined to reflect the concept in the Hebrew Scriptures of how forgiveness takes place. In sixteenth-century early modern English there was no single word that could reflect and explain this Hebrew understanding of the process of forgiving or pardoning a transgression by and before God, an understanding from which issued the atonement theories of the disciples, the Apostle Paul, and the early church—post resurrection. Christ's sacrifice reconciles as it forgives: therefore atonement must explain the simultaneous reconciliation of humanity to God, and the remission of sin, taking into account the question or need of satisfaction.[7] Atonement theories are therefore more than explanations of reconciliation because of an element of justice. It is the conflicting and often contradictory propitiatory elements in doctrines of atonement that have been, and still are, the cause of profound disagreements amongst the churches. The term here is from the verb to propitiate, and relates to traditional concepts of obedience to a monarch, that is, to win or regain favor, to appease. This is from the Latin *propitiat-, propitiare,* "render favorable," "win over," "sooth." See: ARMINIAN(ISM).

AUT DEUS AUT MALUS HOMO

A two-thousand year old tradition focusing on the actual nature of Jesus of Nazareth, the Christ, which culminated in the so-called Lewis trilemma in the mid twentieth century, *aut Deus aut malus homo* ("Either God, or a bad man") is the position we are forced to consider if someone claims to be God. If they are not God, then we are forced to make a moral judgment of them. Therefore, according to Lewis, Jesus is either God, or a bad man, or a mad man: we are forced to make a decision, or hide from the question. The earliest use is in the work of the fourth-century patristic theologian Gaius Marius Victorinus. Other examples of this proposition are found in the sixteenth-century writer Thomas More ("If Christ were not God, he would be no good man either"), the nineteenth-century Anglo-Catholic churchman and theologian, Henry Parry Liddon ("*Christus, si non Deus, non bonus*"—"Christ, if not God, is not good") and the nineteenth-century American preacher and theologian Mark Hopkins who wrote on the condition, character, and claims of Jesus. However, the root of this proposition is in Jesus's question to Peter ("But who do you say that I am?" Matt 16:15), and the opinions of those who knew and heard Jesus as recorded in John's Gospel: he was an unbalanced liar, or possessed, or he was the God of Israel descended to dwell with his people (John 8:49 and 10:21). *Aut Deus aut malus homo* relies on Lewis's use of the "Law of Excluded Middle": whatever our beliefs and apologetics, Jesus confronts us with the need to make a decision. This "either-or" is at the heart of Lewis's most popular and in some ways controversial, apologetic: that Jesus was "Mad, Bad or God" (that is, *aut Deus aut malus homo*—Jesus was God, or he cannot be considered a good man). See: REDUCTIO AD ABSURDUM, AND, "LAW OF EXCLUDED MIDDLE".

CATEGORICAL IMPERATIVE, THE

The categorical imperative implies a transcendent reality; further, that morals

---

[7] Satisfaction is defined by questions over propitiation (to win or regain the favor of, to appease; from Latin, *propitiati, propitiare*—*make favorable*), but also questions of punishment, debt, etc.

and ethics that affect and appear to issue from our will, are grounded in this transcendent reality. From Immanuel Kant's *Groundwork for the Metaphysics of Morals* (1785) the categorical imperative is the standard of rationality on which all moral requirements are based; it is a fundamental philosophical concept in Kant's moral philosophy. Morality is derived from an imperative, a commandment grounded in reason. A categorical imperative is an unconditional requirement; it is absolute. Kant so defined the categorical imperative that we should act only according to that maxim whereby we can simultaneously resolve that it should become a universal law.

COMMUNICATIO IDIOMATUM

The *communicatio idiomatum* (the communication of attributes) is about the divine nature as in Jesus of Nazareth. Traditionally, the divine attributes are considered to be in two groups: God's infinite powers (immanence, immutability, impassibility, impeccability, incorporeality, incomprehensibility, infinity, omnipotence, omnipresence, omniscience); and God's "personality" attributes, such as holiness, love, and (from the Old Testament) jealousy, wrath, freedom, incomprehensibility, *et al.* The *communicatio idiomatum* is in part about the communicable attributes, those that humanity, made in the image of God, possess, as compared to those attributes that are incommunicable, and reside in the divine nature alone. For Lewis, attributes of the divine nature are *transposed*, translated, diminuted, which is why if we had been in Galilee two thousand years ago we would have seen what appeared to be an ordinary man walking around, preaching, teaching, healing. But if we had met him, would we then have sensed something different about him? What was it that made many who met Jesus realize that he was indeed the God of Israel descended, incarnated? What was it that stopped others from realizing this? So, what are the divine attributes of the second person of the Trinity that are translated into Jesus as fully human and fully divine? What is reduced, hidden, veiled, according to Philippians, "emptied"? See: KENOSIS; PLATONISM; and, TRANSPOSITION.

DEISM

Deism emerged in Western Europe in the later seventeenth century, as an amorphous philosophical religion, ill-defined, that questioned the principle of revelation, essentially repudiated ecclesial authority, dogma, and traditional Christianity, replacing with what was considered to be rational religion. Such religion was naturally occurring and perceivable by all humanity—in theory. God became a remote creator who created a mechanistic universe that could exist and continue without any involvement or interference from God. Deism therefore situates and separates God from humanity and creation, and "exists" utterly outside of creation. Only the (philosophically) right-minded can ideally perceive this "god." Deism relates closely to the Age of Reason and the Enlightenment, also to theism, though they are not synonymous. See: AGE OF REASON, THE, AND THE ENLIGHTENMENT; and, THEISM.

DOCETISM

Docetism (from the Greek verb δοκέω, *dokeo*, which meant *to appear* or *to seem to be*): the Docetists believed Jesus was not really human, his humanity was only an appearance—hence the title, Docetism. The Docetists believed that Jesus's human body of flesh was a chimera, and so in the crucifixion he only seemed or appeared to suffer and die, that he was really incorporeal, a pure spirit, and hence could not physically die. So, to the Docetists, Jesus only appeared to suffer, and therefore from an orthodox perspective we are still lost in original sin: the atonement was not really real. With a Docetic Christ, the true nature is out of balance: Christ is not equally fully human and fully divine. This imperils our salvation. The heterodox concept of Docetism was invoked in the Pittenger-Lewis debate. See: APOLLINARIANISM; ARIANISM; and, EUTYCHIANISM. See also: DEISM; and THEISM.

ECCLESIA VISIBILIS-ECCLESIA INVISIBILIS

See: ECCLESIOLOGY.

ECCLESIOLOGY

Ecclesiology is the doctrine or study of the Church (from the Greek for congregation, a gathering of people: ἐκκλησία, *ekklesia*). Ecclesiology is about the foundation and origin of the church, or churches often characterized by pertinent questions: "Did Jesus found the church?", "What is the function of the church?", "Why are there different denominations?", etc. A crucial question is, "What is the relationship between Jesus and the churches?" Do the churches actually control salvation any longer? Therefore a fundamental axiomatic encompassing question is, "By what authority do Christians speak—both in word and action?" Lewis's ecclesiology is relatively broad and numinous; he is often seen as being more concerned with individual salvation, within a communal context, than with church orders and structures. In *The Screwtape Letters* (ch. 2), as in other instances, Lewis invoked the Augustinian distinction (*ecclesia visibilis/ecclesia invisibilis*) between the church we see—buildings, church goers, all the explicit church activities—as distinct from the invisible church, the community of the saved, in the world and in eternity, as God defines and perceives it. This is inevitably Platonic, and in many ways reflects Lewis's life, conversion, and his relationship with the church(es). See: PLATONISM.

ELECTION

See: ATONEMENT.

ESCHATON/ESCHATOLOGY

The *eschaton* (from the Greek for last or final things: ἔσχατος, eschatos; ἐσχάτη, eschatē; ἔσχατον, eschaton) is, in Christian theology, the last things or end-times: that is, the four last things—death, judgment, heaven, and hell. Whether applied individually to people as they die, or to the end of the world is debatable, but we will all face death, followed by judgment, which decides our eternal fate: heaven or hell. Eschatology is the doctrine or study of the eschaton.

EUTYCHIANISM

Eutyches (c.380–456 CE) was a presbyter at Constantinople. He was zealously opposed to Nestorius, whose teachings were condemned as the heresy of Nestorianism because they over separated the human nature and the divine nature, creating effectively two persons. However, Eutyches' over-reaction spawned its own heresy, Eutychianism, which was an early example of the heresy of Monophysitism (from the Greek μόνος, monos, alone or one, and φύσις, physis, nature), claiming that Christ's nature was a synthesis of the human and divine and thus Christ had but one nature, which subsumed the human nature, effectively denying Christ's full humanity. Even after censorship Eutyches continued to claim that there was only one nature (*physis*) and denied that Christ's manhood was consubstantial (of the same substance) with ours, which imperils our salvation. The heterodox concepts of Eutychianism and Monophysitism were invoked in the Pittenger-Lewis debate. See: APOLLINARIANISM; ARIANISM; and, DOCETISM. See also: DEISM; and THEISM.

EXISTENTIALISM

Existentialism is a belief system, or philosophy, which begins with the human as both subject and object, the human observing itself, and the human predicament; but this is not just the philosophical human, but the acting and loving, the emotional existing human, in all its chaos. Theological existentialism is the explication of the character and nature of the relationship between God and humanity: human existence before God. This is often seen from an individual perspective—the crisis of faith of an individual characterized by decision-making. Humanity is not alone without knowledge or understanding of God and the nature and purpose of life, neither is humanity without understanding as to its fate, *post mortem*. This knowledge is independent of the contingent nature of religious knowledge (contingent in the sense of geographical, educational or ability to comprehend). The atonement wrought by Christ may be a topic of religious knowledge and it is important for people to know what God has done for them, but even if they have not come across this knowledge in religious terms the reality is still there. The event of the crucifixion, death and resurrection of Christ has still happened and will impinge on the life of each and everyone—whether she or he knows about it or not, that is in terms of cognitive knowledge and understanding. The primacy of this event should be at the heart of the sound theological understanding. See: THEOLOGICAL ANTHROPOLOGY.

FALL, THE (ORIGINAL SIN)

See: ARMINIAN(ISM); and, ATONEMENT.

FIDES QUAERENS INTELLECTUM

The proposition, *fides quaerens intellectum*, "faith seeking understanding," comes from the medieval theologian Anselm of Canterbury (1033–1109). This is derived from Anselm's prayer in *The Proslogion*. It is not philosophical speculation that leads to prayerful enquiry, but accepting in the first instance what God has done for humanity. Hence: it is faith that leads to the prayer of Anselm, "Let my mind meditate on you, let my tongue speak of you, let my heart love you, let my soul hunger for you, until I enter into the joy of the Lord, who is God, Three in One, blessed for ever." Therefore faith seeks to understand. See: *ANALOGIA ENTIS AND ANALOGIA FIDEI*; FOUNDATIONALISM; and, REVELATION AND REASON.

FOUNDATIONALISM

Foundationalism is the view that the justification of all non-basic beliefs (i.e., beliefs that do not require arguments or evidence in order to be rationally justified) can be derived from basic beliefs that are either universal truths of reason or derived clearly from the senses and are thus incorrigible, persistent, and irrefutable. Foundationalism is, therefore, the view that rational beliefs are either basic (unquestionably true) or legitimately deduced or induced from basic beliefs. In its classical form this creates problems for religious claims because, it was said, they are not unquestionably true (so cannot be basic) but nor can they be safely deduced or induced from basic beliefs. Thus they are irrational. Do religious beliefs require such foundations in order to be rational? This issue has been much debated by philosophers. What is the foundation of your faith? This is a question that is at the heart of Lewis's writings. In terms of epistemology (theories of knowing) foundationalism claims that non-basic beliefs are justified if they are founded on basic, or foundational, beliefs. Foundational beliefs, statements, or propositions are in effect irrefutable, and end the problem of infinite regress. According to the problem of infinite regress, any statement or argument or proposition requires an explanation or justification, a reason or a ground, in some cases, proof. But this can be endless: a proposition can be endlessly, questioned. The classic example is of a child who keeps asking, "Why?," to every explanation given by a parent . . . over and over again. A foundational belief or statement—a response—would then be a categorical "No!" (provided the child is exercising reason and obedience to the parent!). The situation from which the "No!" issues is non derivative, and is characterized by a non-inferential warrant, though it does not constitute evidence in itself. The statement that "Jesus Christ is Lord" should be foundational, non-derivative, but that does not stop people hiding in their own religious world—as we can see from Lewis's painfully slow path towards conversion, or the example of the dwarves, after the end of all things in Narnia.[8] See: IDEALISM; NATURALISM/SCIENTISM; and REVELATION AND REASON.

Gnosticism

Gnosticism, from the Greek γνῶσις, *gnōsis*—knowledge— was a complex mythology with various levels of "gods" or "aeons," a multiplicity of divine beings in a strict hierarchy. This "chain of command," or "pecking-order," so to speak, primarily denied the unity of God, the indivisibility, equality, yet distinctiveness as persons, of the Father, the Son and the Holy Spirit: the Trinity. Within Gnostic sects Christ the Son became a lesser god, often only partially human, in varying degrees, as different Gnostic sects emphasized. Knowledge of these "gods" and "aeons" was esoteric and secretive, it was complex and individualistic; by comparison Christian knowledge and truth was universally available. Our salvation is not dependent upon mastering a body of secret knowledge and initiation. Within Gnosticism salvation is available only to an elite with special access to clandestine and private, furtive and surreptitious, religious understanding. The Gnostic Christ was essentially Docetic because, with varying degrees according to different Gnostic sects, the full humanity of Jesus, and hence the incarnation, was denied. Irenaeus of Lyons (died, 202) who countered the Gnostics, asserted that humanity received corruption and death as a penalty for original sin; God is incorruptible and immortal: incarnation is

---

8 Lewis, *The Chronicles of Narnia: The Last Battle*, Ch. 13, 135–140.

essential for atonement, the uniting of God with humanity. The heterodox concept of Gnosticism was invoked in the Pittenger-Lewis debate.

Heaven

See: Arminian(ism); and, Atonement.

Hell

See: Arminian(ism); and, Atonement.

Idealism

Idealism is ancient, and in many ways contradicts the materialism of much Western Modernism. Idealism has seen something of a revival in Postmodernism. Idealism asserts the priority of the mind. Idealists in effect emphasize that what we take for reality is, in essence, "of the mind"; it is a mental construct. Therefore, *it is only the perception of the mind that is real*. The question is therefore asked, "Can we really know anything that is distinct from the mind? In terms of the nature of reality, all so-called entities are composed of mind or spirit. Idealism is commonplace in a religious mind-set where it asserts this priority. Ancient Indian religions did so; the Neo-Platonists likewise, who had, it may be argued, a profound effect on patristic theology. The eighteenth-century Irish philosopher George Berkeley (1685–1753), Bishop of Cloyne, is credited with instigating a revival, of sorts, of Idealism in Western European thought. Lewis subscribed to a form of Platonic Idealism influenced by the seventeenth-century Cambridge Platonist Henry More and Bishop Berkeley. From Berkeley he learns of the relationship between revelation and imagination, as such Lewis placed fundamental importance and value on Berkeley's dictum, "*esse est percipi*" ("to be is to be perceived") whereby Berkeley argued that we can only know sensations and ideas of objects; ideas (Idealism) were of primary importance, more than sense perception in many ways, ideas and the faculty of imagination were symbiotic. Continental Idealists are often considered to be Kant, Hegel, and Schelling, among others. See: Platonism.

imago Christi/imitatio Christi

The *imago Christi* is the image of Christ, essentially issuing from the cross and the resurrection. At its simplest level, this is the example of Christ Jesus, but more than that, it is in many ways the *imprint* of the true humanity that was masked and nearly obliterated by the *fall* into original sin. The cross and resurrection brings this image back, perhaps like a photograph developing and emerging. If we allow the Holy Spirit to work in us it will bring us back to this true image, it will make us more and more Christ-like, whatever the cost, whatever it takes. Christlikeness can be seen in other religions, but only the person and office of Christ subsist in the Christian religion. If we speak of "image" we must avoid the contemporary Western obsession with personal appearance, with projecting a lifestyle image. The *imago christi*—the image of Christ—is not an affectation we project for the benefit of others, it does not issue from our vanity, it is the essential nature and character that is deep within us, it is the ground from which everything that constitutes us emerges. Prior to the *fall* (Genesis 3) this image was complete and untainted—we were as God intended. After the *fall* it becomes corrupted, tarnished, prey to evil, self-justifying in its corruption. But it is not lost completely. Christlikeness, issuing from the atonement wrought for us by the blood of the lamb will gradually restore us by drawing out the *imago christi*. Christlikeness is not about mimicry—only Christ can be truly Christ. We cannot achieve Christlikeness for ourselves by our own efforts. However, people can in a haltingly limited way, through being *in Christ*, begin to be drawn into Christlikeness: beauty of character, graceful compassion, self-denying, altruistic love, joyous yet suffering, they may radiate an inner Christlikeness despite manifold difficulties and oppression. In his mature writings, Lewis focuses at length on the *imago christi*—Christlikeness—in humanity.

This raises importance questions about the *imitatio Christi* (the imitation of Christ), which relates closely to the *imago Christi*, though the two are not synonymous. Often the *imitatio Christi* issues from the *imago Christi*; however any imitation of Christ must be unself-conscious, or it is likely to be a feign. How does the Holy Spirit recover the image of Christ buried deep within us? Our feeble halting imitation, if it is conscious, can only, perhaps, be Christlike when it involves self-denial, and leads us to self-sacrifice, which every fiber of our being rebels against, yet we must submit gracefully. See: PREVENIENT GRACE; and, TRINITY.

IMAGO DEI

The image of God—a fundamental concept in a doctrine of creation: human beings are created in the image of God. The *imago Christi*, is therefore part of the *imago Dei*, as Christ is the second person of the Trinity. See: COMMUNICATIO IDIOMATUM; *IMAGO CHRISTI*; and, TRINITY.

KENOSIS

Kenosis is about the full or partial renunciation of the divine nature by Christ in the incarnation; from the Greek κένωσις, *kenosis*, "an emptying," from the verb κενόω, *kenóō*, to empty. Kenotic theories are derived from Phil 2:7, Christ "emptied himself" (ἀλλὰ ἑαυτὸν ἐκένωσεν). According to kenotic theology God literally emptied himself in the incarnation; others will claim Christ veiled many of the divine attributes; Lewis asserts that the attributes are transposed, translated, diminuted. See: COMMUNICATIO IDIOMATUM; and, TRANSPOSITION.

LIBERAL NEO-PROTESTANTISM

Liberal neo-Protestantism was essentially a movement in theology, and to a degree philosophy, that claimed freedom not only from traditional dogmas and creeds but also in the analysis of and value accorded to Scripture; such theology was to a large degree formulated in the light of advances in the natural sciences and philosophy. Nineteenth-century Liberal neo-Protestantism interpreted God's revelation as humanity's self-revelation or self-discovery; furthermore it is this thinking that is formative, in part, on Lewis as a young apostate, which then is turned on its head after his conversion.

LIBERAL/MODERN

C. S. Lewis's writings are set against the background of liberal culture and society in Britain specifically, the United States and Europe generally. Liberalism is often seen as a contentious and problematic word—often it appears to generate an emotional response, may be considered pejorative, and may also be invoked in an equally subjective manner. Theological Liberalism in the church is part of this; it is a position that more often than not denies the incarnation and resurrection, that seeks to promote Jesus of Nazareth as an ordinary human being; furthermore, a Liberal theological position may not believe in God (with a capital "G") but happily allow people to believe in "gods" of their own making, their own invention. Lewis often referred to this as a modernist tendency. Characterized by a liberation from tradition and dogma, creed, and the value accorded to Scripture, such Liberal theology was to a large degree formulated in the light of what were considered advances in the natural sciences and philosophy—the spirit of the Age of Reason and the Enlightenment. Liberalism in society and culture generally, in ethics and morality in the twentieth century, has often been to do with sexual behavior, but is also seen in culture, the media, entertainment, etc. Therefore, a distinction needs to be drawn between Liberalism as a theological movement or belief system and what is often euphemistically called a liberal perspective in Western society generally. Today those who subscribe to ethical liberalism (particularly in the area of sexuality and marriage) may or may not to a greater or lesser degree subscribe to Theological Liberalism. For example, there are East Coast American Episcopalians today who support the legitimization of homosexual behavior within Christian ethics who are strongly orthodox and creedal in their doctrinal beliefs, but then there are also those who subscribe to this ethical liberalism whilst simultaneously denying Christ's divinity and regarding him as just another ordinary man, therefore these two liberals cannot be seen as identical, or as completely separate from each other. Lewis uses the term Modernism/Modernist very much in the same context as L/liberalism—he was often scathing about Modernist tendencies in the Church of England, tendencies which essentially were Theological Liberalism, which argued that all our ideas about God were wrong, that there was no supernatural God beyond the ideas in our minds, our deepest desires and wishes. See: POSTMODERN.

LOGOS ASARKOS/LOGOS ENSARKOS

If only the divine nature is uncreated this could be taken to apply only to the Father; asserting that the incarnate Son is uncreated appears to mingle the two natures—a concept that led to thousands of words being exchanged by theologians in the fourth to fifth centuries, a debate that was resolved through the Chalcedonian declaration (to a degree): that the two natures were equal—Jesus was equally fully human and equally fully divine. However, this raises questions about the *logos asarkos/logos ensarkos* (λόγος ἄσαρκος – λόγος ἔνσαρκος; the Greek for flesh is σαρξ, *sarx*). Is the eternal Word (λόγος, *logos*), the second person of the Trinity, unfleshed (*asarkos*) as the pre-incarnate Word of God? By contrast the word (Word) becomes fleshed (*ensarkos*) as the incarnate Jesus (John 1:14a). Why is this relevant? Because an aspect of Lewis's Christology is that the Aslan-Christ (the feline, lionized, creator in *The Magician's Nephew*) is perpetually incarnate, enfleshed, uncreated, the Aslan-Christ does not appear to have had a time when he was the *logos asarkos*.[9] Nothing is written by chance or ignorance in Lewis's theology and perhaps Lewis could see that this issue was to do with Platonic forms, temporality—or more

---

9 For those unfamiliar with the *logos asarkos-logos ensarkos* debate see, Colin E. Gunton, *The Barth Lectures*, London: Continuum, 2007, 167–70

pertinently a temporal paradox in the form of the relationship between eternity and our reality of time-space, and "the lamb that was slaughtered from the foundation of the world" (The Revelation to John 13:8). See: PLATONISM.

NATURALISM/SCIENTISM

Throughout most of his apologetics, and in particular in the 1940s, Lewis worked tirelessly against Naturalism. Naturalism encompasses several philosophical positions (for example, naturalism in the philosophy of mathematics, in legal philosophy, methodological naturalism, naturalized epistemology, ontological naturalism, or metaphysical naturalism); however, one essential aspect of Naturalism is that it declares all phenomena or hypotheses named supernatural to be either false or explicable as naturally occurring phenomena or hypotheses. To this end, nature or the universe is self-contained and self-originating, and does not require any relationship to anything "outside" or "other." From a philosophical viewpoint (as distinct from those of art, literature and moral philosophy), "Naturalism claims that everything arises from natural properties and causes, and supernatural or spiritual explanations are excluded or discounted." (OED.) This mechanistic perception, driven by Naturalism and Scientism, has led to reductionism, where humanity has killed nature, exploited her and dissected and analyzed her for humanity's benefit. For Lewis we must at the very least acknowledge a relationship between the supernatural (or super-nature) and nature. Naturalism denies this relationship. If Naturalism is, in effect, an atheist worldview, Scientism, which relates closely to a Naturalist perspective (and to a degree issues from it), is expounded as a quasi-religion. Lewis often uses the term Scientism to identify something of a pseudo-religious worldview derived from Naturalism. Scientism has often been described as a religion, or a substitute for true religion. In general terms, and issuing from a Naturalist perspective, Scientism identifies and describes the salient characteristics of a belief system that often involves an excessive belief in the power of scientific knowledge and techniques and is often used to assert the authority of Naturalized Philosophy of Science, as the pre-eminent explanation of life. This leads to a belief in the omnipotence of such scientific methods and techniques, which are then deemed applicable to theology and philosophy. Therefore the belief that scientific knowledge is the foundation of all knowledge becomes a dogma, akin to religious dogmas, whereby Scientism is seen as the absolute and only justifiable means of attaining truth. Naturalism is important to understanding Lewis on reason and revelation. During the 1940s, a refutation of Naturalism becomes a central motif in Lewis's apologetic defense of the supernatural, of miracles, and specifically of miraculous revelation. Naturalism denies the miraculous; Naturalism denies the incarnation and resurrection. Lewis, consequently, defends the miraculous generally, and the incarnation and resurrection specifically, through a refutation of Naturalism. This is apologetic in method. Naturalism does not necessarily deny the religious: Naturalists acknowledge the religious impulse in people, but see such religiosity and spirituality as self-contained, self-referential (often self-reverential)—humanity will invent "gods" and "idols" of their own making. However, Naturalism must by default exclude the idea of a real God existing, particularly a God who then comes into creation, is incarnated, and raised from the dead, when such an incarnation (through parthenogenesis) and resurrection (as an actuality) contradict the laws of nature identified by Naturalism. It must deny a God who exercises control that interferes through the miraculous. In terms of technique, Lewis employs *reductio ad absurdum* in combating this view; he demolishes the opponent's argument by reducing it to the absurd, excluding compromise: Naturalism is either-or; there is no ambiguity. There is no middle ground between Naturalism on the one hand and belief on the other. Lewis argues that it cannot be true because it is self-contradictory (*reductio ad absurdum*); he then argues that being self-contradictory, there is only one alternative, namely belief (excluding the middle ground, the centre position, of, say, agnosticism).

Naturalism is about causation, it is about the relationship of cause and effect in all we take for the universe, and how everything interconnects and relates simply because, according to Naturalist, there is no other cause and effect operating on nature. Sometimes within nature things are just so, other times they are key developments in evolved relationships. Nonetheless it is causation, self-contained causation, within a self-generated universe that Naturalists of various persuasions appeal to. Naturalism relates closely to determinism, which is the thesis that the laws of physics are deterministic, everything that is today issues from, is the result of the sequence and order of event since the big bang. Therefore, the thought in your mind at this precise moment issues from, was determined by, the clockwork working out of events through measurable and observable time. Where this leaves free will is, of course, an apposite question. The question of the validity of Naturalism is at the heart of the famous debate between the young don, G. E. M. Anscombe and C. S. Lewis in 1948. See: Ontology; and, reductio ad absurdum, and, "Law of Excluded Middle".

Natural Theology

Natural theology relates to what is considered to be a naturally occurring understanding of God, where the existence of a "god" is speculated from evidence internal to the human mind. Natural theology is in effect philosophical speculation about the existence of a "god," or even *a priori* reasoning about the very nature of God, and God's relation with humanity, but often this is speculation derived from the world and nature (trying to *read* a "god" from nature, or identify the action of God from the world, can lead to belief, but just as often to unbelief—scientific atheism). The aim of natural theology is to generate knowledge and understanding about God (or what is often considered to be the "god" of the philosophers), and therefore to establish truths about God using only our natural cognitive resources. Therefore the method and data for what we may term, naturally occurring theology lies with the human mind. The technique of reasoning things out, of perceiving *a priori* truths about God are the basis and ground of natural theology, as indeed, so it can be argues, with Naturalism and a naturalized philosophy of science. Natural theology, as philosophical speculation about g/God(s), is not the same as a theology of nature, though often the two are mistakenly conflated. See: analogia entis and analogia fidei; Deism; Foundationalism; Naturalism/Scientism; Revelation and Reason; and, Theism.

New Atheists, The

The so-called New Atheists (a title they do not own, and in some cases repudiate) are unofficially led by the Oxford scientist and media atheist Richard Dawkins, author of *The God Delusion*, the title of which builds on Lewis's preparedness to invoke insanity in the form of delusion to criticize and denigrate one's opponents. Other New Atheists include the children's novelist Philip Pullman, the journalist and literary critic Christopher Hitchens (who described himself as an "anti-theist"), the philosopher A. C. Grayling, the journalist-writer Sam Harris, the novelist Martin Amis, and the author and screen writer Ian McEwan. All are united to a greater or lesser degree in an attempt to raise the public profile of atheism, and, as many see it, to convert people to their particular form of anti-theistic "religion," and often to, in effect, declare war on religion generally, Christianity specifically.

Ontology

Ontology is defined as a branch of philosophy (also metaphysics and theology) concerned with the very nature of being, of actual existence, and what there is to the intrinsic nature of entities. From the Greek ὤν ὄτος, *ōn ontos*, "being, that which is," ontology as the philosophical study of the nature of what we take to be reality investigates the basic categories of being and the relationships between things in the created order, but also how such bodies, entities, persons, can be grouped often through identifiable similarities and differences. For example, the human. We may ask, is there a uniquely God-given human nature, and either way, what is it that characterizes the human as distinct from the rest of creation. Indeed what is the very nature of creation itself? Is the human as created?—or is it changed by the *fall*? Is Jesus of Nazareth defined ontologically as merely human, or as fully human and fully divine—the very nature of his being is divine and human. Therefore ontological questions were at the heart of the Pittenger-Lewis debate. The question of ontology also relates to the human capacity to know, to the very nature of language, and how we speculate on God: this involves the study of being or existence, of a thing's very nature. See: Theological Anthropology.

Pagan

Lewis's theological writings, as indeed with his conversion, are played out against the backdrop of what is termed pagan religion or paganism. A pagan is essentially someone holding beliefs from outside of the world's main religions. Pagan therefore refers to this form of religion and religious myths from outside of, in our instance, the Jewish and Christian traditions. It is important to remember that the term pagan was used by Lewis, and is likewise used here, with no derogatory intent, nor as a term of abuse. Lewis used the term simply to refer to those peoples and cultures outside of the Jewish and Christian traditions; that is, Oriental, Middle Eastern, Indian, and European tribes and nations, but particularly in the ancient world (Greek and Roman philosophy and literature, religion and mythology) and especially the religion and mythology of the North European tribes (Celtic, Norse, etc.), with whom the name Pagan is most often associated. In comparison to the post-Christian world in the West today where it often being asserted that Britain is slipping, descending, regressing into paganism, Lewis was quite adamant the ancient pagan was someone who could be converted to Christianity. The ancient pagan was pre- or sub-Christian. By comparison, for Lewis, the post-Christian pagan differs as, in Lewis's words, a divorcée does from a virgin. Essentially the difference between a pre-Christian pagan and the contemporary post-Christian pagan is one of movement: the pre was moving towards God in his/her theistic beliefs, the post is moving away from God in his/her beliefs.

Pantheism/Panentheism

Pantheism is a doctrine or belief that identifies God with the universe, or regards creation as a manifestation of God; the universe and God are the same thing. Pantheism is also related to polytheism as the worship or tolerance of many "gods" (for pantheists, creation may not be just one "god"). Pan*en*theism is where God is not reducible to the universe, is not simply identical with creation, but is irrevocably and indelibly situated in creation, tied to the world. Creation is located "in" God but there is more to God than creation. Yes, God is Emmanuel, with us, Christ is tied into humanity, and Christ is God. Does this mean God is tied panentheistically into creation, the world? Such a risk is countered by a doctrine of the Trinity: the Father is "separate" from creation, yet sustains creation; the Son is situated through incarnation yet ascended; the Holy Spirit is active in the world, yet is not in it or of it. The doctrine of three persons equally co-existing denies the risk of panentheism. A monist "god" the idea of God as a singularity, is at risk of being panentheistic. By contrast God is for humanity, but loves humanity in freedom (Barth): at any moment creation could dissolve away at a glance from his "eye."

Pantocrator

The term Pantocrator is one of the titles given to God. It was probably first used when the Hebrew Bible, the Old Testament, was translated into Greek around the second century BC (the translation was called the Septuagint). *Pantokratōr* (παντοκράτωρ) was used to translate one of the ancient Jewish titles for God—*El Shaddai* ("Almighty One," "God-who-is-All-Sufficient," sometimes, "Magnificent One," and "the God of the Mountain"); in the New Testament it refers to "He who holds sway over all things," "The ruler of all," and "Almighty One, God." The Apostle Paul used the term in his second letter to the Corinthians, and the writer of the book of Revelation uses the Greek term on several occasions. The early church immediately gave this title to Christ raised, ascended and reigning in majesty, ruler of the universe, sustainer of all creation, and the concept of *pantokratōr* was used in much patristic art: mosaics in early Christian basilicas show Christ Pantocrator, risen, ascended reigning on high over humanity, often with a page from the Bible in his hand.

Parousia

From the Ancient Greek παρουσία, *parousia*, means "presence," "arrival," "official visit." Parousia in the early church, and in theology, refers to the second coming, the *return* of Christ, for he will be "present." The parousia will be the visible and manifest *return* from eternity, heaven, of the Christ, to inaugurate the general resurrection, to judge all, and to initiate the kingdom of God. The parousia, the *return*, will initiate the eschaton.

Patristic

The patristic era is from the time of Christ's resurrection through to the mid-eighth century. The church leaders and theologians of this period of over 700 years are called patristic—from the Greek for father, πατήρ, *patēr*, hence the theology of these centuries is patristic, formed by the early church fathers. The immediate years after Christ's resurrection is called the apostolic era—the era or period of the Apostles, essentially the people who knew Jesus of Nazareth or were of his generation, all of whom had died by around the year 100 AD. We then have the sub-apostolic era, which is essentially the second century, then fully the patristic era.

Platonism

Platonism is the name given to the philosophy of Plato (c.424/423BC–348/347BC), and his writings. The term also applies to systems of philosophy derived from Plato's work and ideas, for example, Neo-Platonism or Platonic Realism. Central to Platonism is the theory of forms. The forms are transcendent archetypes; what we take for reality is in some way a pale imitation of the forms—reality relates to the forms as an imperfect copy does to an original. The forms tell us that what we take for reality is perceivable but not intelligible, but that there is another higher reality that is intelligible but not perceivable. Lewis was a trained philosopher; indeed early in his career he taught philosophy. Platonism is a type of philosophy that he not only subscribed to but which characterized his work throughout his life. Most patristic theologians were Platonists, to varying degrees; Neo-Platonism was in many ways part of patristic theology. Many Protestant, Reformed, or Evangelical supporters of Lewis's work today object strongly to his Platonism, not realizing that it is fundamental to Lewis's interpretation of the gospel and is at the heart of his understanding of revelation. As a young don, Lewis was profoundly influenced by Henry More (1614–87) who was one of the most prominent of seventeenth-century British philosophers. More's parents were both Calvinists; however, the severity of their faith was eschewed as More moved towards Anglicanism. More served as an honorary canon at Gloucester Cathedral for a time; however, he devoted himself to the study of philosophy. In his youth he espoused skeptical philosophy, until he became absorbed by the study of the Plato and Neo-Platonism. More was a leading member of the Cambridge Platonists emphasizing mystical and philosophical theology. The highest form in Neoplatonism is the One or the Good (falling short of identifying God); however, Lewis is in effect a *Christian* Platonist.

The relationship between Platonism and the gospel—which is, in effect, defined, in limited terms, as the mechanism whereby the Holy Spirit relates to and acts in our world, our reality—is set out by Lewis, in a limited and intentionally incomplete and flawed manner, in his doctrine of transposition. See: Idealism; and Transposition.

Pneumatology

Pneumatology is the name for the study, and actions of, the Holy Spirit, the third person of the Trinity. Derived from two Greek words πνεῦμα, *pneuma*, spirit, and λόγος *logos*, word. Pneumatology refers to theories about the Holy Spirit, but also the effects of the action perceivable by Christians of the Spirit, including the prevenient action, inspiration, and sanctification of the Holy Spirit. See: PREVENIENT GRACE.

POSTMODERN

It is perhaps too early to formulate a precise definition of Postmodern, or when it started. What is perhaps characteristic is the lack of confidence in the human capacity to solve its problems through its own efforts. Gone is the belief that humanity was progressing to ever greater heights and perfection, which to a greater or lesser degree characterized Modernism. Some will argue that the delusions of Modernism collapsed in the carnage of the First World War; others cite the dropping of the atomic bombs on Japan in 1945. Others, the social, cultural, and sexual revolutions of the 1960s (from this point on does Western humanity lives for indulgence and pleasing its individual self?). Postmodernity is by its name and character to be taken as a reaction to "Modernism" (where "Modernism" is essentially focused on the philosophy, science, and culture of the late nineteenth and early twentieth centuries); such modernity was defined by scientific objectivity, advancement, rejection of old superstitious belief systems, but essentially in progress, all of which was taken to have issued from the Age of Reason and the Enlightenment. Postmodernism is therefore in essence a philosophical movement that eschews objective truth, sees relativity as the norm, all realities are to be seen as pluralistic, relativistic social constructs, where truth is defined by the dominant interest. People's perception of the world, and the mental model of reality they construct, is subjective: to the Postmodernist there is no absolute truth (except the apparently absolute truth that there is no absolute truth), and even then no two Postmodernists would subscribe to the same doctrine or dogma.

PREVENIENT GRACE

Grace as the free unearned blessing of God is the real and actual influence, or illumination, of the Holy Spirit on the mind. Any good we can do does not issue from our own intentions, our will, it issues from the prior action of the Holy Spirit, the illuminatory action of the Holy Spirit on the mind *prior* to any decision we make: hence prevenient—prior—grace. For Lewis, the degree to which we recognize how the Holy Spirit is illuminating our minds for our good is of profound importance. Prevenient grace (or preceding grace) is a philosophical concept derived from a Christian doctrine of God, which was formulated and rooted in Augustinian theology. Prevenient grace is the divine action of the Holy Spirit that *precedes* human decision and action, and hence validity. Prevenient grace is prior to and does not rely on anything people do or have done. For Augustine, because of the corrosive and corrupting effects of original sin where we can no longer make free will decisions unimpeded and not influenced by a wealth of factors around us, prevenient grace allows us to choose salvation and to live for and follow God's will. Prevenient grace precedes our conscious impulses and decisions.

PROCESS THEOLOGY

The Pittenger-Lewis debate, that raised questions of orthodox or heretical Christology, is defined, on Pittenger's side of the debate, by Process Theology. Process theology is typical of much twentieth-century Western theology in its reliance upon what some would see as esoteric modern philosophy. It is also known as neo-classical theology, and is heavily influenced by the philosopher Alfred North Whitehead. Process Theology is characterized by the proposition that "becoming" characterizes life more than "being." Hence, the process of becoming is more important than how we are. Process thinking has influenced a number of Jewish theologians. A basic principle is that it is part of God's essence to give freedom—this is loving act. God does not withdraw creaturely freedom or override free will. Key ideas in Process Theology are: (1) God is not omnipotent if he is not coercive but persuasive; (2) Reality consists of serially ordered events, which are experiential in nature and interrelate to the process of reality. (3) The universe is characterized by process and change, by free will—God influences our use of free will; (4) God contains the universe but is not identical with it (which has led some to accuse Process Theologians of Panentheism, because God is reliant upon the universe); (5) Therefore God is changeable, God is affected by the actions that take place in the creation.

Purgatory/Purgation

See: Arminian(ism); and, Atonement.

Quest for the Historical Jesus, The

The so-called "Quest for the Historical Jesus" was part of the German Liberal Protestant tradition starting in the eighteenth century with Reimarus and Lessing and culminating with the work of Strauss, at the end of the nineteenth century. The "Quest for the Historical Jesus" was/is an attempt to use historical-critical methodology, driven often by an hermeneutic of suspicion, to construct an accurate biography of Jesus (faith and revelation did not, it would appear, come into the study). Albert Schweitzer coined the term "Quest for the Historical Jesus" in the early twentieth century to refer to this first quest. There have been other quests in the twentieth century culminating in the so-called "Jesus Seminar" dominated by white liberal American scholars who attempted to classify from the Gospels what were the genuine words of Jesus and what had been added/altered afterwards. Many exponents of the "Quest"—with the exception of scholars such as N. T. Wright and Richard Bauckham—are using a hermeneutic of suspicion, driven by a concept of rationalism usually associated with the Age of Reason and the Enlightenment, but all appear to be unaware of their cultural conditioning, their prejudices and believe themselves to be writing universal truths when—certainly with the late twentieth-century "Quest"—they operate within a cultural Zeitgeist of postmodernist relativity. Lewis noted how these people knew virtually nothing of genre, in addition, Mark, as the author of a gospel, was no longer around to contradict and disprove their theories, therefore there was no way of verifying their destructive propositions regarding Scripture.[10] See: Skepticism and The Scandal of Particularity.

Redemption

See: Atonement.

---

10 Lewis, "Modern Theology and Biblical Criticism", *Christian Reflections* (1967), 161.

REDUCTIO AD ABSURDUM, AND, "LAW OF EXCLUDED MIDDLE"

In terms of how he presented his apologetics Lewis relied on two identifiable philosophical techniques. First, *reductio ad absurdum* (reduction to the absurd), which is a type of argument used in formal disputation and logic—especially in legal matters—that refutes an opponent's proposal by demonstrating that it is either rooted in, or leads inevitably to, an absurd or self-contradictory conclusion. If such a proposition is shown to be absurd and untenable then the advocate has so to speak, won the day. Lewis excelled at reducing the opposition's arguments to nothing, demolishing their case and showing what they believed to be absurd: *reductio ad absurdum*. Second, the "law of excluded middle" (C. S. Lewis is mortal, or he is immortal, there is no third option, logic excludes that Lewis is neither mortal nor immortal). Grounded in philosophical logic the "law of excluded middle" is the technique used to show that an argument or proposition is either true or not true. In its purest form, because truth can appear ambiguous, this is expressed as "either-or." Ambiguity is then dismissed by fact. Lewis excelled at excluding the grey, nuanced, middle ground where ambiguity thrived; he excluded this in favor of the "either-or." He did not necessarily insist on one option being acknowledged as truth, but left the defeated opponent to see that if absurdity was to be avoided they had to make a decision. See: AUT DEUS AUT MALUS HOMO.

REGULA FIDEI

The rule of faith (*regula fidei*), which was established in Lewis's apologetics from early on, is that which evaluates theological opinion and the life of the church by measuring against what has been firmly established and believed. This is the aim; the objective was in Lewis's content driven method. The objective of the *regula fidei* in Lewis's case was specifically defined by two theologians: the Patristic theologian Vincentius of Lérins ("*quod ubique, quod semper, quod ab omnibus*": "what has been held always, everywhere, by everybody"[11]) and the seventeenth-century Puritan Richard Baxter, his "mere" core of orthodoxy ("I am a Christian, a Meer Christian, of no other Religion; and the Church that I am of is the Christian Church"[12]). The *regula fidei* as the rule of faith was rooted in Scripture, in Paul's comments in Romans, where all is to be seen in proportion to faith (in the Greek New Testament, ἀναλογίαν τῆς πίστεως: literally, the "analogy of faith" Rom. 12:6).

REVELATION AND REASON

Revelation is personal, as in the realization of perception and understanding many people will have—a eureka moment when one finds something, or when something is revealed to us. But it is also more than that, more than the personal and subjective. Revelation is about God's self-disclosure to humanity. Lewis understood and accepted how God had revealed of God's self to humanity in multifarious and diverse ways down the millennia and across vast geographical and cultural eons, but as an orthodox Christian he knew both as fact and from personal encounter that Christ was the unique, the highest, form of self-revelation of the one true living God. So to talk about Christ is to talk about God; to speak of Christ is to speak of revelation. Over recent centuries revelation has often been pitted against reason. Because

---

11 Vincentius of Lérins, *The Commonitory of Vincent of Lérins* (c.434, 214), 207–60.
12 Baxter, *Church-History of the Government of Bishops and their Councils* (1680) xvii.

of the confidence emanating from the Age of Reason and the Enlightenment, a confidence issuing from the belief that the human capacity to reason things out for itself was all that was needed, revelation became in certain quarters, obsolete. Lewis seeks to try to hold both revelation and reason in balance; as a trained philosopher he knew and understood the background against which he was writing.

Romanticism

The term Romantic, with an initial capital letter, has nothing to do with romantic novels or magazines, or romance! The term Romantic represents a movement in art and culture—poets such as Longfellow, Wordsworth, and Keats were considered Romantics, as were painters such as Constable and Turner, and composers such as Beethoven, and to a degree Wagner. As an artistic and cultural term Romantic is to do with feeling, with expressing oneself, with responding to the innate beauty in landscape and the natural world. Romanticism was in some ways a reaction against the scientific rationalism of the Age of Reason. The Romantic Movement was often associated with the cult of the individual—of emaciated, troubled, artists, starving in garrets and producing works of genius entirely by themselves without any input and involvement from anyone else.

Salvation

See: Atonement.

Skepticism and the Scandal of Particularity

Hermann Samuel Reimarus (1694–1768) was a German New Testament scholar and critic, and a philosopher, a proponent of the Enlightenment and of deism. He claimed that the human mind can, through reason alone, know of God. Therefore, revelation was unnecessary. Gotthold Ephraim Lessing (1729–81) was a German writer, philosopher, publicist, and art critic, and representative of the German Enlightenment and spokesperson of the bourgeoisie. Together they formulated and established much of a doctrine of Scripture that was adopted by many skeptics in the eighteenth century through to today. In Britain, contributing to this skepticism, Thomas Woolston (1668–1733), theologian, cleric, and English deist, asserted that all Scripture was allegorical, that the resurrection narratives were a fabrication. In keeping with the deistic belief that denied miracles as an interference with the self-governing nature of the universe, Woolston had published a work in 1727 entitled, *A Discourse on the Miracles of our Saviour, in View of the Present Controversy Between Infidels and Apostates*, which effectively dismissed the miraculous in the Gospels, arguing for an allegorical interpretation. By contrast, the Bishop of Bangor, the Right Revd Thomas Sherlock, in 1729 published an apologetic defense of the Gospel entitled, *The Trial of the Witnesses of the Resurrection of Jesus*. This work was a defense of the apostles, those who witnessed Jesus's resurrection. Sherlock sets the powerful arguments of the apostles against the skepticism of Thomas Woolston among others. A characteristic of the Age of Reason, and the Enlightenment that followed, and the Modernism that Lewis was so critical of, was the principle that a respectable intellectual must be suspicious, skeptical of any religious truth claims, especially when dealing with, in this case, the Bible, and only allow to exist as truth that which could be measured, quantified, and controlled in principle by the human intellect. Thus the argument championed by Reimarus and Lessing that it all happened too long ago for there to be any reliability in the Scriptural accounts. Lessing coined the phrase "ugly broad ditch," which was applied to the time elapsed since the New Testament era. Lessing argued that we could not trust the contingency of history because there was this ugly broad ditch between then and now; therefore we could not accept the New Testament accounts as fact or truth; further, this ditch lay between the contingent truth of history and what Lessing claimed to be the universal truth of reason. Lessing was convinced that rationalism was the universal mode of understanding available to humanity for comprehending the world, therefore the Bible could not be considered to be an acceptable source of truth: the church's account of Jesus was flawed with what was called the scandal of particularity: only the universal was true, the universal available to all humanity through reason, not the particular (i.e., the incarnation) enacted in the contingency of history. His argument was that if God was to come and reveal God's-self to humanity it would be through the *universal*—everybody would "know"—not through a *particular* event such as the incarnation. (However, such a universal principle was in itself a particularity: the understanding of Lessing, Reimarus, and their skeptical followers, especially in the Quest for the Historic Jesus, was *particular*: that is, it issued from a white-European-male-patriarchal-bourgeois-liberal-mindset, that was not *universal*, it was not available to all, universally.) By the mid twentieth century the approach initiated by Reimarus and Lessing dominated debate in certain quarters of the church (especially Lewis's C of E). Lessing may have invented the concept of the contingency of history (as a "broad ugly ditch") to repudiate the church's story of Jesus; however, for two centuries the followers of Lessing have ignored this contingency of history in attempting to proclaim their story of Jesus as the one true version (for example, the so-called "quest" for the one true Jesus, outside of the church's account), grounded in an overinflated concept of reason and universalism, which Postmodernism has done away with. See: Quest for the Historic Jesus, The; Deism; Theism; Naturalism/Scienticism; and, Postmodernism.

Sehnsucht

The Oxford-Duden German Dictionary defines *Sehnsucht* (pronounced *zein-zukt*) as a longing, a yearning for somebody or something. However, although this craving may be for an object—a relative, one's home, a landscape, childhood memories—such longing, such a wistful desire, may be objectless. Lewis wrote at length on *Sehnsucht*—which he termed "Joy"—in his autobiography: a sudden stab of a yearning, a craving ache, that caught him unawares, but the moment he recognized its presence it had gone, dissipated. He saw it as a crucial part of his atheistic wanderings, and how he came back to faith. Lewis, along with many literary writers, saw *Sehnsucht* as a wounding disabling, a craving with almost mystical qualities where the experience of *Sehnsucht* itself replaces the object of desire. Christologically, perhaps *Sehnsucht* is the Holy Spirit pressing upon the individual to convict an individual of sin, where the Spirit begins to draw the person out of himself or herself and into a new God-ward life in Christ; this would apply whether the person has access to explicit knowledge of Jesus Christ or not, and is the action of the Holy Spirit pressing on an individual. Although Lewis never explicitly defined his experience of *Sehnsucht* in such terms, this is a reasonable interpretation of how it applied to him: the disabling longing, this "Joy" as he termed it, lessened in its significance after his conversion. See: PREVENIENT GRACE.

SOLA SCRIPTURA

Solely by Scripture, or Scripture alone: the doctrine that the Bible contains all knowledge necessary for salvation and holiness, therefore only church teachings read from Scripture, to a degree, are considered valid, is defined by Protestants of varying persuasions as *sola scriptura*. Therefore, in principle, all Christian authority is considered subordinate to Scripture as the written word of God. By contrast, Lewis as an Anglican did not subscribe to *sola scriptura*: he held to Richard Hooker's (1554–1600) tripartite defense of authority through Scripture, Revelation (church tradition), and Reason. Furthermore Lewis emphasized that Jesus Christ is the true Word of God.

SOTERIOLOGY (A DOCTRINE OF SALVATION)

See: ATONEMENT.

SUBSTITUTION

See: ATONEMENT.

THEISM

Theism postulates the existence of a God (or in some cases at least one "god") and creator. Theists may, or may not, allow this "god" to interfere with the natural order through miracles; likewise they *may*, or *may not*, believe this "god" to be personal and active in human affairs. In general terms most people anywhere in the world might claim to be theists—that they believe in some sort of God; however, many philosophers see Theism as a distinct belief emerging in the seventeenth century in response to scientific progress, which then developed into Deism; this proposition of a creator God is shared with Jews and Christians. Nevertheless, many theists and deists dismiss the idea of such a "god" being involved personally with people (the work of the Holy Spirit), or, in some cases, appearing to interfere with the natural order (i.e., miracles as an interruption of nature), thus we have later the notion of this "god" as a blind-watchmaker. In a marginalization, or repudiation, of the miraculous, a chief objection among theists and deists is the idea of incarnation. The German philosopher Kant effectively denied the possibility of "god" being involved in the creation. He regularly, indeed liberally, quoted from Scripture in support of his ethics, but never John 1:14a ("and the word was made flesh . . .) Lewis's protracted conversion was in two stages: first to theism, a personal God that cared for and expected a response from people; second, to the Christ, and therefore to Trinitarian revelation. See: DEISM; also, NATURALISM/SCIENTISM.

THEODICY

How do you justify belief in a *good* God when there is so much evil in the world? This is the basic question of theodicy. Can God be good and righteous, holy and wise, when evil stalks the world and wastes people? Hence theodicy often relates to questions of pain and suffering (cf. the book of Job). Lewis's first work of apologetics tackled these thorny question (*The Problem of Pain*, 1940) but also one of his last (*A Grief Observed*, 1961), but the shadow of such issues was always cast over his work because of their nature as apologetics. Theodicy is essentially about the vindication of divine providence in view of the existence of evil. The word is from the eighteenth-century French, *théodicée*, devised by the philosopher and mathematician, Gottfried Leibniz—from the Greek θεος (*theos*, God) and δικη (*dikē*, justice)—for the title of a book of his purporting to answer the question. Theodicy is not primarily about pain and suffering, but, these questions are related: to what extent do we connect bad things, sickness and disease, with evil, and why is justice so uneven, why do good people suffer while bad people thrive? See: ATONEMENT; ONTOLOGY; and, THEOLOGICAL ANTHROPOLOGY.

THEOLOGICAL ANTHROPOLOGY

As distinct from scientific or humanist anthropology, theological anthropology is essentially the human condition as defined by God and in relation to the crucified and resurrected Christ. If Transposition is the key to Lewis's work, then theological anthropology is the measure, the ground from which he works. Theological anthropology is the relationship between humanity and God, whereby humanity must realize the full depravity of its sinfulness and be prepared, facing this crime (the *fall*, original sin, and the selfish human history that issues from it), to accept forgiveness given in judgment, forgiveness given as a free pardon by Christ, because without this forgiveness humanity is *fallen*, corrupt and irretrievably lost. Humanity's understanding of its theological anthropology varies: sometimes naively confident and optimistic, other times darkly despairing and pessimistic. Given that the human condition is defined before God there is hope through the cross and resurrection. But can humanity turn? The turn to repent is often the hardest part. A true and sound theological anthropology states the utter necessity of the cross and resurrection as the solution to the human problem, to the contagion of sin: the answer and solution is in God. Theological anthropology (the condition) is therefore measured by theological existentialism (the relationship), which is about the association and affiliation between human existence and God. It is only from without that any sense of the human condition can be gleaned; any future for humanity is in the relationship of sin (inward) and grace (outward, from without). Lewis characterized this in *The Chronicles of Narnia*: individuals come face-to-face with Aslan; in this meeting they must accept the depravity and delusions that their selfishness has brought about—in a word, sin—and in the judgment, the terrifying judgment of the Aslan-Christ, can they be forgiven. For example, Edmund after his rescue from the White Witch in,[13] or Puzzle the Donkey.[14] Forgiveness is given in measure, in proportion, to the repentance in the individual. This can only be fully understood in the light of the grace of God in the forgiveness proffered by the Aslan-Christ. See: ONTOLOGY; TRANSPOSITION; PREVENIENT GRACE; and EXISTENTIALISM.

---

13 Lewis, *The Lion, the Witch and the Wardrobe*, 126.
14 Lewis, *The Last Battle*, 157 and 171.

Theosophy

Theosophy is a distinct study of religion, philosophy, and metaphysics which developed from the late nineteenth century (though is rooted in many ancient religious and philosophical systems). As a belief system it holds that all religions are equal and are an effort by the so-called spiritual hierarchy to show people how to develop excellence. Reincarnation is believed by them to be universal, the human spiritual self is known as the monad: this is the higher self. Originating in the seventeenth century, Rosicrucianism was a secretive order where inner realms or worlds aided people in their spiritual development. Both Theosophy and Rosicrucianism contain what appears to many to be an unhealthy element of Gnosticism. Lewis was exposed to this system of belief as a teenager at Malvern College; he described it as part of the Anglo-American Occultist tradition.[15] See: GNOSTICISM.

Transposition

Described by Lewis as his contribution to the philosophy of the incarnation, transposition relates closely to kenosis and the *communicatio idiomatum*. The relationship between God and humanity in revelation is defined, for Lewis, by transposition. Lewis sets out a doctrine of transposition in detail.[16] The knowledge and understanding that is imparted, revealed, is transposed: it is changed, diminuted, diluted, through our reception of revelation, like a symphony for full orchestra transposed for solo piano. This is "how" revelation is imparted. As a key to all of Lewis's work, a flawed doctrine of transposition is itself transposed, reduced, lessened, and changed, but essentially still true to the original. This is broadly Platonic in the manner in which the transposed is defined by the truly real in eternity. Lewis's doctrine is designed to explain how revelation works, how it is communicated, and, paradoxically, why revelation can never be fully imparted. At the centre of transposition is the incarnation, which is represented by a transcription, a diminution (Phil 2:6–11)—this can be traced to the *communicatio idiomatum*, the nature and relationship that is the Trinity, and limits to the capacity of humans to know and understand. See, COMMUNICATIO IDIOMATUM; and, KENOSIS.

Trinity

Most people if pressed would acknowledge belief in God, or some sort of "god," subscribing to a vaguely defined monotheism. The truth about God revealed is that God is trinitarian: the Father is God, the Son is God, and the Holy Spirit is God—but there is only one God. This is the teaching of the church; it is the core of Christian doctrine. Three-in-one requires distinctness yet simultaneity. Humanity could not have invented such a concept as the Trinity for itself. The innate religious impulse in humanity is to conceive of a "god" as a single unity, a pure oneness, unknowable, distinct from creation. The idea that such a "god" could be three "persons" in "one God," become incarnate, be simultaneously born into creation while remaining God distinct and outside of creation, is often beyond comprehension. Immediately, theological talk about the Trinity raises questions about incarnation, redemption, the invisible power and

---

15 Lewis, *Surprised by Joy*, 56.
16 Lewis, "Transposition," a sermon from Whit Sunday, May 28, 1944, then reworked and extended into an academic paper in, *They Asked for a Paper*, 1962.

influence of the Holy Spirit, and so on. The realization that God was "Three-in-One" dawned slowly in the early church. There was evidence in the Old Testament, there was evidence in the sayings of Jesus, and the emerging documents we now call the Gospels and the New Testament. This realization, or understanding, became the bedrock of Christian doctrine and was summarized in the earliest of the creeds—the Apostles' Creed. The Trinity is one God in three persons, not three separate gods, and not one God expressed in three different ways or modes. Therefore, the perennial danger with theological talk is to slip into Modalism (God appears, is active towards humanity, in three different, often subsequent, modes: God is Father, then God is Son, then God is Spirit, but not simultaneously yet distinctly One) or Polytheism (too much individuality creates three separate "gods"). See: APOLLINARIANISM; ARIANISM; DOCETISM; and, EUTYCHIANISM.

TRINITY: IMMANENT AND ECONOMIC

Central to Lewis's Christology and his perception of the workings of God is an understanding of the *economic Trinity*, as distinct from the *immanent Trinity*. The *economic* Trinity is our understanding of the *presence* and *action* of God in our reality, the world of human affairs (economic: management of resources, interaction—supervision, administration, and controlling—of persons within a social context; origin: fifteenth century, from French *économie*, via Latin from Greek οἰκονομία *oikonomia*—"household management," often, "the rule or law of the house"). By contrast, the *immanent* Trinity is God's "life," "existence," *within God's triune self*, the three persons of the holy and indivisible Trinity that subsist and persist in love (immanent: existing or operating within God, from sixteenth century Latin *immanent-*, *immanere*, "remain within"). For example, the opening of John's Gospel is about the Trinity: it sets out the immanent—"In the beginning was the Word, and the Word was with God, and the Word was God. He was in the beginning with God (John 1:1–2)." This then proceeds into the economic—"And the Word became flesh and dwelt among us, and we have seen his glory, the glory as of the only Son of the Father, full of grace and truth (John 1:14)," and, "For God so loved the world that he gave his one and only Son, that whoever believes in him shall not perish but have eternal life" (John 3:16). Immanence is also witnessed to by the apostle Paul: "For the Spirit searches everything, even the depths of God." (1 Cor 2:10b) The Christ event is about the economic Trinity, how God interacts with the world, to redeem humanity and raise us up in our *fallenness*: a classic example is in the baptism of Jesus (the Father declares: "This is my beloved Son with whom I am well pleased," as the Holy Spirit descends upon Jesus: Matt 3:13–17, Mark 1:9–11, and, Luke 3:21–23). Many modern theologians will argue that the distinction between *immanence* and *economic* is invalid: one is the other. Lewis's Platonism argues for a distinction. For Lewis this distinction is at its greatest in kenosis (Phil 2:1–11): God descends to reascend with humanity, where triunity defines the reality of God.[17]

UNIVERSALISM

See: ARMINIAN(ISM); and, ATONEMENT.

---

17 See: Lewis, *Miracles* and *The Broadcast Talks*.

Zeitgeist

Literally the Spirit of the Age, the current vogue, fashion, the collective thought and ideas of a given period of time, culture, by its rulers whether political or intellectual. The Spirit of the Age is too often mistaken for the spirit of Christ, the action of the Holy Spirit, and has led to many instances of appalling action by humanity, which is claimed to be in accordance with the will of God.

Index of Names

Adam 11, 18, 24, 32, 95, 128, 132
Aeschliman, Michael D. 75, 103
Alexander, Samuel 33, 71, 119, 123
Alexandria 20–23, 142
Anscombe, G. E. M. 36–37, 38, 103, 105, 120, 136, 141, 153
Anselm of Canterbury xiv, 123, 147
Aquinas, Thomas xiii, xvi, 119, 123, 141
Arians 141
Aristotle 26
Arius 20–22, 142
Arminius, Jacobus 142
Arnett, John David 134
Aslan 32, 90, 95, 126–27, 151, 163
Athanasius of Alexandria 21–22, 32, 47, 76, 123
Augustine of Hippo 23, 24, 70, 119, 141, 157
Aulén, Gustaf 120–22
Austen, Jane 57

Barfield, Owen xvii, 76, 81–82, 86, 92, 115, 128, 130–31
Bates, Percy 47, 134
Baxter, Richard 90, 94, 120, 122, 159
Beethoven, Ludwig van 160
Bennett, J. A. W. 128, 132
Berkeley, George, Bishop of Cloyne 120, 123, 149
Beversluis, John 76, 91
Bunyan, John 63
Byron, George Gordon, Lord 43

Calvin College 125
Calvin, John 76, 79, 101, 125
Cambridge, University of xiv, 48, 57–59, 61, 62–65, 68, 70, 81, 83, 91, 95, 97–99, 101–102, 105–106, 119, 113–17, 119–21, 129, 149, 156
Campbell, Joseph 95
Campbell, Roy 134
Carpenter, Humphrey 77, 124
Caspian, Prince (Narnia) 55, 78
Cecil, David, Lord 50, 128, 132
Chalcedon 24, 25, 26, 27, 29

Chaucer, Geoffrey 39, 43
Chesterton, G. K. 83–84, 92–93, 94, 97–100, 102, 106–108, 114–15, 121, 123, 137
Christensen, Michael J. 77
Church of England, The xiii, xiv, 2, 28, 36, 47, 49–50, 151
Cicero xv
Clerk, N. W. (pseudonym for C. S. Lewis) 62
Coghill, Neville 128, 131
Coleridge, Samuel Taylor 43, 111, 115, 123, 130
Constable, John 160
Constantine 21
Cranmer, Thomas xiv
Cyril of Alexandria 22, 32, 123

Damascus 18
Dante Alighieri 42, 53, 59
Davidman, Helen Joy 71–73, 86, 107, 122, 135
Davis, Stephen T. 50, 63, 89, 91
Dawkins, Richard 154
Docetists 15, 16, 145–46
Donne, John 40
Dorsett, Lyle W. 70, 72, 78, 107
Dostoevsky, Fyodor Mikhailovich 28
Downing, David C. 78, 96, 107
Dundas-Grant, James 134
Duriez, Colin 78, 92, 96
Dyson, Hugo 128, 132

Eagle and Child, The 127–28
Ebionites 15
Eddison 59, 134
Elijah 11
Eliot, T. S. 41, 43, 98
Emmaus 18
Eutyches 141, 146–47
Evans 90, 108, 123

Fox, Adam 128, 132
Frazer, Sir James George 121

Fromke, Jon 134

Gabriel, Angel 6
Gnostics 17–18, 148
God xiv–xvi, 1–2, 5–14, 16–18, 19, 20–30, 32, 36, 42, 45–46, 48, 51, 53, 60, 64, 66, 72, 77, 80–81, 84, 89–92, 94, 100, 103, 112, 114–16, 119–21, 127, 135, 139–51, 152–55, 156, 157–61, 162, 163, 164–66
   Christ xv–xviii, 1–3, 5–15, 16–19, 20, 21–28, 29, 30–32, 35–36, 55, 75, 83–84, 87, 89–91, 112, 120, 122, 124–25, 139–41, 142, 143–44, 146–50, 151, 155–56, 159, 161–63, 165–66
   Christos (χριστός) 6, 7
   Christus 144
   Deus, Dei 20, 30, 47, 76, 89, 119–20, 144, 150, 159
   Father, God the 7, 9, 11, 17–21, 24–25, 30, 32, 112, 133, 142, 148, 151, 155, 164, 165
   Holy Spirit 2, 7, 9–10, 12, 19, 30, 37, 85, 143, 148–150, 155–56, 157, 161–62, 164–66
   Immanuel 29–30, 32, 145
   Jehovah 6
   Jesus xv, 1–3, 5, 6–11, 12–18, 19–30, 31, 32, 55, 89, 91, 140–46, 148, 149, 151, 154, 156, 158, 160–62, 165
   kurios (κυριος) 11, 147
   l/Lord 2, 8, 11, 16, 18, 19, 21, 24, 25, 57, 58, 124, 128, 132, 147, 148
   l/Lordship 11, 147
   m/Messiah 6–11, 13, 15, 16, 19
   Nazareth, Jesus of 1–2, 6–14, 28–29, 30, 143–45, 151, 154, 156
   Son, the xv, 7, 9–11, 13, 17–22, 24–25, 27, 36, 91, 142, 148, 151, 155, 164–65
   Yeshua 6
Green, Roger Llancelyn 33, 61, 80, 105, 128, 131
Greeves 66, 69
Gregory of Nazianzus 22–23, 26, 32
Gresham, Douglas 70, 73, 133, 135

Haggard, Ryder 62
Haldene, J. B. S. 50, 104
Hamilton, Clive (pseudonym for C. S. Lewis) 38–39
Hamlet 44
Hardie, Colin 134
Havard, R.A. "Humphrey" 128, 132
Heck, Joel 107, 114
Hegel, Georg 149
Hitchens, Christopher 154
Homer xv

Hooker, Richard xiii, xiv, 121, 162
Hooper, Walter xiii, xvi, 61, 64, 65–66, 67, 69–70, 76, 80–81, 92, 94–96, 98, 104, 115–16
Hosea 8
Hoyle, Sir Fred 142

Ignatius of Antioch 13
Inklings, The 3, 77, 79, 82, 89, 91, 108–109, 124, 126–28, 135
Irenaeus of Lyons 17, 148
Isaiah 8

John, Apostle 13
Jerusalem 7, 12, 14, 18, 32, 123
John the Baptist 11
Justin Martyr 16–17, 32, 33

Kant, Immanuel 105, 145, 149, 162
Keats, John 43, 160
Kierkegaard, Søren 28, 102
Kilby, Clyde S. 65, 69, 82, 98–99, 108, 113, 115
Kipling, Rudyard 53
Klinger, Max 16, 32
Kreeft, Peter 81, 82, 109

Laodicea 22
Leibniz, Gottfried 163
Lessing, Gotthold Ephraim 158–161
Lewis, Warren ("Warnie") Hamilton 69, 128, 131
Liddon, Henry Parry 144
Longfellow, Henry Wadsworth 102, 160

MacDonald, George 50–51, 81, 83, 86, 99, 121, 123–24, 136–37
Magdalen College 46, 58, 63, 127
Malory, Thomas, Sir 52
Mansfield College xiv, 37, 48
Mary 6, 8, 12–13, 18–19, 23, 25, 27, 41, 43, 53, 69, 105, 109–10
Mary Magdalene 12–13
Mathew, Gervaise 86, 134
Matthew xiv, 52, 78
Maximus the Confessor 26, 27, 32
McCallum, R. B. 134
Milton, John 43, 80–81, 87–88, 98
More, Henry 120, 149, 156
More, Sir Thomas 144
Morris, William 40

Index of Names

Narnia 29, 30, 32, 37–38, 54–58, 68, 70, 76–80, 81, 82, 83–88, 90, 94–95, 97–98, 100–102, 105, 112, 126–27, 133, 143, 148, 163
Nestorius 146
Nygren, Anders 120, 122

Oxford, University of xiv, xvi–xvii, 30–32, 36, 38–39, 40–42, 44–47, 48–51, 53–55, 56–57, 73, 77, 80, 82, 85–86, 88, 89–91, 97, 99, 100–106, 108, 109–12, 114–16, 119, 123, 126–128, 129–30, 134, 154, 161

Parker, Matthew xiv
Paul, Apostle 15, 144, 155
Pelagianists 24
Pelagius 24
Peter, Simon, Apostle 11–13, 20, 81–82, 85–86, 90, 95–97, 98, 99–105, 109–12, 114, 144
Pittenger, W. Norman 5, 22–23, 32, 60, 89, 90, 141, 146–47, 149, 154, 157
Plato 17, 122, 156
Polycarp of Smyrna 13
Pullman, Philip 154

Reimarus, Hermann Samuel 158, 160–61
Reppert, Victor 85, 104, 126
Rome xv, 9, 13, 18, 20, 28, 31–32, 78, 123

Sayers, Dorothy 60, 81, 86, 99, 124, 135, 136
Schakel, Peter J., 85–86, 95–100, 101, 102–103, 110–12
Schelling, Friedrich Wilhelm Joseph 149
Schweitzer, Albert 158
Scott, Sir Walter 59, 77, 86, 106, 112, 120
Shakespeare, William 40, 43–44, 99, 100

Shelley, Percy Bysshe 41, 43
Sherlock, Thomas, Right Revd 160
Sibley, Brian 73, 86
Sophocles xv
Spenser, Edmund 43, 57, 62, 64–65, 80
Stevens, Courteney Edward 134

Tennyson, Alfred, Lord 43
Thomas, Apostle 12, 18
Tolkien, Christopher 78, 95, 102, 109, 113, 115, 128, 132, 154
Tolkien, J. R. R. 30, 57–58, 63, 77, 79–82, 84, 86–87, 95–97, 99–102, 105–6, 108–9, 115, 124, 128–29, 131–34
Turner, J. M. W. 160
Tyrrell, George, S. J. 28, 33

Vaus, Will 87, 110, 127, 135
Vincentius of Lérins 122, 159
Virgil xv

Wagner, Richard 69, 160
Wain, John Barrington 133
Westfield College 43
Whitehead, Alfred North 158
White Witch (Narnia) 32, 163
Williams, Charles xvi, 32, 42, 52–54, 77, 79, 81–82, 84, 86–87, 93, 95, 97, 99–100, 102–103, 105, 108, 115, 124, 128, 129
Wirt, Sherwood E. 63, 93
Wolterstorff, Nicholas 91, 105
Wordsworth, William 43, 99–100, 111, 160
Wrenn, Charles Leslie 63, 134
Wright, N. T. (Tom) xvii, 7, 55, 91, 101, 110, 158

169

Index of Subjects

absolute 30, 99, 111, 145, 152, 157
academic xiv, 35, 36, 38–41, 42, 44–45, 46–49, 50, 52, 53–57, 58, 59, 61–63, 65, 68, 72, 75, 124, 133, 141–42, 164
actuality 121, 153
    actualize 142
    actualized 143
    actualizing 143
Adoptionists 15
affliction 36.
    See: pain; suffering.
Age of Reason 28, 140, 145, 151, 157–58, 160.
    See: Enlightenment.
a/Agnosticism 51, 153
Alexandrian(s) 22–23, 142
a/Allegory 39, 84, 97, 99–100, 102–103, 108, 115
    allegorical 39, 46, 160
amateur 139
American 5, 46, 65, 69, 72–73, 107, 109, 116, 128, 135, 137, 144, 151, 158, 164
analogia entis and *analogia fidei* 140–41, 147, 153
    analogia entis 140–41, 147, 153
    analogia fidei 140–41, 147, 153
    analogy of being 140
    analogy of faith 140, 159
analogy xv, 140, 141, 159.
    analogical 30, 32
    See: m/Metaphor
anguish 36
Anhypostasia/Enhypostasia
    (ἀνυπόστασις–ἐνυπόστασις) 25, 26
anoint 6
    anointed 6, 13
    Anointed 8–10
    anointing 6
anthropology 163
Antiochene 22–23
Apollinarianism 5, 141–42, 146–47, 165
a/Apologist(s) xvi, 5, 23, 32, 36, 60, 77, 90, 91, 92, 93, 97, 100, 105–107, 110, 114, 141

a/Apologetic(s) 5, 8, 11, 20, 23, 30, 32, 36–37, 50, 79, 101, 103–104, 119, 121–22, 126, 139, 141–42, 144, 152, 159, 160, 163
apologia (ἀπολογία) 141
a/Apology 16, 17, 36, 39, 46
apostasy 150.
    See: a/Atheism.
    apostate 150
a posteriori 7
a/Apostle(s) 1, 7, 9, 13–15, 19–20, 87, 107–108, 114–15, 139, 144, 155–56, 160, 165
    Apostle's 19, 20
    apostolic 14–15, 156
    See: disciple.
a priori 153
archetypal 95
argue 89, 141, 157, 165
    a/Argument(s) xiv, xv, 85, 89, 92, 103–104, 114, 115, 141–42, 148, 153, 159, 161
Arian 21–22
    Arianism 15, 20–22, 141–42, 146–47, 165
Arminian 142–44, 147, 149, 158, 165
    Arminianism 142, 143, 165
ascend(ed) 10, 12–13, 19, 21, 29, 155
    ascension 6–7
a/Atheism 120–21, 143, 153, 154
    atheist(ic) 121, 143, 152, 154, 121, 161
a/Atonement 16, 18, 30, 102, 115, 120, 142–44, 146–49, 158, 160, 162–63, 165
    atoning 9, 24
Augustinian 121, 146, 157
aut Deus aut malus homo 89, 144, 159
    God, or a bad man 11, 144–45
authority 2, 11, 13, 28–29, 30, 32, 121, 125, 140, 145–46, 152, 162

baptism 13, 124, 165
    baptized 89, 124
    Baptized 102–103, 124
    See: c/Church(es)
beauty xv, 30, 150, 160

Index of Subjects

becoming xv, 158
begotten 11, 20, 21, 25, 27, 30, 142
b/Behaviour xiv, xvi, 45–46, 55
being xiii, xv, 2, 5, 10–11, 13, 15, 17, 21–23, 25–27, 28–29, 38, 75, 140, 146, 150–51, 153–54, 155, 158–59, 162
belief(s) 2, 14–15, 17–20, 22, 24, 36, 141–44, 147, 148, 151–55, 157, 160, 162, 164. See: faith.
    believe xv, xvi, 8, 14, 19, 21–22, 140–41, 143, 151, 158, 162
Bible xv, xvii, xviii, 7–8, 28, 52, 84, 111, 114, 139, 142–43, 155, 160–62.
    biblical xiv, xvii, 13, 36, 139, 142
    See: Scripture.
blasphemy 14
blind-watchmaker 162
books xvi, 1, 3, 6, 8, 12, 14, 35, 38, 55, 102, 130, 133, 139

Cambridge Review, The 58, 59
Categorical Imperative 144, 145
Catholic Art Quarterly, The 61
causation 153
Christian(s) xiii, xiv, xv, xvi, xvii, xviii, 1–3, 5, 7–9, 11–13, 15–17, 20, 28, 30, 32–33, 35–36, 37, 40–42, 43–45, 46–48, 50–51, 53–56, 59–60, 61– 62, 64–65, 67– 69, 76, 79, 80–82, 85,–87, 89–90, 91, 93–94, 96–104, 105, 107–108, 109, 111–16, 119–20, 125, 127, 136–37, 139, 141, 146, 148–49, 151, 154–59, 162, 164, 165
    Christendom xiii
    Christianity xiv–xvi, 1–2, 16–17, 21–22, 28, 33, 37, 39, 40–41, 46, 48, 51, 55, 66, 68, 72, 87, 90–91, 94, 96–97, 100, 104–109, 114, 120, 129, 133, 139, 143, 145, 154–55
Christian Century, The 5, 32, 60, 90, 93, 103, 111
Christian Herald, The 60
Christlikeness 38, 149–50
Christology 3, 5, 7–9, 11–16, 18–30, 32, 35–36, 38, 75, 89–90, 115, 151, 157, 165
    christological 3, 5, 8, 11, 17, 19–20, 23, 29–30, 89, 121, 142
    christologically 161
Christus Victor 120, 122
c/Church(es) xiii–xiv, xv, xvii–xviii, 1, 2–3, 5, 6–9, 10–15, 17, 18–20, 21, 22, 24, 26–28, 29, 31–32, 33, 36, 41, 43, 44, 47, 49, 50–52, 53–54, 60, 68, 78, 81, 85, 87–88, 94–95, 96, 115–16, 120–23, 124, 125–26, 139, 140–142, 144, 146, 151, 155–56, 159, 161–62, 164–65
    Anglican(s) xiii, xiv, 1, 2, 90, 94, 109, 121, 139, 162
    Baptist 1, 11
    Calvinism 143
    Calvinistic 143
    Calvinists 156
    demonination(s) 2, 146
    e/Ecclesiology 13, 94, 146
        ecclesia 13, 139, 145–46
        ekklesia (ἐκκλησία) 146
        ecclesia visibilis-ecclesia invisibilis 146
    Ecclesiastical xiv, 121
    Evangelical(s) 1, 2, 28, 91, 98, 110, 113–14, 122, 125, 139, 156
        Evangelicalism 110, 115–16
        Evangelism 114
        Evangelist 116
    Methodist 1
    neo-Protestantism 150
    o/Orthodox 1, 5, 7, 8, 16, 21–23, 28–29, 32, 36, 87, 94–95, 120, 139, 141, 146, 151, 157, 159
        o/Orthodoxy 14, 21, 24, 87, 100, 112, 114, 123, 136, 141–42, 159
    Presbyterian 1
    Protestant(s) xiii, 28, 72, 120, 156, 158, 162
    Roman Catholic xiii, 1, 2, 28, 30, 47, 125
        Catholic xiii, 1, 2, 19, 28, 30, 36, 47, 61, 85, 121–22, 125, 136, 144
        Catholicism 94, 137
Church of England Newspaper, The 47, 49
Church Times, The 60, 120, 139
c/Classical xv, 16, 101, 143, 148, 158
coeternal 20, 142
communicatio idiomatum 145, 150, 164
    communicated 164
    communication of attributes 145
communion 10, 19
compassion 150
comprehension 164
consubstantial 20, 142, 147
c/Conversion 5, 30, 36–37, 83, 89, 91, 93, 119, 122, 146, 148, 150, 154, 162
    convert 2, 17, 119, 154
    converted 9, 16, 30, 119, 155
correspondence xv, 35–36, 38, 42, 69, 70
    corresponded 70
    correspondent 69, 102
corruption 18, 24, 148–49
c/Creation 10–11, 29, 96, 104, 139–40, 142, 145, 150, 153–54, 155, 158, 162, 164
    created 20, 22, 25–26, 139, 142, 145, 150, 154
    c/Creative 95, 103
c/Creed 2, 11, 18, 19, 20, 21, 24, 25, 30, 124, 151, 165
    creedal 18–19, 22, 28, 36, 151
    creeds 1, 19–20, 150, 165
crime 163

171

crucifixion 16, 19, 139, 146–47
    cross 7, 9–10, 12–13, 18, 24, 30, 142–43, 149, 163
c/Culture 16, 41, 78, 99, 111, 150–51, 157, 160, 166
cultural 6, 28–29, 157–60

d/Death 10, 18, 23, 24, 30, 35, 36, 37, 47, 64, 69, 82, 139, 140, 143, 146, 147, 148
debate xiii, xv, 5, 12, 22–23, 36, 38, 41, 54, 89, 120, 141, 146–47, 149, 151, 153–54, 157, 161
defence 37, 141–42
Deism 28, 140–41, 142, 145–47, 153, 161–62
    deists 162
descend 7, 8, 22
    descended 7, 9, 13, 18–19, 29, 144–45
    descending 22, 154
    See: reascend
desire 28, 92, 112, 114, 116, 161
determinism 153
    deterministic 153
devotional 38
dialectic 27, 30.
    dialectical 30
    See: Paradox
dilemma 111
diminuted 145, 150, 164
    diminution 164
disciples 7, 11–12, 19, 144.
    See: apostles.
distinction xv, 22, 25, 28, 119, 121, 142, 146, 151, 165
divine 7, 8, 10, 12–17, 19–23, 25–26, 28–29, 111–12, 141–42, 145, 146–48, 150–51, 154, 157, 163
    divinity 14–15, 20, 22–23, 25, 140, 142, 151
Docetism 5, 15, 141–42, 145–47, 165
    Docetists 15–16, 145, 146
    dokeo (δοκέο)
d/Doctrine xv, 8, 14–15, 17, 20, 24–27, 32, 35–36, 89, 116, 119, 121–22, 127, 141–43, 146, 150, 155, 156–57, 160, 162, 164–65
    doctrinal 8, 14, 17–18, 20, 151
dogma(s) 140, 145, 151–52, 157
drama xvi, 56
dualism 95
    duality 95

Ebionite(s) 15, 16
    Ebionitism 15
economic 10, 165
ecumenical 27–28, 94, 100, 105, 112, 114
election 143

El Shaddai 155
enchantment 100–101
Enlightenment 28, 140, 145, 151, 157–58, 160.
    Enlightened 140
    See: Age of Reason.
epistemology 96, 102, 148, 152
    epistemic 98
    e/Epistemological 96
Eros 113, 120, 122
e/Eschaton 31, 140, 146, 155
    e/Eschatology 77, 89, 91, 146
    eschatē (ἐσχατη) 146
    Eschatological 95
    eschatos (ἔσχατος) 146
    Four Last Things, the 139, 140, 146
eternal(ly) 11, 16, 19–21, 27, 30, 142–43, 146, 151, 165
ethics xiv, 14, 127, 144, 151, 162
    moral 23, 29, 144–45, 152
    m/Morality 46, 98, 145
Eutychianism 5, 24, 141–42, 146–47, 165
event xvi, 7, 30, 147, 153, 161, 165
evil 10, 18, 24, 42, 81, 85, 90, 111, 116, 149, 162–63
evolution 139–40
e/Existentialism 147, 163
    existence 29, 143, 147, 153–54, 162–63, 165
ex nihilo 29

f/Faith xiii, 1–2, 11, 13, 15–19, 21–22, 25, 27–30, 32, 36–37, 46, 53, 60, 68–69, 78, 83–85, 88, 90–91, 92–93, 98–99, 101, 104, 109, 111–13, 120, 122, 127, 139–43, 147–48, 156, 158–59, 161
f/Fantasy 58, 60, 77, 87, 95–97, 99, 101
    fantastic 78, 86, 99, 135, 137
fides quaerens intellectum 147
    faith seeking understanding 147
forgiveness 19, 30, 46, 52, 144, 163
foundation xiii, 125, 140, 146, 148, 152
    foundational 148
    f/Foundationalism 147–48, 153
freedom 30, 111, 145, 150, 155, 158
fundamental xiii, xiv, 89, 116, 142, 145–46, 149–150, 156

glory 165
Gnostic 17–18, 21, 36, 148
    gnōsis (γνῶσις) 17, 148
    Gnosticism 5, 15, 19–20, 98, 148–49, 164
good xiv–xv, 2, 10, 18, 24, 28–29, 36, 48, 61, 81, 90, 95, 144, 156–57, 162–63
    goodness 81, 116, 143

Index of Subjects

g/Gospel(s) 2, 11-13, 14, 16-18, 20, 28-29, 37, 79, 84, 87, 89, 90, 92, 97, 99, 100, 102, 108, 113, 115, 116, 121, 124, 139, 141-44, 156, 158, 160, 165
g/Grace xiii-xv, 18, 24, 94, 113, 142-43, 150, 157, 162-63, 165
    graceful 150
    gracefully 150
Greek xv, 6, 7, 9-11, 13, 15-17, 20-21, 23-25, 26, 27, 139-41, 145-46, 148, 150-51, 154-56, 163, 165
g/Grief 62, 76, 84, 92-93, 163

happiness 11
h/Heaven 1-2, 8, 11, 19, 21, 56, 63, 76-77, 82-83, 87, 93, 100, 113, 122, 139-40, 143, 146, 149, 155
h/Hell 19, 82-83, 89-90, 100, 139, 140, 143, 146, 149
    damnation 143
heresy 5, 13-14, 17, 20, 22, 29, 146
    heresies 17, 122
    heretical 14
    heterodox 5, 141, 146-47, 149
history xv, 1, 8-9, 12-13, 16-17, 21, 28, 32, 53, 161, 163
    historical 5, 8, 9, 12, 17, 28, 158
    historicism 55
holy 10, 18, 19, 23, 25, 29, 162, 165
holiness 10, 18, 19, 30, 102, 145, 162
holon (ὅλον) 27
    holos (ὅλος) 27
homoiousios (ὁμοιούσιος) 24
homoousios (ὁμοούσιος) 21, 24
h/Human xv, 1-2, 6, 8, 10-12, 14-18, 19, 20, 22-24, 25-26, 27-29, 30, 69, 77, 89-90, 111-12, 120-21, 140, 141, 143, 145-48, 150-51, 153-54, 157, 160-61, 162-65
    humanism 76, 111
    humanist 111, 136
    h/Humanity 1, 7-10, 11, 12, 15, 18, 22-25, 26, 27, 28, 29-30, 32, 139-141, 142, 143-45, 147, 148-50, 152-53, 155, 157, 159, 161, 163-66
    man 1, 11, 14, 16, 18, 20-21, 24-26, 28-29, 56, 121, 139, 142-144, 145, 151
hypostasis (ὑπόστασις) 25-26

Idealism 104, 148-49, 156
    Idealists 149
ideology 82
illumination 12, 89, 112, 157
    illuminatory 157

i/Image 28, 30, 64, 88, 90, 98, 103, 123, 145, 149-50
i/Imagination 59, 79, 83, 85-86, 88-89, 97-99, 101-103, 107, 109, 112-13, 115, 124, 149
    imaginary 66
    imaginative xv, 86, 96
imago Christi 149, 150
    image of Christ 149, 150
imago Dei 30, 150
    image of God 30, 145, 150
imitatio Christi 149, 150
    imitation of Christ 149, 150-51
immanence 10, 145, 165
    immanent xiv, 10, 165
immediate animation 26-27
immutability 145
impassibility 145
impeccability 145
i/Incarnation xv, 7, 17-19, 22-23, 26, 27, 29-30, 47, 76, 91, 122, 139, 140-41, 148, 150-51, 152-53, 155, 161-62, 164
    incarnate 2, 11, 13-14, 21-23, 25-26, 28-29, 30, 89, 151, 164
    incarnated 10, 11, 27, 140, 145, 153
in Christ 8, 10-11, 16, 22-23, 26, 30, 32, 36, 139-41, 142-43, 150, 161
incognito 11
incomprehensibility 145
incorporeality 145
indivisible 10, 165
infinity 145
Inklings, The 3, 77, 79, 82, 89, 91, 108-109, 124, 126-28, 135
inspiration 157
intellect xv, 27, 139, 161
    intellectual xv, 22, 36, 160, 166
intertestamental 6, 15
invisibility 164
    invisible 21, 121, 146, 164
Israel 6, 11, 144, 145
    Hebrew(s) 6-8, 14-15, 16-17, 29, 144, 155
    Jew(s) 6, 9, 12, 14, 28, 162
    Jewish 6-9, 10, 15-16, 29, 31, 154-55, 158
    Judaism 6, 12, 143
    Judaistic 6

Jesus Seminar, The 158
j/Joy 57, 68, 70-73, 83, 86, 92-93, 97-99, 106-107, 114, 119, 122, 135, 143, 147, 150, 161-62, 164
    joyous 150
    See: *Sehnsucht*
judgement
judgment 30, 31, 139-40, 144, 146, 163

justification 147–48
   justified 147–48
   justify 17, 36, 141, 162

Kantian 89, 120
k/Kenosis (κένωσις) 145, 150, 164–65
   kenóō (κενόω) 150
   kenotic 150
   Kenotic 150
Kingdom of God, the 155
   the k/Kingdom 124, 143, 155
   king(s) 6
   kingship 6
knowledge 1, 3, 5, 8, 10, 17–18, 30, 140–41, 147–48, 152–53, 161–62, 164
   Knowing 93

language xiv, xvi, 20, 38, 119, 139, 154
l/Law xiii, 9, 15–17, 24, 44, 93, 112, 115, 144–45, 153, 159, 165
   Law of Excluded Middle 144, 153, 159
l/Liberal 2, 5, 28, 150–51, 158, 161
   liberalism 151
   liberally 162
libraries 123, 130, 135
l/Light 21, 26, 30, 77, 79, 90, 92–93, 99, 107, 109–11, 112, 114–15, 116, 150, 151, 163
literary 39–40, 41–42, 43, 50, 52, 55–57, 62–63, 65, 80, 88, 94, 97–99, 103, 115, 123, 130–31
literature xiv–xvi, 36, 83, 39–40, 42–43, 48, 51, 53, 56, 59–63, 64–65, 68, 90–91, 93–95, 96, 98–100, 103, 111, 113, 121, 127, 137, 152, 137, 154
logic 22, 119, 142, 159
   logical 119
l/Logos (λόγος) 16–17, 20, 22, 25–27, 141, 151, 156
   logos asarkos/logos ensarkos (λόγος ἄσαρκος–λόγος ἔνσαρκος) 151
   logos spermatikos (λόγος σπερματικός) 17
l/Lord 2, 8, 11, 16, 18–19, 21, 24–25, 57–58, 124, 128, 132, 147, 148
   l/Lordship 11, 19
l/Love xv, 2, 10, 11, 29, 32, 39–40, 69, 73, 76, 84, 87, 103, 109, 114, 115–16, 120, 122, 145, 147, 150, 165
   agape (αγαπη) 10, 120, 122
   altruistic 150
   self-denial 150
   self-denying 10, 150

Manichee 27
martyrdom 11, 17
materialism 149
m/Medieval xv, 39, 42–43, 53, 59–61, 62–64, 65, 98, 120, 141, 147
mere Christianity, xiv, 1, 120
   meer Christian 120, 159
   mere 2, 16, 38, 159
Messiah 6–11, 13, 15–16, 19
   messiahship 6–7, 15
   messianic 6, 15
m/Metaphor 21, 109, 114, 140.
   metaphorical 140
   See: analogy, analogical
method 122, 141–42, 152–53, 159
   methodology 158
m/Miracle(s) 37, 44, 50, 52, 61, 84, 105, 152, 160, 162, 165
   miraculous 152–53, 160, 162
Modalism 27, 165
m/Modern xvi, 5, 22, 26–27, 28, 31–32, 49–52, 53, 61, 73, 82–83, 87, 97, 104–105, 110, 120–21, 130, 135, 143–44, 158, 165
   Modernism 81, 149, 151, 157, 160
   Modernist 151
   modernity 157
m/Monophysitism 15, 24, 146–47
mystical 119, 121, 156, 161
m/Myth(s) xv, xvi, 17, 30, 47, 62, 65, 77, 84, 89–90, 97, 99–102, 107–109, 112, 115, 121, 148, 154
   Mythological 95
   mythology xv, 17, 148, 154
m/Mythopoeia 102
   mythopoeic 128
   Mythopoeic 62, 128
   Mythopoetic 112

Narnia 29–30, 32, 37–38, 54–58, 68, 70, 76–88, 90, 94–95, 97–98, 100–102, 105, 112, 126–27, 133, 143, 148, 163
   Narnian 32, 77, 102, 114
Narrative 65, 90, 95, 99, 101, 109
nature xiii–xv, xvii, 5–7, 9–11, 13, 15–16, 20, 22–25, 27, 30, 35, 37–38, 120, 140–42, 144–47, 149, 150–54, 158, 160, 162–64
   natural xiii, xiv, xv, 150–52, 153, 160, 162
   naturalism xv, 152
   n/Naturalism 103–105, 141, 148, 152–53, 161–62
   naturalists 140, 152, 153
   natural law 93
Nestorianism 15, 23, 146

Index of Subjects

New Testament xviii, 6–8, 11, 14, 21, 52, 139, 155, 160–61, 165
Nicene 17, 21, 24, 33, 122, 123
nihilism 90
    nihilistic 90
    nothingness 90
novels 35, 38, 160
numinous 146

Occultist 164
Old Testament 6–7, 11, 19, 145, 155, 165
omnipotence 145, 152
omnipresence 145
omniscience 145
o/Ontology 152, 153, 154, 163
    o/Ontological 89, 152, 154
    ontos, ὢν ὄτος, ōn ontos 154
ousia (οὐσία) 20, 25

p/Pagan(s) 9–10, 13, 16–17, 30, 87, 111, 121, 124, 141, 154, 155
pain 23, 32, 36, 41, 75, 81, 91, 162–63.
    See: suffering.
p/Panentheism 155, 158
    panentheist 155
    panentheistically 155
    pantheism 155
    pantheist 155
Pantocrator 29–31, 155
    Pantokratōr (παντοκράτωρ) 29, 155
paradox 23, 27, 152.
    See: d/Dilemma.
parousia (παρουσία) 155
p/Patristic 5, 14–15, 25, 29–31, 32, 119–120, 122–23, 125, 141–42, 144, 149, 155–56, 159
Pelagianism 23–24
perception 6, 13, 32, 140, 143, 149, 152, 157, 159, 165
person xvii, 6–13, 15, 17, 20–21, 23, 25–27, 29, 141, 145–46, 148–51, 154–55, 156, 161, 164–65
    Personal 40, 48, 106
    personhood 10
p/Philosophy xiv–xv, 16, 23, 27, 36, 38, 68, 76, 83, 89, 101, 103–105, 109, 112, 116, 120, 122, 124, 130, 136, 145, 147, 150–57, 158, 164
    philosopher 16, 26, 28, 38, 42, 91–93, 97, 100, 105–107, 114, 116, 136, 140–41, 149, 154, 156, 158, 160, 162–63
    philosophers 16–17, 28, 119–20, 136, 140, 148, 153, 156, 162

philosophical xv, 11, 32, 36–38, 83, 85, 89, 103, 112, 119–20, 123, 139, 145, 147, 152–54, 156–57, 159, 164
    philosophies 17, 36, 141
p/Platonic 17, 29, 122, 146, 149, 151, 156, 164
    platonically 122
    Platonism 16–17, 37, 89, 105, 113, 122, 145–46, 149, 152, 156, 165
    Neoplatonism 62, 105, 156
    Neo-Platonists 149
Pneumatology 156
    pneuma (πνεῦμα) 156
    See: Holy Spirit (Name Index)
Poems 53, 64–65, 67, 71–72, 99, 116
Poetry xv–xvi, 40, 47, 56, 62, 73, 99, 135
Polytheism 27, 165
Postconversion 99
Postmodern 83, 151, 157
    Postmodernism 96, 149, 157, 161
    p/Postmodernist(s) 110, 157–58
praeparatio evangelica 107
prayer xiv, 12, 38, 49, 52, 56, 61, 64, 92–93, 116, 147
    pray 92
    prayerful 147
Preconversion 99
predicament 26, 140, 147
prefigurement 17, 89, 121
prefigured 17
prevenience 143
    prevenient 143, 150, 157, 162, 163
    See: g/Grace
priests 6, 28
process theology 157, 158
professional 29, 106, 139
    professionals 139
propitiation 144
    propitiare 144
    propitiati 144
    propitiatory 144
proposition 22, 144, 147, 148, 158, 159, 162
    propositional 5
Providence 111
p/Purgatory 2, 158
    purgation 30, 89, 158

Quest for the Historical Jesus, The 158
quod ubique, quod semper, quod ab omnibus 159
    what has been held always, everywhere, by everybody 159

radio broadcasts 36–37, 44–46, 48, 50, 54, 63
reascend 22, 165

175

reascending 22
See: descend
r/Reason xiii–xv, 2, 7, 12, 14, 16, 17, 28, 30, 38, 39, 46, 83, 85, 86, 89, 102, 104, 111, 112, 140, 145, 147, 148, 151–53, 157–59, 160, 161, 162
    rational 26, 76, 104, 142, 145, 148
        irrational 148
    rationalism 158, 160–61
    r/Rationality 16, 93, 103, 145
    rationally 147
    r/Reasoning 13, 30, 86, 140, 153
reconciliation 144
redeemed 6, 142
    redemption 6, 10, 22–23, 30, 158, 164
reductio ad absurdum 153, 159
Reformation xiv, 28, 79, 120–21, 140
regula fidei 141, 159
    rule of faith 141, 159–60
    analogy of faith (ἀναλογίαν τῆς πίστεως) 159
reign 155
    reigning 29, 155
r/Religion(s) xvi, 1, 2, 6, 13, 17, 21, 30, 43, 44–45, 49, 51, 55, 60, 62, 76–77, 82, 87, 94–95, 97, 102–104, 106, 111, 116, 120–21, 135, 136, 140–41, 145, 149, 152, 154, 159, 164
    religiosity 152
    r/Religious xiv, 6–7, 8, 15–17, 29–30, 36, 87, 99, 140, 147–49, 152, 154, 160, 164
repentance 30, 163
r/Resurrection xv, 6, 7, 9, 12, 14, 17–19, 30, 122, 139–40, 144, 147, 149, 151–53, 155–56, 160, 163
    resurrected 1, 9–10, 12, 17, 140, 163
    risen xvi, 12–13, 29, 155
r/Revelation xiii–xvi, 1, 3, 5, 7, 12–13, 17, 19, 26, 30, 35, 36, 38, 75, 89, 111–13, 139–41, 145, 147–49, 150, 152–53, 155–56, 158–60, 162, 164. See: reason.
    intimation(s) 17
    realization 6, 11, 159, 165
    revealed 7, 11, 28, 30, 140, 159, 164
    revealing 69
    self-disclosure 159
revolution 140
Roman(s) xiii, 1–2, 6, 9, 12–13, 15–17, 20–21, 28, 30, 47, 88, 125, 141, 154, 159
Romanticism 39, 46, 140, 160
    Romance 42, 107, 121
    Romantic 96, 99, 105, 160
Rome xv, 9, 13, 18, 20, 28, 31–32, 78, 123
Rosicrucianism 164

sacrifice 16, 22, 24, 120, 141, 144, 150

sacrificial 9
salvation 1, 6–7, 8–9, 11–14, 17, 18, 21–25, 27, 30, 32, 82, 141–43, 146–48, 157, 160, 162
save 2, 6–8, 11, 22, 24, 141
savior 6, 12, 18
s/Soteriology xiv, 162
sanctification xiv, 30, 157
sarx (σαρξ) 151
satisfaction 144
science xvi, 112, 125, 140, 153, 157
    science fiction 57, 58, 60, 63
    scientific xvi, 26, 142, 152–53, 157, 160, 162–63
    Scientism 75, 103–104, 141, 148, 152–53, 162
    Scientists 104, 140, 142
s/Scripture xiv, 7, 13, 21, 28, 77, 112–13, 116–17, 122, 150–51, 158–60, 162
    scriptural 161
    sola scriptura 162
    See: Bible; biblical
second coming 108, 139, 140, 155
secular xiv
Sehnsucht 104, 108, 112, 119, 161–62
    longing 161–62
s/Shadowlands 30, 73, 82–84, 86, 90, 92–93, 107, 109–12, 114–16
    shadows 32, 77, 81, 87
silence 81
s/Sin(s) 2, 8–9, 10, 14, 16, 18–19, 22, 24–25, 30, 46, 139–42, 144, 146–48, 149, 157, 161, 163.
    original sin 8, 10, 16, 18, 24, 139–42, 146, 148–49, 157, 163
    fall 8, 10, 18, 24, 119, 139–40, 142–43, 149, 154, 163
    fallen 24, 26, 28, 30, 141–43, 163
    fallible 141
    postlapsarian 142
    prelapsarian 142
    selfish 163
    sinfulness 163
    sinlessness 22
    sinners 94
skeptical 156, 160–61
    skepticism 158, 160
    skeptics 87, 108
society 126–27, 129, 150–51
    social 157, 165
Socratic Digest, The 38, 43–44, 47, 51, 56, 103
Sonship 19
Space 30, 60, 63, 75, 83, 93, 119
Spectator, The 42, 45–47, 49, 58
spirit xv, 16, 25, 28, 146, 149, 151, 156, 166
    Spirit of the Age 166

Index of Subjects

spiritual xiv, 17, 77–78, 80, 83, 87, 94, 96, 143, 152, 164
spirituality 32, 80, 152
spiritually 32
statements 11, 18, 148
sub-apostolic 15, 156
sub-creation/sub-creator 99
Substitution 162
s/Suffering 17, 36, 77, 81, 91, 150, 162–63
    See: pain
Summa Theologica xiii
Sunday Telegraph, The 63
supernatural xiv–xv, 37, 151–52
symbolic 30
symbolum apostolorum 19
    See: creed

temporal 152
Ten Commandments 72
testament(s) 6
Theism 28, 56, 76, 117, 141–42, 145–47, 153, 161–62
    theistic 154–55
    t/Theists 162
theodicy 36, 162–63
t/Theology xiii–xiv, xv, xvi, 1, 2, 5, 8, 11–13, 15, 17, 28, 32, 36–38, 41, 43, 47, 61, 66, 77, 81–82, 87, 89–90, 91–93, 96–97, 100–103, 105, 107, 110–16, 119, 124, 139–42, 146, 149–50, 151–58
    natural theology 153
    t/Theologian(s) xiii–xiv, 2, 7, 12, 15, 16, 22, 26, 28–29, 37, 43, 82, 91–93, 97, 100, 105–106, 107–108, 114, 119–20, 122, 136, 140–42, 144, 147, 151, 156, 158, 159–60, 165
    t/Theological xiii, xiv, 13–14, 22, 29, 32, 78, 86, 89–91, 95, 98, 111, 113–14, 120, 125, 139, 141, 147, 151, 154, 159, 163–65
    theological anthropology 147, 154, 163
    Theological Liberalism 151
    theologies 87
    Theologische 84
theory 27, 141–43, 145, 156
Theosophy 164
Theotokos (θεοτόκος) 23, 25
t/Time 41–45, 47–49, 51, 53, 57–59, 62, 77, 79, 83, 85, 119
Time and Tide 42–45, 47, 49, 51, 53, 57–59, 62
Times Literary Supplement, The 41, 52
Transcendence 100
    transcendent xiv, xv, 29, 144, 145, 156
transcription 164

t/Transposition, doctrine of xiv, xvi, 37, 41–43, 48, 50, 54, 63, 89, 122, 145, 150, 156, 163, 164
translate(d) 23, 32, 47, 55, 70, 76, 90, 92–93, 107, 110–12, 114–16, 119, 122, 145, 150, 155
translation 52, 116
transposed 145, 150, 164
Trinity 6, 10–11, 13, 17, 20–21, 25, 27, 29–30, 32, 48, 100, 145, 148, 150–51, 155, 156, 164–65
    economic Trinity 10, 165
    immanent Trinity 10, 165
    t/Trinitarian 6, 7, 9, 19, 27, 162, 164
    triune 6, 10, 165
t/Truth(s) xv, xvi, 12, 14, 16–17, 18, 28, 30, 37, 83, 89, 103, 110, 112–13, 114, 141, 148, 152, 157, 159, 160–61, 164–65
    true xiii, xv, 5, 11, 16, 27–30, 121, 141, 146, 148–49, 152–53, 159, 161–64

ugly broad ditch 161
uncreated 21, 30, 151
understand(ing) xiii, 1, 3, 5, 7–9, 10–11, 13–15, 17, 21, 23–26, 29–30, 35, 37, 75, 89, 122, 125, 139–42, 144, 147–48, 152–53, 156, 159, 161, 163–65
u/Universal 8, 12, 16–17, 30, 103, 140, 142–43, 145, 148, 158, 161, 164
    u/Universalism 161, 165
    universality 122, 140
    universe xiv, 16, 20, 27, 29, 32, 44–45, 56, 139–40, 142, 145, 152–53, 155, 158, 160

via media xiii, xiv, 94, 121
visibility 164
    visible 21, 120–21, 155, 164
vivisection 52

wilful 141
wisdom 162
    wise 16, 162
w/Witness 1, 7, 12, 14, 28, 36, 51, 84, 90, 92, 94, 96–98, 101, 103–104, 109, 111–12, 116
Word 16, 20, 22, 25–27, 47, 76, 81, 112, 141, 151, 162, 165. See: Bible; Scripture.
Works 36, 37–38, 42, 52–53, 61–62, 79, 81, 85, 87, 91, 92–93, 95–100, 101, 102–103, 105–108, 109, 110, 113–15, 122–23, 124, 133, 134
    address(es) 35, 37–38
    article(s) xvii, 37, 89–90, 100, 128, 130, 135–136
    essay(s) xv, 35, 36–38, 39, 40–47, 49–50, 51, 52–59, 60–66, 67–68, 72, 83, 86–87,

89, 93, 94–98, 99, 100–101, 103–104, 107–109, 110, 111–12, 113, 115–16
letter(s) 9, 13, 30, 32, 35, 37–38, 41, 44, 52, 61, 64–67, 68–69, 70, 73, 81, 93, 102, 104, 113, 117, 120, 123–24, 130, 139, 146
pamphlet(s) 41, 43, 46, 51–52, 55, 57, 60
paper(s) 35–36, 38–39, 40, 41– 45, 46, 48, 49–50, 51, 52, 53–54, 55, 56–57, 58–61, 62, 63, 65, 68, 72, 83, 92–93, 97–98, 99, 103, 106–107, 114, 130
sermon(s) xiv, 35, 37–38, 41, 42–43, 44, 46, 48, 49–50, 52–53, 55–58, 60, 63, 106, 123, 164,
story(ies) 35, 38–42, 44–46, 49–50, 52–60, 61, 62–63, 65–66, 68, 72, 83, 97, 102, 135
study(ies) 32, 39, 40–43, 53, 59–61, 62, 63–65, 78–79, 81, 83, 85–86, 88, 92–93, 97–98, 105–107, 113, 114–15, 117, 121, 124
writing(s) xv, 2, 8, 13, 17, 26, 29, 30, 32–33, 35–36, 38, 76, 78, 84, 86, 88, 115, 122–25, 141, 148, 150, 154, 156

world xiii, 1, 2, 12, 17–18, 20, 28, 30, 32, 37, 139–41, 146, 148, 152–54, 155, 156–57, 160–62, 165
worldview 76, 104–105, 152

yearning 161
See: *Sehnsucht*

Zeitgeist 107, 158, 166

Index of C. S. Lewis's Works
An index of Lewis's works cited or quoted

C. S. Lewis: Books

Abolition of Man, The. Or, Reflections on Education with Special Reference to the Teaching of English in the Upper Forms of Schools, xiv, 45
All My Road Before Me: The Diary of C. S. Lewis 1922-27 67
Allegory of Love, The. A Study in Medieval Tradition, 39
Arthurian Torso, Containing the Posthumous Fragment of The Figure of Arthur and a Commentary on the Arthurian Poems of Charles Williams and C. S. Lewis 53

Beyond Personality: the Christian Idea of God xiv, xvi, 46, 48.
    See: *Broadcast Talks*, and, *Mere Christianity*.
Beyond Personality: The Christian View of God 48
Boxen: The Imaginary World of the Young C. S. Lewis 66
Broadcast Talks xvi, 36, 44-46, 48, 55, 165.
    See: *Right and Wrong, What Christians Believe, Christian Behavior*, and, *Beyond Personality*.

C. S. Lewis: Letters to Children 70
Christian Behaviour xiv, xvi, 45, 46, 55.
    See: *Broadcast Talks*, and, *Mere Christianity*.
Christian Reflections 35, 40-43, 45-46, 54-56, 59, 61-62, 64-65, 68, 158
Christian in Danger, The 41
Christian Reunion 35, 47, 67
Chronicles of Narnia, The 30-32, 38, 54-58, 76, 79, 80-81, 84, 90, 94-95, 98, 100-102, 105, 143, 148, 163.
    See: individual titles.

Collected Letters, Vol. I: Family Letters 1905-1931 68, 70
Collected Letters, Vol. II: Books, Broadcasts and War 1931-1949 68, 70
Collected Letters Vol. III: III: Narnia, Cambridge and Joy 1950-1963 68, 70
Collected Poems of C. S. Lewis, The 67.
    See: *Poems*, and, *Narrative Poems*

Dark Tower and Other Stories, The 38, 40, 61, 66
Discarded Image, The. An Introduction to Medieval and Renaissance Literature 64
Dymer 39

English Literature in the Sixteenth Century xiv, 48, 56, 103, 121
Essay Collection and Other Short Pieces 68
Essay Collection: Faith, Christianity and the Church 68
Essay Collection: Literature, Philosophy and Short Stories 68
Essays Presented to Charles Williams 42, 52
Experiment on Criticism, An 62

Fern Seed and Elephants and Other Essays on Christianity 52, 61, 66
Four Loves, The 61, 114

George MacDonald: An Anthology 50-51, 123
God in the Dock (UK, 1979) 36, 66
God in the Dock: Essays on Theology and Ethics (US, 1971) 36, 66. (UK *Undeceptions*, 1971)
Great Divorce, The 30, 37, 49, 50, 77, 100-102
Grief Observed, A 62, 84, 92, 163

Guardian, The (weekly Anglo Catholic newspaper) 36, 41–42, 44, 45, 50, 102, 133

Horse and His Boy, The 56.
    See: *Chronicles of Narnia, The.*

Last Battle, The 58, 148, 163.
    See: *Chronicles of Narnia, The.*
Letters of C. S. Lewis 65–67, 69, 70, 102
Letters to an American Lady 65, 69
Letters to Malcolm: Chiefly on Prayer 38, 64
Lion, the Witch and the Wardrobe, The 54, 76, 96, 102, 130, 163.
    See: *Chronicles of Narnia, The.*
Literary Impact of the Authorized Version, The. The Ethel M. Wood Lecture Delivered before the University of London on Mar. 20, 1950 55

Magician's Nephew, The 29, 32, 57, 143, 151.
    See: *Chronicles of Narnia, The.*
Mere Christianity. A revised and amplified edition, with a new introduction, of the three books Broadcast Talks, Christian Behaviour, and Beyond Personality xiv, xvi, 55.
    See: *Broadcast Talks.*
Miracles: A Preliminary Study (1st ed.) 37, 50–52, 84, 105, 165
Miracles (2nd ed.) 37, 61, 84, 105
Miserable Offenders: An Interpretation of Prayer Book Language 52

Narrative Poems 65.
    See: *The Collected Poems of C. S. Lewis*, and, *Poems.*

Of Other Worlds. Essays and Stories 50, 56–58, 60–63, 65
Of This and Other Worlds 41, 47, 51, 54, 57–60, 62, 66
Out of the Silent Planet 36–37, 40, 96.
    See: *The Space Trilogy,* also, *Perelandra,* and, *That Hideous Strength.*

Perelandra 37, 45, 96, 97.
    See: *The Space Trilogy,* also, *Out of the Silent Planet,* and, *That Hideous Strength.*
Personal Heresy, The. A Controversy 40

Pilgrim's Regress, The. An Allegorical Apology for Christianity, Reason and Romanticism 36–37, 39, 46, 98.
    See: "Preface" to *The Pilgrim's Regress* (3rd ed.)
Poems 53, 64–65, 67, 71–72, 99, 116.
    See: *The Collected Poems of C. S. Lewis*, and, *Narrative Poems.*
Preface to Paradise Lost, A 44
Present Concern: Ethical Essays 35, 42, 45–47, 49, 51, 53, 56, 58–59, 63, 67
Prince Caspian: The Return to Narnia 55.
    See: *Chronicles of Narnia, The.*
Problem of Pain, The 23, 32, 36–37, 41, 75, 163

Reflections on the Psalms 37–38, 59, 93
Rehabilitations and Other Essays 38–41
Right and Wrong Wrong: A Clue to the Meaning of the Universe xiv, xvi, 44.
    See: *Broadcast Talks,* and, *Mere Christianity.*

Screwtape Letters, The 30, 37, 44, 61, 113, 117, 146
Screwtape Proposes a Toast 43, 58, 61, 64, 67
Screwtape Proposes a Toast and Other Pieces 64
Selected Literary Essays 39–41, 43, 50, 55–56, 57, 62–63, 65
Shall We Lose God in Outer Space? 60
Silver Chair, The 56, 96.
    See: *Chronicles of Narnia, The.*
Space Trilogy, The 30.
    See: *Out of the Silent Planet, Perelandra,* and, *That Hideous Strength.*
Spenser's Images of Life 65
Spirits in Bondage 38, 99
Studies in Medieval and Renaissance Literature 39, 42–43, 53, 59, 60–62, 64–65
Studies in Words 61, 106
Surprised by Joy: The Shape of My Early Life 57, 92, 98, 119, 122, 143, 164

That Hideous Strength. A Modern Fairytale for Grown-Ups 37, 49, 96–98, 100.
    See, *The Space Trilogy,* also, *Out of the Silent Planet,* and, *Perelandra.*
They Asked for a Paper: Papers and Addresses 43, 44, 47–48, 54–55, 57, 59, 63, 164
They Stand Together: The Letters of C. S. Lewis to Arthur Greeves 1914–1963 66, 69
Till We Have Faces: A Myth Retold 30, 37–38, 58, 85, 86, 95, 99, 101–103
Timeless at Heart 42, 67

Index of C. S. Lewis's Works

Transposition and Other Addresses xiv, 37, 41–43, 48, 50, 54, 63, 89, 122, 145, 150, 156, 163–64

Undeceptions 35–36, 41–47, 49–53, 55–56, 58–60, 62–64, 66, 68, 103. (US, *God in the Dock: Essays on Theology and Ethics*, 1971.)

Vivisection 52
Voyage of the Dawn Treader, The 56.
See: *Chronicles of Narnia, The*.

Weight of Glory and Other Addresses, The 42, 54
What Christians Believe xiv, xvi, 44–45.
See: *Broadcast Talks*, and, *Mere Christianity*.
Will We Lose God in Outer Space? 60
World's Last Night and Other Essays, The 55, 57, 60–61

Yours, Jack: The Inspirational Letters of C. S. Lewis 70

C. S. Lewis: BBC Radio Broadcasts

"Answers to Listeners' Questions." *The Broadcast Talks*. The First Series, *Right and Wrong*. Fifth Talk, 6 September 1941 xiv, 36–37, 44

"Common Decency." *The Broadcast Talks*. The First Series, *Right and Wrong*. First Talk, 6 August 1941 xiv, 36–37, 44

"Faith (1)." *The Broadcast Talks*. The Third Series, *Christian Behaviour*. Seventh Talk, Nov. 1, 1942 xiv, 46
"Faith (2)." *The Broadcast Talks*. The Third Series, *Christian Behaviour*. Eighth Talk, Nov. 8, 1942 xiv, 46
"Forgiveness." *The Broadcast Talks*. The Third Series, *Christian Behaviour*. Fifth Talk, Oct. 18, 1942 xiv, 46

"Good Infection." *The Broadcast Talks*. The Fourth Series, 1944, *Beyond Personality: The Christian View of God*. Third Talk, Mar. 7, 1944 xiv, 48
"Great Sin, The." *The Broadcast Talks*. The Third Series, *Christian Behaviour*. Sixth Talk, Oct. 25, 1942 xiv, 46

"Introduction to The Great Divorce, An." Home Service, May 9, 1948 50

"Invasion, The." *The Broadcast Talks*. The Second Series, *What Christians Believe*. Second Talk, 18 January 1942 xiv, 45
"Is Christianity Hard or Easy?" *The Broadcast Talks*. The Fourth Series, 1944, *Beyond Personality: The Christian View of God*. Sixth Talk, Mar. 28, 1944 xiv, 48

"Let's Pretend." *The Broadcast Talks*. The Fourth Series, 1944, *Beyond Personality: The Christian View of God*. Fifth Talk, Mar. 21, 1944 xiv, 48

"Making and Begetting." *The Broadcast Talks*. The Fourth Series, 1944, *Beyond Personality: The Christian View of God*. First Talk, Feb. 22, 1944 xiv, 48
"Materialism or Religion." *The Broadcast Talks*. The First Series, Right and Wrong. Third Talk, 20 August 1941 xiv, 36–37, 44
"Morality and Psychoanalysis." *The Broadcast Talks*. The Third Series, *Christian Behaviour*. Third Talk, Oct. 4 1942 xiv, 46

"New Man, The." *The Broadcast Talks*. The Fourth Series, 1944, *Beyond Personality: The Christian View of God*. Seventh Talk, Apr. 4, 1944 xiv, 48
"Novels of Charles Williams, The." BBC, the Third Programme, Feb. 11, 1949 54

"Obstinate Toy Soldiers, The." *The Broadcast Talks*. The Fourth Series, 1944, *Beyond Personality: The Christian View of God*. Fourth Talk, Mar. 14, 1944 xiv, 48

"Perfect Penitent, The." *The Broadcast Talks*. The Second Series, *What Christians Believe*. Fourth Talk, 8 February 1942 xiv, 45

"Practical Conclusion, The." *The Broadcast Talks*. The Second Series, *What Christians Believe*. Fifth Talk, 15 February 1942 xiv, 45

"Rival Conceptions of God, The." *The Broadcast Talks*. The Second Series, *What Christians Believe*. First Talk, 11 January 1942 xiv, 45

"Scientific Law and Moral Law." *The Broadcast Talks*. The First Series, *Right and Wrong*. Second Talk, 13 August 1941 xiv, 36–37, 44

"Sexual Morality." *The Broadcast Talks*. The Third Series, *Christian Behaviour*. Fourth Talk, Oct. 11, 1942 xiv, 46

"Shocking Alternative, The." *The Broadcast Talks*. The Second Series, *What Christians Believe*. Third Talk, 1 February, 1942 xiv, 45

"Social Morality" *The Broadcast Talks*. The Third Series, *Christian Behaviour*. Second Talk, Sept. 27, 1942 xiv, 46

"Three Parts, The" *The Broadcast Talks*. The Third Series, *Christian Behaviour*. First Talk, Sept. 20, 1942 xiv, 46

"Three-Personal God, The." *The Broadcast Talks*. The Fourth Series, 1944, *Beyond Personality: The Christian View of God*. Second Talk. Feb. 29 1944 xiv, 48

"What Can We Do About It?" *The Broadcast Talks*. The First Series, *Right and Wrong*. Fourth Talk, 27 August 1941 xiv, 36–37, 44

"Vision of John Bunyan, The." BBC Home Service 63

C. S. Lewis: Articles, Essays, Addresses, Sermons, etc.

"Addison" 50
"After Priggery—What?" 49
"After Ten Years" 61
"Alliterative Metre, The" 39
"Answers to Questions on Christianity" 46
"Anthropological Approach, The" 63
"Avant-Propos a l'édition Française" 55

"Before We Can Communicate" 62
"Behind the Scenes" 58
"Blimpophobia" 47
"Bluspels and Flalansferes: A Semantic Nightmare" 41

"Christian Apologetics" 50
"Christian Hope – Its Meaning for Today" 55
"Christian Reply to Professor Price, A" 51
"Christian Reunion" 47
"Christianity and Culture" 41
"Christianity and Literature" 40

"Cross-Examination" 63

"Dangers of National Repentance" 41
"Dante's Similes" 42
"Dante's Statius" 59
"Dark Tower, The" 40
"De Audiendis Poetis" 61
"De Descriptione Temporum" 57
"De Futilitate" 46
"Death of Words, The" 47
"Decline of Religion, The" 51
"Delinquents in the Snow" 59
"Dethronement of Power, The" 57–58
"Difficulties in Presenting the Christian Faith to Modern Unbelievers" 53
"Dogma and Science" 45
"Dogma and the Universe" 45
"Donne and Love Poetry in the Seventeenth Century" 40
"Dream, A" 46

Index of C. S. Lewis's Works

"Edmund Spenser, 1552–1599" 57
"Efficacy of Prayer, The" 61
"Empty Universe, The" 56
"'Establishment Must Die and Rot, The . . .' C. S. Lewis Discusses Science Fiction with Kingsley Amis" 63
"Equality. 45
"Evil and God" 42

"Fern Seed and Elephants" 61. See: "Modern Theology and Biblical Criticism."
"Fifteenth-Century Heroic Line, The" 40
"Forms of Things Unknown" 65
"Founding of the Oxford Socratic Club, The" 44
"Four-Letter words" 62
"Funeral of a Great Myth, The" 65

"Genesis of a Medieval Book, The" 60
"Genius and Genius" 39
"George Orwell" 57
"God in the Dock" 53
"Gods Return to Earth, The" 57–58
"Good Work and Good Works" 61
"Grand Miracle, The" 50. See: "Miracles," *Miracles* (1st ed.), and, *Miracles* (2nd ed.)

"Haggard Rides Again" 62
"Hamlet: the Prince or the Poem" 44
"Heaven, Earth and Outer Space" 63, 93
"Hedonics" 49
"Hero and Leander" 56
"High and Low Brows" 41
"Historicism" 55
"Hobbit, The" 41
"Horrid Red Things" 47
"Humanitarian Theory of Punishment, The" 54

"I was Decided Upon" 63, 93
"Imagery in the Last Eleven Cantos of Dante's Comedy" 53
"Imagination and Thought in the Middle Ages" 59
"Inner Ring, The" 48
"Interim Report" 58
"Introduction to The Great Divorce, An" 50
"Introduction" in *St. Athanasius, The Incarnation of the Word* 47
"Is English Doomed?" 47
"Is History Bunk?" 59
"Is Progress Possible?" 60
"Is Theism Important? A Reply" 56

"Is Theology Poetry?" xv–xvi, 47
"It All Began with a Picture . . ." 62

"Kappa Element in Romance, The" 42
"Kipling's World" 53

"Language of Religion, The" 62
"Laws of Nature, The" 49
"Letter to Corbin Scott Carnell, Oct. 13, 1958" 120
"Letter to Dom Bede Griffiths, April 24, 1936" 120
"Letter to Dom Bede Griffiths, May 23 1936" 120
"Letter to *The Church Times*, Feb. 8, 1952" 120, 139
"Lilies that Fester" 57
"Literary Impact of the Authorized Version, The" 55

"Man Born Blind, The" 38
"Man or Rabbit?" 51
"Meditation in a Toolshed" 49
"Membership" 50
"Metre" 62
"Ministering Angels" 60
"Miracles" 44, 50. See: "The Grand Miracles," *Miracles* (1st ed.), and, *Miracles* (2nd ed.)
"Miserable Offenders" 52
"Modern Man and his Categories of Thought" 51
"Modern Theology and Biblical Criticism" 61, 158. See: "Fern Seed and Elephants."
"Morte D'arthur, The" 52
"Must Our Image of God Go?" 64
"My First School" 45
"Myth Became Fact. 47

"Neoplatonism in the Poetry of Spenser" 62
"New Learning and New Ignorance" 48. See: *English Literature in the Sixteenth Century.*
"None Other Gods: Culture in War Time" 41
"Note on Comus, A" 39
"Note on Jane Austen, A" 57
"Notes on the Way" 42, 43, 44, 45, 47, 51, 53
"Novels of Charles Williams, The" 54

"On Church Music" 54
"On Criticism" 65

"On Ethics" 42
"On Forgiveness" 52
"On Juvenile Tastes" 60
"On Living in an Atomic Age" 53
"On Myth" 62
"On Obstinacy in Belief" 57
"On Punishment: A Reply" 54
"On Science Fiction" 57
"On Three Ways of Writing for Children" 56
"Onward, Christian Spacemen" 64

"Pains of Animals, The" 42
"Panegyric for Dorothy L. Sayers, A" 60
"Peace Proposals for Brother Every and Mr Bethell" 41
"Period Criticism" 51
"Petitionary Prayer: A Problem without an Answer" 56
"Poison of Subjectivism, The" 45
"Preface" in, *Essays Presented to Charles Williams* 52
"Preface" in, *How Heathen is Britain?* 51
"Preface" in, *Letters to Young Churches* 52
"Preface" to *The Pilgrim's Regress* (3rd ed.) 46
"Priestesses in the Church?" 53
"Private Bates" 47
"Prudery and Philology" 58
"Psalms, The" 59

"Rejoinder to Dr Pittenger" 5, 32, 60
"Religion and Rocketry" 60
"Religion and Science" 49
"Religion without Dogma?" 51
"Reply to Professor Haldene, A" 50
"Revival or Decay?" 60

"Scraps" 49
"Screwtape Proposes a Toast" 61
"Seeing Eye, The" 64
"Sermon and the Lunch, The" 49
"Sex in Literature" 63
"Shelley, Dryden, and Mr. Eliot" 41
"Shoddy Lands, The" 58
"Sir Walter Scott" 59
"Some Thoughts" 53
"Sometimes Fairy Stories May Say Best What's to be Said" 58
"Spenser's Cruel Cupid" 64

"Talking about Bicycles" 51
"Tasso" 42
"Thoughts of a Cambridge Don" 58
"Three Kinds of Men" 45
"Tolkien's *The Lord of the Rings*" 57–58
"Transposition" (1st ed.) xiv, xvi, 37, 48, 54, 89, 122
"Transposition" (2nd ed.) xiv, xvi, 37, 63, 54, 89
"Tribute to E. R. Eddison, A" 59
"Trouble with 'X', The" . . . 53
"Two Lectures" 49
"Two Ways with the Self" 42

"Unreal Estates" 63

"Variation in Shakespeare and Others" 40
"Vision of John Bunyan, The" 63
"Vivisection" 52

"We Have No 'Right to Happiness'" 64
"Weight of Glory, The" 37, 43, 111
"What Are We to Make of Jesus Christ?" 55
"What Chaucer Really did to *Il Filostrato*" 39
"What Christmas Means to Me" 59
"Who was Right – Dream Lecturer or Real Lecturer?" 49
"Why I am not a Pacifist" 42
"William Morris" 40
"Willing Slaves of the Welfare State" 60
"Work and Prayer" 49
"World's Last Night, The" 55, 142

"Xmas and Christmas: a Lost Chapter from Herodotus" 58

Sectional Contents

Introduction C. S. Lewis—An Annotated Bibliography and Resource | 1
1. Why C. S. Lewis | 1
2. Aims and Objectives | 2

Chapter 1 Lewis . . . and The Christ | 5
1. Who or What is the Christ? | 6
    i. The Messiah | 6
    ii. Expectations | 6
    iii. Trinitarian | 7
    iv. Witness | 7
2. A Developing Christological Tradition | 7
3. The Study of The Christ | 8
    i. Trinitarian Considerations | 9
    ii. "But, Who do You Say I Am?" | 11
    iii. The Gospels | 13
4. The Development of Patristic Christology | 14
    i. Humanity and Divinity | 15
    ii. Justin Martyr and Logos Christology | 16
    iii. Irenaeus and the Gnostics | 17
5. Creedal Christology | 18
    i. The Proto Creed | 18
    ii. The Apostles' Creed | 19
6. Arianism | 20
7. Church Councils | 21
    i. The Nicene Creed | 21
    ii. "What has not been assumed has not been healed" | 22
    iii. Antioch and Alexandria | 23
    iv. The Council of Ephesus | 23
8. Constantinople, Augustine, and Pelagianism | 23
9. The Chalcedonian Creed | 24
10. The Moment of the Incarnation | 26
11. Modern Christology | 27
12. Lewis's Christ; Lewis's Christology | 29
    i. Christ Pantocrator | 29
    ii. Christ in the Shadowlands | 30

Chapter 2 C. S. Lewis: An Annotated Historical Bibliography of Primary Sources | 35

The Early Works: 1931–44 | 36
The Middle Works: 1941–47 | 37
The Later Works: 1948–63 | 38

1. The Early Period Works | 38

1919	38	1933	39	1938	40
1920s	38	1935	39	1939	40
1926	39	1936	39	1940	41
1932	39	1937	40	

2. The Middle Period Works | 42

1941	42	1944	46	1947	52
1942	44	1945	49	
1943	45	1946	50	

3. The Later Period Works | 53

1948	53	1954	56	1960	61
1949	54	1955	57	1961	62
1950	54	1956	58	1962	63
1951	55	1957	59	1963	63
1952	55	1958	59	
1953	56	1959	61	

4. C. S. Lewis: Publications—*Post Mortem* | 64

1964	64	1977	66	1991	67
1965	64	1979	66	1994	67
1966	65	1982	66	1998	67
1967	65	1985	66	2000	68
1969	65	1986	67	2004	68
1970	66	1987	67	2007	68
1971	66	1988	67	
1975	66	1990	67	

Chapter 3 C. S. Lewis: Correspondent | 69

1966	69	1985	70	2007	70
1967	69	1988	70	2011	70
1979	69	2004	70	

Chapter 4 Helen Joy Davidman: An Annotated Historical Bibliography | 71

1. Primary Sources | 71

1938	71	1944	71	1951	72
1940	71	1949	72	1954	72
1943	71	1950	72	

2. Secondary Sources | 72

Sectional Contents

Chapter 5 C. S. Lewis: Revelation And The Christ: Secondary Sources—Books | 75

Chapter 6 C. S. Lewis: Revelation and the Christ: Secondary Sources—Articles and Essays | 89
1. Christology and Eschatology | 89
2. Conversion and the Christian Life | 91
3. Ecclesiology | 94
4. Literature and Analogical Narrative | 95
5. Philosophy and Naturalism, Scientism and Rationality | 103
6. Preacher and Apologist, Teacher and Professional | 106
7. Religion and Culture, Liberalism and Humanism, Secularity | 111
8. Revelation and Reason | 111
9. Theology and Biblical Studies | 113

Chapter 7 Secondary Sources—Related to Lewis's Development | 119
1. Books Cited by Lewis | 119
2. Works Relating to Lewis's Patristic and Philosophical Development | 123
3. Works Relating to Lewis's Defence of Pagan Mythology | 124
4. Inklings Related | 124

Chapter 8 Web Resources | 125
1. C. S. Lewis on the Web | 126
2. The Inklings | 127
   i. The Inklings | 128
   ii. J. R. R. Tolkien | 128
   iii. Charles Williams | 129
   iv. Owen Barfield | 130
   v. Warren "Warnie" Hamilton Lewis | 131
   vi. Nevill Coghill | 131
   vii. Roger Lancelyn Green | 131
   viii. Hugo Dyson | 132
   ix. Lord David Cecil | 132
   x. R.A. "Humphrey" Havard | 132
   xi. J.A.W. Bennett | 132
   xii. Adam Fox | 132
3. A Younger Generation | 132
   i. Christopher Tolkien | 132
   ii. Douglas Gresham | 133
4. Other Members & Guests | 133
   i. John Barrington Wain | 133
   ii. Percy Bates | 134
   iii. John David Arnett & Jon Fromke | 134
   iv. Courteney Edward Stevens | 134

  v. Colin Hardie | 134
  vi. R. B. McCallum | 134
  vii. Gervase Mathew | 134
  viii. Roy Campbell | 134
  ix. James Dundas-Grant | 134
  x. Eric Rucker Eddison | 134
  xi. Charles Leslie Wrenn | 134
 5. Writers Valued by the Inklings and Associated with Their Work | 135
  i. Joy Davidman | 135
  ii. Dorothy Sayers | 135
  iii. G. E. M. Anscombe | 136
  iv. George MacDonald | 136
  v. G. K. Chesterton | 137

Chapter 9 Glossary | 139

 Age of Reason, the, and the Enlightenment | 140
 analogia entis and *analogia fidei* | 140
 Apollinarianism | 141
 Apologetics | 141
 Arianism | 142
 Arminian(ism) | 142
 Atheism | 143
 Atonement | 143
 aut Deus aut malus homo | 144
 Categorical Imperative, The | 144
 communicatio idiomatum | 145
 Deism | 145
 Docetism | 145
 ecclesia visibilis-ecclesia invisibilis | 146
 Ecclesiology | 146
 Election | 146
 Eschaton/Eschatology | 146
 Eutychianism | 146
 Existentialism | 147
 Fall, the (Original Sin) | 147
 fides quaerens intellectum | 147
 Foundationalism | 147
 Gnosticism | 148
 Heaven | 149
 Hell | 149
 Idealism | 149
 imago Christi/imitatio Christi | 149
 imago Dei | 150
 Kenosis | 150
 Liberal Neo-Protestantism | 150
 Liberal/Modern | 150

Sectional Contents

logos asarkos/logos ensarkos (λόγος ἄσαρκος–λογος ἔνσαρκος) | 151
Naturalism|Scientism | 152
Natural Theology | 153
New Atheists, The | 154
Ontology | 154
Pagan | 154
Pantheism/Panentheism | 155
Pantocrator | 155
Parousia | 155
Patristic | 156
Platonism | 156
Pneumatology | 156
Postmodern | 157
Prevenient Grace | 157
Process Theology | 157
Purgatory/Purgation | 158
Quest for the Historical Jesus, The | 158
Redemption | 158
reductio ad absurdum, and, "Law of Excluded Middle" | 159
regula fidei | 159
Revelation and Reason | 159
Romanticism | 160
Salvation | 160
Skepticism and the Scandal of Particularity | 160
Sehnsucht | 161
sola scriptura | 162
Soteriology (a Doctrine of Salvation) | 162
Substitution | 162
Theism | 162
Theodicy | 162
Theological Anthropology | 163
Theosophy | 164
Transposition | 164
Trinity | 164
Trinity: Immanent and economic | 165
Universalism | 165
Zeitgeist | 166

www.ingramcontent.com/pod-product-compliance
Lightning Source LLC
Chambersburg PA
CBHW082039230426
43670CB00016B/2708